Foreign Intelligence

· Foreign Intelligence ·

Research and Analysis in the Office of Strategic Services 1942–1945

Barry M. Katz

Harvard University Press
Cambridge, Massachusetts
London, England
1989

Library of Congress Cataloging-in-Publication Data

Katz, Barry M.
  Foreign intelligence : research and analysis in the Office of Strategic Services,
  1942–1945 / Barry M. Katz.
      p.   cm.
  Includes bibliographical references and index.
  ISBN 0-674-30825-5
  1. United States. Office of Strategic Services. Research and Analysis Branch.   2. World
War, 1939–1945—Secret service—United States.   3. World War, 1939–1945—Military in-
telligence—United States.   I. Title.
D810.S7K33   1989   89-31278
940.54′86′73—dc19   CIP

To Deborah

Contents

Figures

Preface

*A real weakness of the R[esearch] and A[nalysis] Branch
was undoubtedly the fact that it was of necessity so largely
academic.*

William L. Langer, Chief

World War II has been called the physicists' war in deference to the
unprecedented recruitment of the scientific community to government
service and the historic pooling of intellectual effort that followed. Seemingly every major scientist in a dozen fields—theorists and experimen-
talists, emeriti and graduate students, the American-born and the
European refugee—joined forces to bring the war explosively to an end.

It was also, however, the economists' war—and the sociologists', the
historians', the philosophers' war—even if, viewed from the perspective
of the human sciences, it ended less with a bang than a whimper. The
social sciences and humanities were called to arms in an intellectual
mobilization that pressed into government service a community of academic scholars that was no less extraordinary than that of their scientific
counterparts. At the same historical moment that General Groves and
Professor Oppenheimer were recruiting the world's most eminent scientists to the Manhattan Project, General William J. Donovan and Professor William L. Langer were conscripting the leading thinkers in a
dozen scholarly disciplines into the Office of Strategic Services.

Like their scientific counterparts, the humanist scholars of OSS's Research and Analysis Branch were challenged to mobilize their academic
training and adapt it to the practical exigencies of the war. They did not,
to be sure, engineer a secret weapon, nor can they be said, by any
stretch of the imagination, to have made a decisive contribution to the
war. As one eminent participant later reflected, the limited influence of
the human sciences was a function not of their importance but of the
nature of their subject matter: the classicist, the anthropologist, the
political scientist is faced with the almost contradictory task of system-

atizing the unique and unrepeatable, "in contrast to the natural chain reaction of an atomic explosion which will happen in the same form according to the same laws whenever the same elements meet under the same circumstances."[1] When called upon not just to explain but to predict the course of future events, the humanist scholars often faltered.

Other factors limited the influence of the Research and Analysis Branch, despite the high quality of its scholarship, the innovative research methodologies which it developed, and its transcendence of the conventionalized academic division of labor. For one thing, there is an inherently political content to these disciplines of a sort that is rarely manifest in the sciences and that soon won for the Branch the reputation of being "a hotbed of academic radicalism."[2] Second, there was no shortage of officials in the Departments of War and State who looked askance at a secret intelligence service which was made up of garrulous professors and which employed some forty-seven of the foreign-born, including more than a dozen enemy aliens. Finally, the ".Chairborne Division" of OSS brought to the war effort a profoundly foreign intelligence in yet another sense: habituated to the library, the seminar room, the research institute, these scholars wrote, spoke, and thought in an idiom frequently at variance with that of officialdom. The discourse of the intelligentsia, one might say, adapted itself most uneasily to the discourse of intelligence.

From the standpoint of intellectual history, the limitations as much as the achievements of the Research and Analysis Branch are equally deserving of examination. The erudite scholars of "R&A" did not paddle ashore in rubber dinghies or drop from the sky into enemy territory; they did not carry the famous OSS L capsule (potassium cyanide), and the only code book used in the Branch was a glossary of the fractured English spoken by the German émigrés of the Central European Section. In the last analysis, however, it was they more than their operational colleagues who laid the foundations of modern intelligence work. It is predictable, then, if unfortunate, that the tasks of research and analysis have received no more than fleeting attention in the many volumes of memoirs, exposés, and spy chillers that have been written about the Office of Strategic Services. But it is astonishing that R&A has been overlooked by professional historians, some forty of whom served in it, including no less than seven future presidents of the American Historical Association. Among humanist scholars of later generations, few are not intellectually indebted to one or more of the outstanding figures of modern thought who worked out of its offices at 23rd Street and E, and fewer still would not benefit from sustained reflection upon the engagement of academic scholarship with the external world that took place there.[3]

Although its intended clients were Secretaries and Generals, the ultimate significance of R&A lies less in the fields of diplomatic or military history than in intellectual history. An international brigade of committed scholars was challenged to contribute its essentially academic skills to a struggle of global proportions, to enter into history not in spite of its academic training but by virtue of it. Fascism was destroyed in Europe and Asia, and the academic scholars of the Research and Analysis Branch contributed, however modestly, to that defeat. More decisive was the contribution of their epic engagement to the postwar world of academic scholarship.

As a study in modern intellectual history, then, *Foreign Intelligence* has two primary objectives. The first is an analysis of the manner in which the discourse of academic scholarship—the philosophies of Hegel and Marx, the historiography of Ranke, Burkhardt, and Meinecke, neo-classical economic theory, the methodologies of the social sciences—was adapted by two generations of American and European-born scholars to the demands of war and peace. The second objective is to follow the careers of certain exemplary scholars as they were intellectually demobilized and returned to the groves of academe. The world-historical events into which they had been thrust transformed them as individuals, and they in turn contributed to the recasting of academic scholarship. I have not been overly preoccupied with the degree to which they were right or wrong in their various predictions, forecasts, estimates, and evaluations. This would have been a relatively easy and extremely tedious chore, which seems to have little to do with my main business: the epistemology of intelligence.

· · ·

I would like to conclude with some explanations and excuses. First, many distinguished scholars participated in the events described in this book but will make no more than cameo appearances. This has in many cases to do with the nature and the extent of the documentation available to me. Even when veterans of the Research and Analysis Branch were generous in their assistance, I have elected to use interview material only to supplement the documentary record.

Second, the Reseach and Analysis Branch of OSS employed, at peak strength, over nine hundred professionals, many of whom contributed in fundamental ways to the war effort but cannot be said to have become leading thinkers in their respective disciplines. The story I have chosen to tell is, I confess, intellectual history "from above," but the narrowness of my interests implies nothing whatever about the large numbers of competent men and women who participated in this remarkable chapter of modern history, often at great professional sacrifice and occasionally at considerable personal risk.

Finally, this was a global war, fought on all fronts, that pressed a bewildering number of academic disciplines into service: anthropology, art history, classical philology, comparative literature, economics, geography, history, philosophy, political science, psychology, sociology, and statistics—to name but a few. A fascinating study awaits anyone qualified to extend this investigation of European intellectual history to the extraordinarily distinguished group of thinkers who applied their specialized academic skills to the Far Eastern theaters—the Sinologist John King Fairbank, the anthropologists Gregory Bateson and Cora DuBois, and many others. To have attempted that here, given my own limitations, would have severely compromised the standards of scholarship I have tried to maintain.

Those standards come, above all, from the scholars of the Research and Analysis Branch themselves, many of whom I have had the privilege to meet in the course of my research; others took the time to respond in writing to my inquiries. Since I do not pretend to have met those standards in every respect, the usual caveats that free one's readers and interlocutors from responsibility must in this case be greatly emphasized: All of the judgments and interpretations offered here are my own, and I have often—imprudently, no doubt—felt compelled to reject the advice of individuals who were generous with their time and patience.

It is a pleasure to thank the following alumni of the Research and Analysis Branch, OSS: Professors Moses Abramowitz, Sidney Alexander, Abram Bergson, Beatrice Braude (deceased), NOB, Gordon Craig, Harold Deutsch, Lorenz Eitner, Franklin Ford, Felix Gilbert, John H. Herz, Edgar M. Hoover, H. Stuart Hughes, Alex Inkeles, Carl Kaysen, Dr. Henry Kellerman, Professors Sherman Kent (deceased), Charles P. Kindleberger, Leonard Krieger, Wassily W. Leontief, Dr. Walter Levy, Professors Edward S. Mason, Henry Cord Meyer, Barrington Moore, Jr., Chandler Morse, William N. Parker, Mr. Albert Phiebig, Professors David H. Pinkney, Walt W. Rostow, John E. Sawyer,

Arthur M. Schlesinger, Jr., Carl E. Schorske, Dr. Sam Schurr, Professors Edward Shils, Paul M. Sweezy, Robert C. Tucker, Wayne Vucinich, and Paul Zinner.

Mrs. Joanne Despres, Dr. Hanna Holborn Gray, Mrs. Anne Kirchheimer, and Dr. Walter Salant made very valuable contributions as well.

A number of younger scholars read portions of this manuscript and were generous with their time and uncompromising with their criticism: Drs. Josef Chytry, Martin Jay, Dominick LaCapra, Carl Landauer, William Pietz, Robert Proctor, and Bradley F. Smith. At Stanford, my distinguished colleagues Kenneth Arrow, Barton Bernstein, Alexander Dallin, Nathan Rosenberg, and James Sheehan helped to reorient me at certain difficult junctures, and James L. Adams kept faith in me during years of distraction from my teaching duties in the Values, Technology, Science, and Society Program. They are, I believe, aware of my appreciation and of my admiration for their own achievements. Once the basic research was completed, Angela von der Lippe and Susan Wallace of Harvard University Press offered expert advice on the preparation of the manuscript.

Finally, anyone who has undertaken primary research owes inestimable debts to the "shadow warriors" of all historical scholarship. It is a pleasure to thank Ms. Terry Hammett, Mr. Lawrence H. McDonald, Ms. Kathy Nicastro, and Mr. John Taylor of the U.S. National Archives. Working under the most difficult conditions and belabored by the unceasing demands of impatient researchers like myself, they made my research possible, and frequently enjoyable.

Foreign Intelligence

Military Disciplines

The arrival of the professors was greeted in characteristic Washington fashion, with some derision and more suspicion, not to say outright and avowed hostility.

William L. Langer, Chief
Research and Analysis Branch

Military metaphors, like military supply lines, can easily become overextended, but seasoned strategists know that at times risks must be taken. This study examines the mobilization of a diverse intellectual community and the adaptation of its essentially academic skills to the exigencies of war. Since it is concerned precisely with the mutual infiltration of scholarly and soldierly forces, it will be inevitable that metaphors will become extended, mixed, and merged with the literal truth it is their sworn duty to represent.

The universal allure of espionage lies undoubtedly in the theatrical license to step outside the constraints not only of law, custom, and morality but of one's ego as well. The career of William Donovan, founding director of America's first central intelligence agency, testifies well to the power of this mystique: he has entered into contemporary folklore as "Wild Bill," "America's Master Spy," and even "the Last Hero," despite his repeated insistence that, the exploits of agents and double-agents notwithstanding, "most of our intelligence came from good old-fashioned intellectual sweat."[1] The mental exertions that occurred at the intersection of intellect and intelligence, so routinely overlooked in histories of the war, are the subject of the chapters that follow. We must begin, however, with an overview of research and analysis as they were conducted in the Office of Strategic Services.

Academic Recruitment

Almost from the beginning of the war, a sense of uneasiness had prevailed in Washington over the degree of American preparedness; for whether or not the United States were drawn militarily into combat, it was clear that this would be a war of global dimensions. In this climate, the inadequacy of the American intelligence apparatus had become conspicuous and critical. Alone among the great powers, the United States had entered the field of global politics without one centralized agency responsible for the collection, evaluation, and distribution of foreign intelligence. The Army and the Navy had their separate military intelligence units (G-2 and the Office of Naval Intelligence, respectively), but these were staffed by officers frequently lacking in specialized training and expertise. The FBI, even under the aggressive J. Edgar Hoover, was statutorily restricted to domestic activities. A Coordinator of Inter-American Affairs (Nelson Rockefeller) had regional jurisdiction over Latin America in the intelligence field; and at least nine other agencies and departments, from State to Treasury, conducted operations that could be classed as "intelligence" and which they pursued with greater or lesser degrees of professionalism. As the United States became increasingly embroiled in developments on the European continent, the need for a coordinated program of information gathering and analysis became acute.

Roosevelt's first move, when he finally began to take steps to create an integrated intelligence service, was to recall from private legal practice the irrepressible William J. Donovan, soldier, statesman, and personal confidant. In order to appraise the emerging situation and survey America's anticipated intelligence needs, Donovan was instructed to conduct a series of overseas missions as personal representative of the President. In July 1940 he traveled to England to assess the British capacity to resist a German invasion and to evaluate their vulnerability to German Fifth Column activities, and at the end of the year Donovan began a second tour that carried him for three-and-a-half months around the Mediterranean basin. He returned reaffirmed in his conviction that a regular channel of strategic information was essential and that political and psychological factors were destined to play a major role in the emerging "total" war. On the basis of these estimations, Donovan submitted to the President a "Memorandum of Establishment of Service of Strategic Information," in which he urged that there be assembled in Washington a corps of "carefully selected trained minds" with a knowledge both of languages and research techniques. A month later, on July 11, 1951, Roosevelt accepted this recommendation and signed an Executive Order creating the office of the civilian Coordinator of Information (COI), responsible directly to the President and the Joint Chiefs of Staff.

Donovan was named to the post and instructed "to collect and analyze all information and data which may bear upon national security," to which end he was given some rooms and borrowed furniture in the old State Department office building, a secret budget of unvouchered funds, and the authority to seek out and hire a staff possessed of the requisite qualifications.[2] Donovan's greatest insight, perhaps, was to recognize that this body of expert knowledge already existed, dispersed throughout the nation's universities, libraries, museums, and research institutes.

When the Bureau of the Budget estimated that the COI would require a staff of 92 to assist him in his designated task, it did not reckon with Donovan's imperial dreams of a superorganization that would spread stealthily across Washington to claim the functions of information gathering, propaganda, espionage, subversion, strategic and postwar planning, and more. Before his wings were clipped at the end of his first year, Donovan commanded a force of 1,852 that was growing fast and causing consternation in many established branches of the government. Accordingly, for much of its first year the COI led a defensive existence in Washington, buffeted by jurisdictional rivalries, lacking in organizational coherence, and unable to develop a unified conception of its mandate. Its essentially dissimilar functions were awkwardly distributed between a Research and Analysis Branch (R&A) and the Foreign Information Service (FIS), whose staffs may have intrigued as much with one another as against the common enemy.

The shock of Pearl Harbor underscored the need for a rational restructuring of American intelligence capabilities. In a major attempt to reorganize this unwieldly apparatus, the overt propaganda functions of the original COI were severed and autonomously constituted as the Office of War Information. Donovan retained control over his intelligence gathering, research, and analysis functions, however, to which was added a clandestine operational branch that would carry out designated activities within enemy and enemy-controlled territory. On June 13, 1942, streamlined and staffed with its first generation of agents and analysts, the American intelligence establishment came into its own as the Office of Strategic Services.[3]

The Research and Analysis Branch, which survived intact the metamorphosis of COI into OSS, was conceived as the heart of the intelligence organization: the other principal branches of OSS—Secret Intelligence and Special Operations—would be as veins and arteries, feeding into and supplied by it, respectively. It may be more suggestive, however, to regard R&A as the "head" of the agency, for it rapidly acquired a reputation, both within OSS and beyond, for the extraordinary intellectual credentials of the personnel attracted to it and for the sophistication with which they adapted the methods of modern scholarship to the discovery and analysis of data.

The director of the Branch, according to the original plan, was to serve as Chair of a select Board of Analysts composed of leading scholars drawn from a range of social scientific disciplines, as well as military experts from the Army and Navy. Their function would be to recruit and then supervise the work of a corps of civilian researchers whose factual reports they would distill into policy alternatives that would be submitted to the President at Donovan's discretion. In practice, however, this body of senior academic mandarins soon came to be looked upon by their colleagues as "a do-nothing aristocracy," superfluous to the work of the independent-minded specialists deployed throughout the agency.[4] As the directive functions of the Board of Analysts narrowed to the trivia of bureaucratic detail, the substantive analytical work of the Branch acquired a quality of academic insularity. The same lack of administrative authority that limited the influence R&A could exert may have actually been a condition of the acknowledged excellence of its work, however, for by being removed at the very outset from any hope of a policy-making role, the scholar-analysts lost whatever inducement they might have had to adjust their findings to meet the approval of prospective "clients," or otherwise to compromise the intellectual integrity of their work.

What is beyond dispute is that this essential tension—between analysis and adminstration, scholarship and policy, theory and practice—remained an inherent feature of research and analysis throughout the history of the Office of Strategic Services. Even in its final phase, a frustrated Division Chief could unload on his crew of displaced academicians the lament that, "for reasons I do not profess to understand . . . it appears easier to get out a 250-page epitome of what Europe will be like in 1986, to be delivered tomorrow morning at 8:30," than "a 2-page summary of what you most want to know about the job you're doing."[5] It is often less instructive, then, to search out the organizational highways and byways that connected R&A to the outer world than to analyze the conditions of intellectual production that prevailed within it. We may begin by attempting a collective intellectual-political portrait of the Research and Analysis Branch and the post-academic division of labor according to which it functioned.

· · ·

At the end of July 1941, Librarian of Congress Archibald MacLeish met in an all-day session with representatives of the American Council of Learned Societies (ACLS), the Social Science Research Council, the National Archives, and leading scholars from several universities to help name a slate of advisors for Donovan's fledgling organization. Shortly thereafter, James Phinney Baxter III was called to Washington to preside over the creation of a Research and Analysis Branch. Baxter, President of Williams College and a respected authority on American diplomatic and military history, was well-connected in academic circles and turned first to his old friend and former colleague, William L. Langer of Harvard, whom he invited to assist him by supervising a staff of research scholars to work with published materials at the Library of Congress. It was never clear who was to be assisting whom, but Baxter's withdrawal in September 1942, ostensibly for reasons of ill health, left Langer the undisputed Chief of Research and Analysis for the duration of the war. During those first months, however, Baxter and Langer managed to lead coordinated assaults on two fronts. In the Washington theater they conducted continuous operations against the fortresses of officialdom, wherein "we spent much time running hither and thither explaining our objectives and our hopes, petitioning for toleration and cooperation, and waving our Presidential order."[6] While their attempts to take the capital by storm were of little avail, they were inordinately successful in their siege of the ivory towers of the Ivy League.

Aided by MacLeish, the ACLS, and above all the dense and time-honored network of academic association, Langer and Baxter set out to recruit an elite professoriate to their newly chartered "College of Cardinals," as the Board of Analysts came to be known. From Harvard they brought two of Langer's close colleagues, the economist Edward S. Mason, who moved over from a wartime assignment with the Office of Production Management, and the French historian Donald C. McKay. They also requisitioned the intellectual services of Edward Mead Earle, a military and diplomatic historian at the Institute for Advanced Study; Joseph Hayden, Chair of the Department of Government at the University of Michigan; and another economist, Calvin Bryce Hoover, Professor and Dean of the Graduate School of Duke University. Although the Board of Analysts comprised a diverse body of mature scholars, influential within the academic world and beyond it, several common themes make it possible to discuss them at least as a corporate entity, if not a general staff.

Most obviously, their very presence on the governing body of R&A indicates that these men were marked by a personal sense of duty in a time of crisis, but several of them clearly believed that civic responsibility extended to the academic scholar as such. Mason had already placed his technical training in the service of numerous commissions and federal agencies, and he was sharply critical of the economics profession to the extent that it had acquiesced throughout the thirties in "the 'business as usual' mentality which has impeded the war effort in all the democracies."[7] If Edward Earle differed, it was only in the degree of stridency with which he rallied his fellow scholars. From the beginning Earle had foreseen that this was a war that would "invade the classrooms of our colleges [and] rustle the thumbed pages of our scholars,"[8] and he argued that only a total academic mobilization could meet the challenges that lay ahead. Drawing upon a legacy that reached backwards from the American Federalists through Machiavelli to Plato and Aristotle, the editor of the classic *Makers of Modern Strategy* argued that America lacked "a reserve of trained scholars" who had addressed themselves professionally to "the study of military problems as an inherent factor in the science of government and politics."[9]

This exhortation was based on an implicit sociology of knowledge that was substantially shared by his colleagues: whereas the military officer is in effect a technician, necessarily excluded from questions of policy and politics, the community of scholars floats free of all particular interests and, as citizens of the transcendental republic of letters, its members can "speak as individuals without fear, favor, or bias."[10] Earle's belief in the independence of the intellectual from any interest but "the cause of scholarship and the welfare of the nation" was characteristic of the academic generation that had come to maturity during the ordeal of World War I. Although it would be challenged by the postwar theoretical labors of their students, under the emergency conditions of war it facilitated the passage across the Great Divide that separated university from government service.

A second, more explicitly political motivation moved these conservative gentlemen to descend from the heights of pure scholarship, namely, an early and unhesitating advocacy of American intervention. The German invasion of Russia would render this position unexceptional, but in the context of the agonized political debates of the 1930s, when their own universities were being shaken by the oddly convergent demands of right-wing isolationists and left-wing anti-imperialists, it represented a highly deliberate stance. The interventionist argument was grounded in a characteristically conservative political disposition that assimilated fascist Germany and the Soviet Union into a single, undifferentiated threat from "totalitarianism," best represented in Calvin Hoover's pre-war writings on comparative economic systems.

Once cured of his youthful socialist proclivities, Hoover too believed himself to have been elevated to "a sort of social extra-territoriality" that enabled him to serve as professor, administrator, government advisor, and publicist "without allegiance to any economic or social class."[11] His politics, he intimated, derived objectively from the empirical researches he had conducted in the Soviet Union (1929–30), in Germany during the first year of the dictatorship, and, as an economic consultant, in the New Deal program of the Agricultural Adjustment Administration. The data indicated to him that, except in periods of acute market instability, state intervention in a national economy leads invariably to authoritarian management of society as well. Whatever may be said of the validity of these conclusions—and of their claims to "free-floating extra-territoriality"—they reflect the experience and the values of a generation of scholars that emerged in the age of Stalin, Mussolini, and Hitler.

Finally, in addition to these sociological and ideological commitments, one may discern in the prewar writings of the Board of Analysts elements of a broadly shared view of the dynamics of the international system. William L. Langer, the original Director of Research and one of the outstanding American representatives of a conservative neo-Rankean diplomatic historiography, most fully articulated a conception of national interest as the invisible hand which, unobstructed by distortions of a "sentimental or ideological" character, acted to maintain the stability of the international political order. Bismarck had been the master of this game, which needed only to be tempered by American democratic ideals to provide intellectual legitimacy to a politics of interventionism: "We who thought once more to wash our hands of responsibility and to stand aloof from the European mess may well in these cataclysmic days return to Woodrow Wilson."[12] The paramount interest of the United States, under the present circumstances, was to prevent—by any means necessary—the domination of Europe by a single power, and this translated into a vigorous call to arms, "lest German dreams come true."[13]

Fortified behind these intellectual and political defenses—and anchored to the larger war effort by the counsel of Army Lt. Col. J. Y. Smith, Naval Commander Frances C. Denebrink, and John C. Wiley of the Treasury Department—the superstructure of the Research and Analysis Branch thus fell into place. From late summer 1941 until its dissolution in November 1943, the Board of Analysts met regularly on Tuesday and Thursday mornings to discuss, in addition to the progress of the war in Europe and Asia, the evolving structure of the Branch, the coordination of the intelligence services it hoped to provide, and the resocialization of the staff of academic researchers they had recruited to carry it out.[14]

· · ·

In the first phase of its campaign, the Board of Analysts set out to recruit a corps of veteran academicians to administer the separate regional and functional subdivisions of the Branch—a delicate process, because one's standing in the academic world, as experience would show, was not necessarily an indication of the intellectual adaptability, political acumen, and practical administrative sense required of these positions. Still, the American universities offered the most obvious pool of expertise in the techniques of research and analysis. From the History Department at Yale, Baxter brought Sherman Kent to organize a Political Group that would grow into the sprawling Europe–Africa Division. Conyers Read was furloughed by the University of Pennsylvania to direct research on the British Empire and Cornell contributed its tough-minded Russian historian Geroid T. Robinson to the USSR Division. Rudolph Winnacker came down from Harvard to organize a "flamboyant and happy-go-lucky outfit" of self-trained Africa specialists; Ralph Bunche moved over from Howard University to handle "the subjects of colonial policy and administration, native problems, and race relations" within the British Empire; and Maurice Halperin, one of the more outspoken leftists in the organization, monitored the political mood of Latin America from an office strewn with back issues of the *Daily Worker*. Before the first year was over, the faculty had mushroomed to over forty professional historians and ultimately came to include such influential scholars as Crane Brinton, John K. Fairbank, and at least six other future presidents of the American Historical Association. A mobile division of distinguished economists, commanded by Mason, Emile Despres, and Chandler Morse, and including five future AEA presidents and a Nobel Laureate, followed not far behind. In time they would be joined in Washington by leading representatives of newly militarized disciplines ranging from geography to philology and represented in a dozen OSS outposts overseas by influential scholars including the anthropologist Gregory Bateson at Kandy, the sociologist Edward Shils at London, and the historian Perry Miller at Wiesbaden in occupied Germany.[15]

If the eastern academic grapevine had provided the sole means of recruitment, the OSS could still have boasted a professoriate of a distinction to which any university might well aspire. It is very much to the credit of these established gentlemen, however, and to their insight into the complexity of the task that awaited them, that they did not set out to construct an organization in their own collective image. To the contrary, as several units of academic irregulars were pressed into service, the Research and Analysis Branch came to shelter a community of scholars without precedent in modern intellectual history.

The elders of the Branch, as tradition dictated, first set out to place their most promising graduate students in positions of responsibility throughout the agency, and it was by virtue of this sustained exercise in intellectual nepotism that a generation of gifted young scholars acquired a unique postgraduate apprenticeship in *Weltpolitik*. From Harvard, Langer drafted his dissenting doctoral student Carl Schorske, McKay recalled to active duty his recent PhDs David Pinkney and H. Stuart Hughes, and Edward Mason hired Walt W. Rostow as his personal assistant and recruited former students of the caliber of Moses Abramowitz, Sidney Alexander, and his radical teaching apprentice Paul Sweezy, who, because of his well-known political position, had first to be interviewed by General Donovan himself: "I told him that I was a socialist more-or-less like Laski and Nye Bevan. The only thing he was interested in was whether I was in favor of throwing bombs and street rioting. I assured him that I was not, which seemed to satisfy him."[16]

When the immediate reserve was exhausted, letters went out from the senior scholars of the Branch to their civilian colleagues around the country inquiring after "a few good boys who will ruin their health for about $2000 *per annum* . . . and who are mentally flexible enough to learn new things rapidly and with enthusiasm."[17] Then, as now, the Old Boys answered the call, supplying "Bill" Langer and "Shermo" Kent with lists of graduate students and recent PhDs whom they deemed to be possessed of the requisite qualities and qualifications. The collapse of the wartime academic job market, the prospect of serving the war effort a safe distance from the front lines, and many shades of intense political commitment enabled the Research and Analysis Branch to conscript an outstanding class of freshman analysts: the historical scholars Arthur Schlesinger, Jr., Gordon Craig, and Franklin Ford, whose provocations to American intellectual life are well known; the economists Charles Kindleberger, Carl Kaysen, and Abram Bergson, who would greatly stimulate their profession both within and outside of the university; and many others—Leonard Krieger, Norman O. Brown, Morris Janowitz, Barrington Moore, Jr.—whose work is familiar throughout the scholarly world. "We find that people with youth, good training, pliability of mind, and a lot of intellectual curiosity can learn the game from scratch in a rather short period of time," wrote Sherman Kent to fellow historian Raymond Sontag at Berkeley," and they are the ones I am most interested in."[18]

In the spring of 1943, as the tide was turning in favor of the Allied armies, OSS began a third recruiting drive whose results were, if anything, even more astonishing. Although Baxter had declared himself to be "personally opposed to the employment of enemy aliens in this branch," Langer recognized at the outset that the community of refugee scholars in America offered yet another reserve of skilled experts, fluent in the European languages, immersed in the intricacies of party politics, sensitive to cultural nuances, and attuned to points of strength, weakness, and resistance in enemy and enemy-occupied countries. Already in 1941 the Germanist Walter Dorn, first chief of the Europe–Africa Division's Central European Section, had taken the initiative of requesting from the exiled scholars of the International Institute for Social Research at Columbia a list of experts on Germany to be found within the refugee community. "That is not an easy assignment," wrote Franz Neumann in reply, "since it is obviously difficult for me to be fully objective," but he was nonetheless quick to nominate an impressive cast of specialists, beginning with his own immediate colleagues: Max Horkheimer, Theodor W. Adorno, Friedrich Pollock, Herbert Marcuse, Otto Kirchheimer, Leo Löwenthal, and Arkadij Gurland, "whose knowledge of the ramifications between business and politics exceeds my own."[19] Reaching outward, Neumann proposed the names of Bertold Brecht and Siegfried Kracauer to cover culture and propaganda, Paul Tillich and Heinrich Brüning of the defunct Catholic Center Party to monitor religious life under the Nazis, Bauhaus director Walter Gropius to analyze wartime housing and urban development, and an illustrious corps of other *Landsmänner* more or less precariously settled in the United States. Although not all of these celebrities found their way into government service, the historical imagination reels at this Who's Who of Weimar luminaries and at the radical tendencies with which the American intelligence establishment flirted in its headstrong youth.

In the following months, these and other members of the antifascist emigration bombarded the OSS with applications, manuscripts, and research proposals calculated, they insisted, to help win the war. Marcuse sent to the Chief of the Psychology Division manuscripts he had written on "The New German Mentality" and "Private Morale in Germany"; Gurland delivered his findings on "Technical Trends and Economic Structure under National Socialism"; Heinz Paechter followed with his pioneering study of "Magic Thought and Magic Grammar in Totalitarian Propaganda"; from his new refuge at Smith College the conservative historian Hans Kohn, not to be outdone, warned that "the time is short [and] the essential thing at present is not to draw up memoranda, to do research, or to sit in committees," and proposed instead a lecture tour designed to prepare the home front "for a war of unprecedented dimensions and consequences." Neumann himself offered to place at the disposal of Colonel Donovan's office his Institute's "rich and up-to-date collection of National Socialist literature," as well as the profiles of German business leaders he had assembled in the course of his own research.

It was many months before matters of politics and nationality made it possible for OSS to draw upon the pool of refugee scholars so obligingly supplied by Hitler, but by mid-1943 the Europe–Africa Division sheltered "a staff of Jewish scribblers"[20] of extraordinary scholarly achievement and political sophistication: Franz Neumann, Herbert Marcuse, Otto Kirchheimer, Friedrich Pollock, and Arkadij Gurland of the International Institute for Social Research; Hajo Holborn and Felix Gilbert, the two outstanding representatives of a tradition of German historiography with its roots in Meinecke, Burckhardt, and Ranke; the art historian Richard Krautheimer, the jurist Henry Kellerman, and the "brilliant but erratic" Marxist economist Paul A. Baran. Occasionally the foreign-born contributed to the Branch skills other than those of the academic scholar: the naturalized American Eugene Fodor (of the famous guidebook series) had listed his operative languages as "Czech, English, French, Flemish, German, Hungarian, Polish, Serbo-Croatian, and Slovak" before he ran out of space on the personnel form. And when the Branch required a specially outfitted War Room, it turned for its design to the Finnish-born Eero Saarinen, tucked away in the Visual Presentations unit and already one of the most daring architects of his generation.[21]

Collectively, the foreign legion that encamped in the corridors of R&A represented an extraordinary coup for the agency. Although they were barred from holding positions of administrative authority—and although at least one German refugee was denounced to the FBI as a suspected Fifth Columnist for producing sobering economic estimates allegedly calculated to undermine the war effort—these loyal enemy aliens were often able to redirect investigations that had veered off course or were hampered by reliance on the obsolete textbook from which an American scholar-analyst might have been teaching for years. Franz Neumann, one of the most sophisticated of the "political scholars" of the emigration, could review a draft on the German Security Service (SD) with a uniquely close eye for detail: "The document contains certain errors. The historical sequence is off . . . The analysis is not quite correct . . . The chart is inaccurate . . . The plural of *Amt* is *Ämter* and not *Amts.*"[22] And when a report on the composition of a committee of jurists appointed by the Military Governor of Frankfurt caught his notice, he proved a more immediate source of intelligence than the most intrepid foreign agent: "In view of the fact that I studied law in Frankfurt-am-Main, spent my *referendar* period there and was, for some months, judge of the legal court, I think it important to add a few notes to the biographies. . . . From this information you may gather that, with [one] possible exception . . . the Committee does not contain one single anti-Nazi."[23] The foreign accent provided by the émigré analysts to this shadow university enriched the intellectual life of OSS as much as it did the various civilian fields of art, science, and scholarship that were exposed to it. They disputed the originality of Cicero in the corridors ("A synthesizer! An elegant synthesizer, but a synthesizer!"), spiced their memoranda with the occasional dash of *Germanistik* ("The report is certainly too sentimental and too naive."), and registered their cultural dislocation in various other ways. "Stupidly enough I am not allowed to give you the name of the author of this report," complained Felix Gilbert about the Anglo-American philosophy of cable security, "but it was written by a participant of the conference and Marcuse's knowledge of dialectics might lead him to discover who the author is." Surveying his cosmopolitan domain, Chief Eugene Anderson was heard to remark that "in the Central European Section the *lingua franca* is broken English."[24]

Three discernible intellectual communities thus merged in the Research and Analysis Branch. First was a body of established American scholars at midcareer, broadly conservative in political outlook but motivated by a fierce detestation of the fascist regimes and a willingness to get "about as close as a civilian can come to the war."[25] They were supported by a disciplined regiment of younger scholars—graduate students and recent PhDs—who would gain in the Branch an extraordinary training in applied social science and who would redirect the course of postwar scholarship in a dozen disciplines. And finally, R&A sheltered an eccentric airborne division raised from what George Mosse has called the "community of the uprooted," refugee scholars of theoretical disposition, leftist orientation, and massive erudition. Other members of the American academic community sought in their own ways to assist in the war effort: Arthur O. Lovejoy and Talcott Parsons were among the "civilian" scholars to submit proposals to R&A that reflected their research priorities, and pressing assignments were on occasion simply subcontracted out to university departments.[26] The diversified in-house staff was generally more than adequate to its tasks, however, for it represented an assemblage of intellectual ability without precedent in the annals of modern government. It is not easy to characterize the international brigade of antifascist scholars who made up the Research and Analysis Branch, but the remark of one alumnus of the German Section seems particularly apposite: "Das Office of Strategic Services war ein seltsames Gebild,"[27] recalled John Herz—the OSS was a singular entity.

The Epistemology of Intelligence

While other branches of OSS were cultivating their public image as coteries of socialites and adventurers, official Washington was more concerned about the Research and Analysis Branch, whose presumed leftist coloration threatened to stain the entire agency. Throughout the government R&A was viewed as a cadre of academic radicals incapable of producing objective intelligence estimates in the context of an intensely politicized war. In Central Europe they were alleged "to care for little but socialist parties and trade unions"; in the Far Eastern theater they were suspected to be "politically unreliable and possibly anti-KMT"; in the Balkans no less than an American ambassador registered his feeling that "R&A reports are slanted toward the left and are anti-British."[28] In actuality, R&A spanned a political spectrum that ranged in hue literally from Stalinism to blue-blooded Republicanism. The documentary evidence, however—and the virtually unanimous testimony of its alumni—suggest that overtly ideological differences tended to be submerged within a shared set of overriding purposes.

From the very outset, Langer had been instructed to regard the Branch as a service organization whose "sole purpose" was to transform raw intelligence data into concise, factual, and rigorously objective analyses for the use of government agencies, and "not to suggest, recommend, or in any way determine the strategy or the tactical decisions of the war."[29] OSS had entered a crowded field, and just as Donovan had been cautioned that the mere use of the word "strategic" in its name could condemn it to a military court-martial, Langer was warned that the established State Department desks entitled to participate in the policy-making process would tolerate no competition from his upstart seminar of displaced academicians.

Even within OSS "the 'cloak-and-dagger boys' felt that the 'long-haired researchists' were owlishly impractical" and altogether too modest in their presentations.[30] Langer's staff had been advised, however, that "there is no future in R&A as a pressure group," and that on the first suspicion of pleading a special cause, "we will very soon lose our entree to all policy-makers other than those already committed to the same special cause."[31] Opportunities to influence policy would arise, but only insofar as those authorized to decide policy had confidence in the quality, integrity, and impartiality of their work. In the face of this hostility, and in order to win a clientele for its goods, it was a matter literally of life and death that R&A gain a reputation for its disinterested professionalism as much as for the sheer excellence of its work.

Without the secure patronage of some entrenched constituency, the only protection available to the Branch was the invisible mantle of social scientific objectivity and the cultivation of "what might be called a clinical attitude." Accordingly, it was on the terrain of methodology and epistemology that the professors fought some of their most decisive engagements. Political disputes and internal tensions existed within the Branch, but they were characteristically transposed from the substantive problems of strategic planning into formal questions of a hermeneutic or "meta-interpretive" character.

Remarkably, a theoretically explicit inquiry into the nature of objectivity, resting on "some basic analysis of the whole process of scientific thought in the social field," was sustained throughout the entire wartime history of the Branch.[32] The "official" position derived precisely from the fields in which the senior American scholars of R&A were such eminent practitioners, namely, "that area of knowledge usually referred to as social science."[33] Across these disciplines the antinomies of fact and value, scholarship and partisanship with which Max Weber had struggled so heroically had been largely resolved and (to paraphrase Edmund Burke) the age of sociologists, economists, and calculators had succeeded. Nor did this purification imply an inherent conservatism, for had not the radical wing of the Vienna Circle itself pointed out how the toleration of "metaphysics" had facilitated acceptance of the irrationalist premises of fascism? Just as the political credibility of the R&A Branch rested upon its image of disinterested professionalism, the epistemological credibility of the disciplines represented in it was held to rest on a positivist standard of objectivity that could be defined in theory even if only approximated in practice.

To an impressive degree, the Research and Analysis Branch appreciated the need to present a common face to the outside world and was able to do so even on such divisive issues as strategic bombing or the prosecution of war criminals. The cautious academics of R&A, unaccustomed to committing themselves in print to a position before all the data had been scrutinized through the magnifying lens of critical scholarship, learned to "accept the fact . . . that you cannot indefinitely postpone the decisions of war" and that finally the "debating society" must be adjourned and decisions made on the basis of the available information.[34] Political battles were indeed fought—between champions of de Gaulle and Giraud, Mihailovich and the Partisans, the USSR and Poland—but as the Research and Analysis Branch consolidated its position, these came increasingly to be displaced to a rhetorical plane. At issue were seemingly "academic" questions of style and substance, authorship and readership, the silent tropes of persuasion and the political limits of scholarship, and other features of what the successor generation has designated "the content of the form."

To safeguard the purity of the neophyte agency and enforce the protocols of language, truth, and logic upon which its reputation depended, a Projects Committee was created in July 1942 as the executive arm of the Board of Analysts. The Committee was chaired by Richard Hartshorne, a hard-headed geographer from the University of Wisconsin whose last book, not insignificantly, had been a massive historical survey intended to secure "a sound basis on which geography may develop" as a rigorous science.[35] Assisted by a grammatical police force of editors, translators, and secretaries, the charge of this tribunal was to determine research priorities, monitor the procedures according to which specific studies were executed, and approve for distribution those finished reports that had been cleared of grammatical "pecadilloes," "stylistic misdemeanors," and outright "crimes against objectivity." Hartshorne's directives to his academic colleagues, models of what has been called "the rhetoric of anti-rhetoric," managed to be simultaneously pointed and blunt: "Intelligence reports find their literary merit in terseness and clarity rather than in expressive description . . . Proust, Joyce, or Gertrude Stein would all be equally out of place in R&A."[36]

Even those members of the faculty most sympathetically disposed toward this flat and dispassionate prose were obliged to abandon enshrined academic practices. Research scholars accustomed to the admittedly limited celebrity of their learned journals had to suffer the anonymity of a report number, the ignominy of a classification stamp, and the indignity of a controlled distribution list. The suppression of footnotes, those most lethal weapons in the arsenal of scholarship, was a security requirement to which the professoriate of the USSR Division in particular was never fully reconciled. And the received division of intellectual labor, which compartmentalized and departmentalized the world into reified academic categories, had to be repudiated in favor of a collaborative and interdisciplinary practice based upon the principle that "in connection with total war, the traditional distinctions between political, economic, and military data have become almost entirely blurred."[37] Already during the war Langer had threatened, in a warning shot fired across the bow of the Social Science Research Council, that "such members of the staff as may return to academic life will never be able to view their teaching or research in the narrow way which was all too common."[38] Indeed, the challenge to the cloistered scholasticism of academic thought may well prove to be the most enduring legacy of the Research and Analysis Branch.

To neutralize the subtle strategies of persuasion with which every writer is familiar, a variety of rather crude and superficial editorial measures were applied. Writing was filtered for the auxiliary verbs 'ought,' 'should,' "and above all 'must' "; subjective inflections posing as the views

of unnamed foreign sources were ruthlessly exposed; impolitic insin-
uations were discreetly withdrawn, and reports were shorn of embel-
lishments of no relevance to officers in the field presumed to be short
on time and philological training. "In the writing of reports, one is expected to turn out thoroughly objective and neutral intelligence," instructed the young Arthur Schlesinger, Jr. "There should be no personal
pronouns, no wisecracks, no slang or clichés, and care should be taken
about the use of color words such as 'reactionary,' 'progressive,' 'left
or right,' etc."[39] The Projects Committee, whose directives seem alone
to have been exempted from the procedures they themselves directed,
reinforced the sentiment: "It may be true that 'with consistency a great
soul has simply nothing to do,' but the less soul in government reports
the better."[40] More recalcitrant than these habitual sleights-of-scholarly-
hand, however, were basic questions pertaining to the rhetoric of analysis
that eluded the stern gaze of the Projects Committee; their survival in
the official documentary record invites a level of analysis to which government reports are not customarily subjected.

At one level, R&A was expected to redress the dearth of strategic
intelligence available to the government through the collection, classification, and evaluation of raw information, and in this they were by all
accounts inordinately successful. One of the early achievements of this
first generation of American intelligence analysts was to demonstrate
that it was possible to secure the greater part of this vital intelligence
not by dropping behind enemy lines but by walking over to the Library
of Congress, where they did what scholars do best, namely, plodding
through journals, monographs, foreign newspapers, and other published
sources. Operations of this sort required nerves of steel,—"Shelves are
empty. Card catalogues indicate that certain books exist, but librarians
are not allowed to say where the books are [or] who is using them"[41]—
but few agents were lost while conducting them. When this procedure
was extended to the network of OSS bases overseas, and supplemented
by censorship intercepts, diplomatic cables, and materials purloined by
the Secret Intelligence Branch, it yielded impressive results. By the end
of 1944, R&A had collected 100,000 documents, assembled perhaps the
finest map collection in the world, and composed on the basis of these
materials a series of up-to-date country handbooks and regional surveys
that were widely acclaimed for their value in strategic planning and
military operations.

It would be remarkable, however, if the innovative research scholars of the Branch did not grow impatient with pedestrian labors of a sort which, in more ordered times, would be assigned to graduate students and research assistants. Moreover, as this spadework proceeded it became clear that there were many analysts who, quite apart from the indignity of such menial labor, "are disdainful of the encyclopedic approach and who insist that the mere gathering of facts is a useless occupation."[42] A significant faction of the professional staff, believing that data do not exist outside of an interpretive framework, resisted the empiricist assumption that the only path to the Holy Grail of objectivity lay in ordering supposedly raw data into an accessible and readily usable form rather than the evaluation of "objective possibilities" inherent in given situations. The implications of this concept can be perceived in the 2,000 R&A Reports produced by the Branch over the course of its four-year history, many of which achieved an extraordinary level of intellectual creativity tempered by scholarly rigor. In contrast with its laborious compilations of "raw" background information, this vast body of "cooked" intelligence, which offers a unique running commentary on the world-historical events of 1941–1945, was largely ignored during the war, as it has been since the end of it.

· · ·

The Research and Analysis Branch prepared analytical reports on a bewildering range of problems: the condition of rail transport on the Russian front, the relation between aggression and business structure during the Weimar Republic, attitudes of the Roman Catholic Church in Hungary, the political ideas of Charles de Gaulle, the looting and damaging of artworks, the location of concentration camps in central Europe.[43] Regional specialists studied the Communist Party of India and the puppet regime in Nanking, inflation in Burma and guerillas in the Philippines, trade routes in the Congo basin and rival cliques in the Japanese Army. Historians searched for precedents in the annals of World War I, while economists extrapolated forward to anticipate the consequences of a "hard" peace. Anthropologists studied Japanese films and psychologists listened in the speeches of Goebbels for parapraxes offering clues to impending military offensives. Many of these reports display daring leaps of logical deduction or ingenious methodological procedures that would be formalized only in postwar economic, sociological, or historiographical theory. Many of them were also dead wrong in their predictions and misguided in their formulations. As limited as their value may have been to the Joint Chiefs of Staff, however, they lose none of their significance for intellectual history, for as Foucault has demonstrated, "a sentence cannot be non-significant";[44] it refers to something—even if no more than the presumptions of its author—by virtue of its very existence.

Those finished papers that passed the scrutiny of the various editorial agencies of the Branch constitute an impressive body of work but reflect little of the process by which they took shape. Fully and fairly to assess the accomplishments of R&A, and to interpret its significance in the careers of the academic scholars it comprised, we must supplement analysis of the finished products by consulting the vast literary residue of the Branch: unedited drafts, memoranda, minutes of committees, cablegrams, administrative files, field reports, cover letters, and more. These residual strata, excavated mostly from the National Archives of the United States, offer documentary testimony to the conditions of intellectual production that prevailed within the Branch—including the production of a new kind of intellectual who, like Emerson's ideal of the American Scholar, "grudges every opportunity of action passed by as a loss of power."

The analysts of OSS were in the business, literally, of inventing a new mode of political writing, and within the United States, at least, neither the universities nor the government were able to offer up any sort of useful models. Their ostensible goal was to survey the political landscape and describe the present situation—with apologies to Ranke— "as it was actually happening." This objectivist program admitted of realization only insofar as their writing could be purified of all elements of subjectivity or, failing that, by settling upon a set of assumptions that were at least grounded in some objective criterion such as stated war aims or published articles of foreign policy. "This view, of course, is founded on a crude conception of the intellectual processes which go into the analysis of events," remarked one dissident, "but somewhat more important than its epistemological naiveté is its practical unworkability,"[45] given the inevitable shifts of American policy and the divisiveness that existed even at the highest levels of government.

No enforceable standard of objectivity ever rose above this "epistemological naiveté," but since the credibility and even survivability of R&A seemed to hang in the balance, controversy over it never fully abated. For example, a writer might estimate that a certain posthostilities program in Germany would likely result in a "serious lack of calorie intake" or "grave deficiency in heating fuel," but even such bland observations as these assumed that all potential readers of the document would be in prior agreement that the citizens of postwar Germany should be well-fed and well-housed and that Germany as a whole should be treated like any other member of the family of nations. *"These assumptions are not permissable,"* thundered the Projects Committee; "We are not concerned with the fact that millions of Germans may not get enough of the right kind of food to be healthy, but are only concerned with what those millions may do in whatever efforts they may make to get more."[46]

The Projects Committee, then, fought a rear-guard battle to enforce in practice the objectivist standard of political reporting called for by the positivist theory to which the directorate of the Branch subscribed. (Not as a mere antiquarian did Langer boast that his most prized possession was a 50-volume set of the writings of Leopold von Ranke, snatched up for a song in Leipzig during the German inflation.)[47] From the trenches, analysts countered that in its eternal vigilance the Committee had come to serve as a check on intellectual initiative and that "its mandatory preoccupation with form often led it to interference with content." "What evidence is there for this damning charge?" demanded Hartshorne, and then provided it himself by deleting the charge of "legalistic and negativisitic censorship" from an internal memorandum.[48] The dream of a pure and presuppositionless logic, abandoned already in the thirties by Husserl and on whose ruins the major positions of postwar philosophy would rise, endured some of its most rigorous reality-testing in the wartime Office of Strategic Services.

Thus was a fierce campaign waged to neutralize political agents operating not behind the lines but between them. Nor was it wholly unsuccessful, and for that reason alone it would be inadmissible to suggest that a finished report has the same authorial status as a signed article published in the *Journal of Modern History* or the *American Economic Review.* It is nevertheless doubtful that even the most professional observer was able to gaze upon the horrific events of the 1940s with what Ruskin called "the innocence of the eye." The weight of a classical humanistic education, training in the epistemology of the social sciences, the urgency of the war, and even "the relative paucity of objective adjectives in our language" were among the factors that conspired to rescue them from the *schlechte Unendlichkeit,* that infinite logical regress that Hegel had dreaded in his private philosophical warfare against an earlier European dictator. Late in the day, when the war in Europe had been won but the struggle to pacify the discourse of intelligence was still raging, the young Stuart Hughes nearly gave away the game. Overt statements of criticism or counsel should be superfluous, he advised; "The report, if written clearly and concisely, can carry its own message."[49]

In R&A a generation of younger humanist scholars gained their first experience of the now-canonical wisdom that facts do not speak for themselves through a language of protocol-sentences that is transparent and politically neutral and that leaves no value-laden residue on the "objective reality" it sets out to describe. This lesson was never fully mastered by the OSS, much less by the CIA, the wayward stepchild born of its ashes in 1947. But by then the lesson was already finding its way back into the academic world of teaching and scholarship to which the professoriate of the Branch was beating a hasty retreat.

The Organization of Research and Analysis

The Research and Analysis Branch was structurally differentiated along several different axes: its internal functional organization, the geographical distribution of its activities, and a temporal axis, determined by the course of the war, along which its work of strategic analysis proceeded. It remains only to describe the organization of the Branch as it developed in space and in time and in spirit.

After R&A had outgrown successive lodgings in the new Library of Congress annex, the Apex Building at the eastern tip of the Federal Triangle, and an abandoned ice skating rink, it settled finally into an apartment house at the corner of 23rd Street and E, not far from the main headquarters of the OSS. From this Washington address, Baxter and then Langer commanded a regiment of professional, clerical, and military personnel that would grow to well over 900 persons before the war was over. The Chief of R&A was responsible to Brigadier General John Magruder, one of four Deputy Directors who reported directly to William Donovan (Chart 1).

Within his own fiefdom, however, Langer reigned with absolute sovereignty and moved quickly to suppress movements toward regional autonomy. Langer's own Deputy Director was Edward Mason—in practice they were co-directors for political and economic intelligence, respectively—and he had a personal staff of four politically astute special assistants: Carl Schorske, his all-around trouble-shooter, pinch-hitter, and point man; William Applebaum for Branch security; John D. Wilson for relations with R&A units in OSS outposts overseas; and Hajo Holborn for military liaison once the planning of the Civil Affairs program was launched in May 1943. Between the Office of the Chief and the regional and functional intelligence divisions sat the governing Board of Analysts and the Projects Committee.

The Research and Analysis Branch survived two major reorganizations in its lifetime. First was the post-Pearl Harbor rationalization that created the streamlined OSS out of its cumbersome predecessor, the COI. A second, begun early in 1943, had the effect of binding the research sections together in ways that reflected the regional theaters of operation rather than the inherited academic division of labor. This was one of the most portentous administrative decisions of its history, but also the most traumatic, for it violated the received wisdom that the world is organized in the manner of a university catalogue. So deeply entrenched was this academic world view that Langer declared himself in retrospect to be "rather astonished that the whole branch did not break down under the strain."[50] In the course of this administrative upheaval, the disciplinary walls behind which the original Economic, Geographical, and Psychological (Political) divisions had been sequestered were battered down, and the "functionalists" were forced into a framework dictated by the patently interdisciplinary realities of the European and Asian theaters. Academic specialists, socialized in the disciplinary heritage as old (or as recent) as Humboldt and von Stein, were a long while establishing an accommodation with colleagues of greater or lesser claims to scientificity, and many of the economists in particular declared that they would not serve under or even with political scientists or historians. By forcing a degree of cross-disciplinary collaboration, however, the reform of January 1943 harnessed the latent epistemological ferment and enabled them to transcend the bounds of traditional scholarship and to bring to bear all types of knowledge on problems of a particular region, with dazzling results.

The warring disciplines thus met each other in an academic no-man's land, and the basic work of research and analysis was henceforth carried out by the staffs of four regional divisions, each of which had functional subdivisions assigned to particular technical matters: the Europe–Africa Division directed by Sherman Kent, who was assisted by Harold Deutsch, Chandler Morse, and E. A. Ackerman for political, economic, and topographic intelligence, respectively; the Far East Division, directed by Charles Remer and subdivision chiefs G. G. Stelle, Charles Fahs, and Joseph Spencer; and smaller divisions responsible for the Soviet Union (Geroid T. Robinson, assisted by Bernadotte Schmitt, Wassily Leontief, and J. A. Morrison) and Latin America (Preston James and Maurice Halperin). Resources for these four regional divisions were provided by four others: a Map Division collected and produced maps and topographic models; the Central Information Division coordinated the collection of reference materials, pictorial records, and biographical data on thousands of foreign notables; a Current Intelligence Staff oversaw the publication of a series of highly regarded periodicals produced by the Branch; and the Interdepartmental Committee handled the coordination of R&A with other agencies (Charts 2 and 3).

The structure of R&A/Washington, as the main campus was called, was recapitulated ontogenetically but on a proportionately smaller scale by about a dozen Research and Analysis units that were attached to the OSS network of overseas outposts. By far the largest of these was the London Outpost (R&A/London), set up in April 1942 to provide Washington with a listening post to the Continent and to establish direct lines of cooperation with the myriad agencies of British intelligence. Its early governance by the investment banker Shepard Morgan helped give it the reputation as a cabal of "eastern and moneyed Republicans" that so delighted Thomas Pynchon, but by the time its direction finally came to rest with Chandler Morse (in February 1944), R&A/London had survived "a period of free-for-all pioneering expansion"[51] and had settled into a program of political and especially economic intelligence reporting that brought the Branch as near as it ever came to influencing actual military strategy (Chart 4). Elsewhere on the European continent, R&A units were operating successfully out of missions in neutral Stockholm and Bern, where Allen Dulles ran a one-man espionage ring about which many yarns have been spun.

The general pattern, as the European war progressed, was for the Research and Analysis Branch to dispatch units into liberated territories as soon as possible after they had been secured, from which agents immediately began to churn out dispatches, cablegrams, and "Field Intelligence Studies" on everything from the attitudes of Catholics and Communists to supplies of fuel and footwear. Starting in the Algiers, where Rudolph Winnacker, Donald McKay, H. Stuart Hughes, John Sawyer, and a few other "applied historians" set up operations under the glow of Operation TORCH, R&A/METO followed the front in the Mediterranean Theater of Operations to way-stations in Bari, Caserta, and Rome, from which two R&A men finally managed to be picked up by the Germans. At the other end of the Mediterranean, outposts had been operating out of Cairo (under Moses Hadas) and Istanbul (under Dean Woodruff) to monitor political developments in the Balkans and throughout the Near East. In August 1944 an R&A office was set up under Harold Deutsch in liberated Paris, from which much of the planning took place for the final penetration of Germany itself, and by May of the following year R&A units were functioning in bases in Wiesbaden, Salzburg, Vienna, and amid the ruins of Berlin.

In the Far Eastern Theater of Operations several more academic stars shone brightly in the firmament of intelligence, although their work must fall outside the scope of this study. The anthropologists Cora DuBois and Gregory Bateson operated an important outpost in Ceylon (R&A/Kandy), Charles B. Fahs ran agents throughout India and Southeast Asia, and Joseph Spencer and John K. Fairbank were among some fifty China hands who shipped out to bases in the wartime capital at Chungking and later Kunming. Closer to home were stations in New York, concerned mainly with securing current information from refugees and returning travelers, and in San Francisco, where materials pertaining to the Far East and the impending occupation of Japan were assembled for transmission back to headquarters. Although the bulk of the finished reports produced by the Research and Analysis Branch were prepared by the teams of specialist scholars in Washington, they were heavily dependent upon the paramilitary research programs being carried out by the foreign intelligence teams overseas. Indeed, the precarious state of "outpost-home relations" under the difficult conditions of war was the bane of Langer's existence throughout his tenure as Chief of R&A, and it is to his efforts to secure regular communications with some 400 iconoclastic professionals scattered throughout Europe, Africa, and Asia that we owe the exceptionally detailed records of the overseas outposts that survive.

This organizational survey—as tedious but necessary as are most things bureaucratic—conveys a superficial sense of efficiency that is belied by the steady stream of complaints, grievances, and at least one collective "Grudge Manifesto" filed with the office of the Chief. "As this agency has increased in size the mechanization has taken on a nightmarish quality, in which the flow of the product over various wheels and travelling belts causes a tragic loss of effective power," warned one disgruntled worker on the academic assembly line, and another stressed the need to consider the special insecurities of professors in an organization that must of necessity be more tightly organized than a university faculty: "If each staff member is to be a cog in a machine, it is necessary to his well-being as a human individual that he feels himself a significant part of the machine, that he understand the purposes of the machine, and have some knowledge of what the machine as a whole is accomplishing."[52]

Even correctives of this sort do not reveal the full picture, however. In addition to the tough administrators and learned scholars whose work is the focus of the following chapters, R&A depended for its most elemental functioning on a clerical staff of whom it made extraordinary demands. The product of an intelligence agency is ultimately information, and the processing of the inconceivable volume of information that flowed into and out of the Branch fell, in the antediluvian age of carbon paper, fountain pens, and mimeograph machines, to a women's army corps of typists, secretaries, and filing clerks whom William Donovan tactfully called the "invisible apron strings of an organization which touched every theater of war."[53] The outpost correspondence to Washington frequently concluded with desperate pleas for clerical relief—"ten girls might not be too many, French and German should be a *sine qua non*"[54]—and a helpless gesture toward the chronically overworked staff of skilled typists was the standard rejoinder to complaints of delayed reports and missed deadlines. Although the initials at the bottom left-hand corner of some 4,000 cubic feet of typescript are frequently their only archival trace, no plausible account of the origins of American intelligence can take for granted the conditions that prevailed at what Marx called the "point of production."

Langer, if only in his memoirs, paid honest tribute to his reliance upon two successive secretaries, Mildred Brockdorff and Frances Douglas, who ran interference for this inexperienced administrator in addition to carrying out "regular" professional duties. Phoebe Morrison performed comparable services for Hajo Holborn, without which it is doubtful that the great historian would have survived his first nontextual encounter with the military. The secretary to Emile Despres, Chief of the Economic Subdivision, was expected to have sufficient technical expertise to prepare regular summaries of work completed and in progress within the department, while drawing up agendas for meetings, drafting correspondence, routing mail, directing inquiries, and more, all for a starting salary of $1,620 per year.[55] And the perils of war affected them no less than their male superiors. In September 1942 Roselene Honerkamp, as Administrative Secretary to Chandler Morse, made the hazardous journey across the Atlantic via Pan Am Seaplane to set up an office staff within the R&A outpost in London. A later flight, carrying Edward Mason and Harold Barnett, crashed at Gander, sparing the economists but killing other passengers seated closer to the front of the plane. Such acknowledgments as may have been accorded to these women, like those that often precede vast scholarly tomes, reveal little of the professional abilities required and expected of them.

Moreover, the women employed by the Research and Analysis Branch were not always relegated to vital if thankless secretarial duties, for it was in the nature of an agency whose history was partly a history of its own self-definition that roles often became inverted and functions fused. Beatrice Braude evolved from secretary to research aide to full participant in the work of the Central European Section, and she recalled her period of wartime service "with nostalgia and affection," even if it was repaid with years of official blacklisting during the McCarthy era. Inge Neumann and Annemarie Holborn, in defiance of a western archetype as old as Hektor and Andromache, accompanied their husbands to battle and fought bravely in the Biographical Records Section of R&A. Women in a number of the regional subdivisions also worked as equals: Helen Fisher on Czechoslovakia, the Russian literary scholar Vera Sondamirskaya Dunham on the USSR. In general, however, amid the many "rituals of cultural inversion" played out in the Branch, the subordination of the female staff was one that remained stubbornly intact. It took the outstanding performance of Janet Burns and Priscilla Redfield Roe, the first "professional women" taken on by the Political Intelligence Staff, to allay the "original masculine misgivings" expressed by their colleagues.[56] And Langer conceded in an unguarded moment that the Harvard anthropologist Cora DuBois "has done a superb job" as acting Chief of the R&A outpost at Kandy, "despite the handicap of her sex which alone makes it impossible to name her as head of the branch in the China–Burma theater."[57] "How explain the anger of the professors?" puzzled Virginia Woolf from a room of her own.

While Donovan's intercession could sometimes secure the reassignment back to OSS of young men who had been drafted out from under him, one of R&A's most vexing problems was that it never exercised sufficient clout to ensure on a regular basis that its best analysts would not be lost to more active military duty. It was a chronic fear that "if the present quality of the staff of R&A is allowed to degenerate in order to provide less than two hundred men for company sergeants, clerks, and junior officers, and their places are filled by women and older men of 2nd rate ability, the justification for the Branch will disappear."[58] Behind this revealing dilemma in the intellectual history of American intelligence lay the fact that specialized skills were required for which training could not be provided. Middle-aged academics, whom tenure had relieved of the burdens of scholarship, "cannot be used effectively in our work [for] they have lost both the aptitude for research and the flexibility to change to new habits of work." At the other end of the academic hierarchy, the ruling patriarchs of the Branch now discovered—to their understandable chagrin—that just the opposite situation prevailed and that "women in these fields have been restricted primarily to teaching rather than research and are not so well prepared for the work required."

Two decades of feminist theory have permanently altered the landscape of historical scholarship by demonstrating that history is not a uniform and passive oracle that pronounces impartially upon all who approach it but a mutable construct that is not only perceived but experienced differently by different classes of historical subjects. This is, of course, precisely the theme that exercised the theoreticians of the Research and Analysis Branch in their ongoing methodological self-examination. To a greater extent than they may have realized, however, it informed their practice as well.

· · ·

The preceding pages have sought to provide the framework of information and ideas that forms the background of the separate studies that follow. Philosophy, politics, and economics provide the central categories of these analyses, along with problems of theory and method and issues relating to the ways in which a disparate group of scholars navigated the sea change from intellectual to intelligence work. It is of the first importance to recognize that we are not dealing with a simple and direct "application" of refined theoretical programs to the exigencies of war but of a heavily mediated process in which the *forms* of academic training were at least as significant as the contents. Research procedures were often guided by intuitions that were only later formalized into coherent theories and methodologies, a significant measure of individual intellectual identity was always sacrificed to the collective work of research and analysis, and that, in turn, was always subordinated—in the last analysis, at any rate—to the official policies of the United States government.

Once this is clearly established, however, it remains possible to follow in detail the wartime careers of certain exemplary cohorts of the American and European intellectual communities that were mobilized by OSS and to locate the R&A episode as a *stage* and not merely an unwonted interruption in the larger careers of some of the most influential scholars of two generations. Just as they could not leave behind them such mentors as Hegel and Ranke, Marx and Keynes, when they were drafted into the intellectual commando outfit that was R&A, neither could they prevent their wartime experience in the Office of Strategic Services from accompanying them back to the university. There was not a uniform pattern to this reciprocal influence, however—although generational affinities seem to exist—and it is the task of the following chapters to analyze the diverse intellectual trajectories that may be traced back to this unprecedented moment in modern intellectual history.

The Frankfurt School Goes to War

*The Central European Section remains its brilliant but
incoherent, Teutonic, and maladministered self.*

Ens. Carl E. Schorske to
Harold Deutsch, October 26, 1944

The extremity of the Second World War fostered an untold number of
ad hoc coalitions, united fronts, and shotgun marriages between mis-
matched political partners: Polish patriots intrigued with Zionist refugees
in London; right-wing nationalists courted communist partisans in Paris;
and Soviet ministers in Moscow affirmed their solidarity with captured
German officers. One of the strangest of the political liaisons of the
1940s took place in Washington, D.C., where a cadre of the most outstanding Marxist scholars of the European emigration forged a tactical
alliance with the executive wing of the United States government. Franz
Neumann, Herbert Marcuse, and Otto Kirchheimer, leading theoreticians of the exiled Frankfurt Institute for Social Research, worked during
the war years in the Research and Analysis Branch of the Office of
Strategic Services—America's first central intelligence agency. Although
the extraordinary community of scholars which they joined would have
at best a limited influence on the prosecution of the war and the administration of the denazification and military government programs that
followed, they did contribute to an indisputably brilliant episode in the
history of ideas, of intellectuals, and of intelligence.

Hegel, Marx, and the Criticism of Arms

Neumann, Marcuse, and Kirchheimer had been drawn by rather different
routes into the orbit of Frankfurt's neo-Marxist Institut für Sozialforschung. All three had been affiliated with the left wing of the German
Social Democratic Party; but as the history of the Weimar Republic

demonstrates, this broadly defined socialist stance could admit of quite dissimilar theoretical and practical commitments. At Freiburg University, Marcuse had evolved an unorthodox synthesis of a Hegelian Marxism with Heidegger's fundamental ontology; it stressed the access provided by philosophy to a transcendent standard with which to criticize the deficient historical reality. By contrast, Neumann and Kirchheimer attacked the deficiencies of the historical world through a normative legal theory and with a degree of activist involvement in the trade-union movement quite uncharacteristic of Marcuse and the other central figures of the Institute.[1]

It would be precipitous, then, to view the three political scholars as simply exponents of a uniform "Critical Theory," as Institute director Max Horkheimer dubbed the theoretical program of the Frankfurt School. At the same time, it is clear that their association served as more than just a refuge when the new International Institute of Social Research reopened under the protection of Columbia University at the onset of the dictatorship. Late in the thirties, when the declining budget threatened Neumann's appointment, he protested that "I have so identified myself with the work of the Institute and with its theoretical foundations that leaving would be a terrible burden."[2] And Marcuse, in a remark that could have applied to all of them, observed in retrospect that within the Institute, "theoretical, political, and personal ties remained inextricably intertwined."[3] Throughout the 1930s, Neumann, Marcuse, and Kirchheimer contributed to the Institute's journal a series of investigations of what Marxists had traditionally regarded as the epiphenomenal realms of philosophy, politics, and the law. These studies reinforced one another and contributed decisively to the Frankfurt School's attempt to grasp the inner dialectics of the transition from the liberal to the fascist stage of monopoly capitalism.

In a series of challenges to the extremes of legal positivism and of a revived natural law theory, Franz Neumann developed a critique of formalistic theories of law and their vulnerability to arbitrariness and politicization. Abstract legal principles, he argued, operated legitimately only in social conditions supporting a large number of free and equal competitors. Under conditions of manifestly unequal competition, a theory that proclaims the legal equality of individual entrepreneur and monopolistic empire becomes a legal mask for the rule of the holders of real political and economic power. Under such circumstances the sonorous phrases of the law ring hollow: "What is decisive," Neumann countered, "is the status which the person actually holds in the society."[4]

Otto Kirchheimer expanded this conception with empirical studies of the functioning of the German courts in the early years of the dictatorship. The Nazis, he conceded ironically, had fulfilled the promises of their own propaganda and "closed the gap which, under the liberal era, had separated the provinces of law and morality."[5] The critique of this premature reconciliation of the antinomies of liberal thought, thematic for the Frankfurt School in general, was expressed with Kirchheimer's characteristic understatement: "The attempt of the [fascist] legislature and the judiciary to use the criminal law to raise the moral standards of the community appears, when measured by the results achieved, as a premature excursion by fascism into a field reserved for a better form of society."[6] More decisive, however, was his demonstration that the seeds of judicial self-destruction had been sown in the legal structure of the liberal order itself. A substantive normative content had already been smuggled into the putatively objective judicial practice of the Weimar Republic, and fascism only completed the politicization of justice by reducing the courts to a mere administrative bureaucracy and replacing jurisprudence with a "technical rationality" geared solely to the expeditious enforcement of Reich policy.

Hebert Marcuse, finally, extended the theory of the negation of the liberal stage of monopoly capitalism to its cultural forms and the logic that sustains them. In studies of leading concepts of philosophy, aesthetics, and even "objective" social science, he attempted to build a bridge of criticism between the positivist empiricism that engages the actual conditions of life but is incapable of transcending them and the concepts of idealist metaphysics that abstract from those conditions to an independent sphere of value from which they are incapable of returning. The consequences of these seemingly antithetical currents of thought were shown to be paradoxically the same: hypostatization of the given, and surrender before the increasingly brutal facts of the established reality. Science and philosophy, precisely because of their commitment to the formal autonomy of reason, became "free" to accept moral and political valuations imposed from outside. They are thus transformed into ideological instruments in the service of a society increasingly requiring the integration and coordination of all spheres of life.[7]

By the beginning of the war, then, a distinctive theory of the inner mechanism of fascism was already in place: politically neutral and ostensibly emptied of normative content, the legal, constitutional, and ideological principles enshrined under the liberal Republic had come increasingly to be applied in the interests of the de facto holders of political and economic power. The fascist attack against "bourgeois" law and philosophy was, then, an attack only at the level of ideology. In reality, the Nazis only called the system by its name and enforced the realities of domination with the unmediated apparatus of the authoritarian state. As Marcuse would write in retrospect, "If there was one matter about which the author . . . and his friends were *not* uncertain, it was that the fascist state was fascist society, and that totalitarian violence and totalitarian reason came from the structure of existing society, which was in the process of overcoming its liberal past and incorporating its historical negation."[8]

· · ·

But the arm of criticism, as every Marxist knows, cannot replace the criticism of arms. Neumann, Kirchheimer, and Marcuse had formulated a powerful interpretation of the *Aufhebung* of German liberalism; but for these philosophers, who had hitherto only interpreted the world in different ways, the point now was to change it. The route from theoretical to practical criticism was not, however, obvious: they were scholars, trained in the European classical-humanistic tradition, and the imperative was obviously to enter into the historical struggle against fascism on the basis of their intellectual calling, not in spite of it.

The unlikely catalyst for this unity of theory and practice, of course, proved to be the executive wing of the United States government. Recruitment to the Research and Analysis Branch of OSS had been conducted in the first year of its existence largely through an informal network of personal contacts, generated by Branch Chief James Phinney Baxter III, his successor, William L. Langer, and their prestigious Board of Analysts drawn from the American academic mandarinate. By mid-1943, however, in an inspired departure from admittedly limited precedent, the R&A leadership finally began to explore the deep reservoir of political, regional, and linguistic expertise to be found among the refugee scholars. Franz Neumann, who had just published his classic study *Behemoth: The Structure and Practice of National Socialism,* was among the first of the émigrés to be called to Washington; an FBI investigation eventually confirmed his political reliability and loyalty to the United States, and efforts were made to expedite his naturalization proceedings. In March he was joined by his friend and colleague Herbert

Marcuse, who, in the words of Section Chief Eugene M. Anderson, "at once became the leading analyst on Germany." On July 3 Anderson reported that Otto Kirchheimer had finally been cleared and would report for duty, initially on a consultant basis, a few days thereafter. The Research and Analysis Branch likewise obtained the occasional services of Friedrich Pollock and Arkadij Gurland, the Institute's theorists of "state" and "monopoly" capitalism, respectively.[9] As one of their younger colleagues would recall, "It was as if the left-Hegelian *Weltgeist* had taken up temporary residence in the Central European Section of the OSS."[10] The Frankfurt School had gone to war.

On the face of it, nothing could be more incongruous than the united front that was struck between the American intelligence establishment and this cadre of German intellectuals who were not only Marxists but, technically speaking, enemy aliens as well. The irony has been savoured by critics of both parties to the alliance, who have observed grimly that only Admiral Canaris had more German intelligence experts at his disposal. Unquestionably, the personal circumstances of the refugee scholars played a role, for by the beginning of the war the privately endowed International Institute for Social Research had lost the means to support them, and they lived in constant insecurity. The positions of Neumann and Marcuse had been extended through 1942 only through the largesse of Columbia University and an outside grant from the Committee in Aid of Displaced Foreign Scholars, but by this time they and other Institute members had begun to supplement their incomes with part-time consulting jobs for various of the new war agencies: Marcuse and Leo Löwenthal with the German Section of the Office of War Information, Neumann, Gurland, and Pollock with the Board of Economic Warfare.[11]

Their entry into the government cannot have been simply a function of difficult financial circumstances, however, for their published theoretical work reveals a fully consistent set of political motivations.[12] The explicit premise of Neumann's *Behemoth*, a landmark in the Institute's analysis of fascism, was that National Socialism could be combatted only as a military and political totality: "The military superiority of the democracies and of Soviet Russia must be demonstrated to the German people," he wrote at the end of 1941, "but that is not enough. The war must be shortened by dividing Germany and divorcing the large masses of the people from National Socialism. This is the task of psychological warfare, which cannot be disassociated from the domestic and foreign policies of Germany's rivals. Psychological warfare is not propaganda.

It is politics."[13] Within a year of this call to arms, Neumann, Marcuse, and Kirchheimer were installed in the Central European Section of R&A / Washington, charged with the task of collecting and assessing information about German intentions and capabilities. Such committed and iconoclastic scholars would inevitably chafe under the restrictions of this modest assignment, resulting in tensions that can be perceived in retrospect and, indeed, that were already evident during the war: "Early in 1943 the Section, now numbering sixteen, had at its core a highly individualistic and incurably academic group," wrote Eugene Anderson, "including Franz Neumann (the recognized intellectual leader), Herbert Marcuse, Sinclair Armstrong, Felix Gilbert, and Edgar Johnson. It was a notable if not always tractable group, and its strengths and weaknesses were often summed up by the one-word description, 'primadonnas.' "[14]

•   •   •

Although it was never to exert a decisive influence on the organization as a whole, much less on American military or diplomatic policy toward Europe, the Central European Section was recognized for a series of distinctive theses regarding the nature of totalitarian rule. In pursuing them, the work of the Section developed along three phases that corresponded to the immediate requirements of events. Throughout 1943 the Senior Analysts were concerned with the functioning of the New Order in Germany and Nazi-occupied Europe. Their studies, based on reports in the European press, radio broadcasts from the Reich monitored by the Federal Communications Commission, cables from the OSS Mission to London and outposts in neutral Lisbon, Algiers, Stockholm, and Bern, prisoner-of-war interrogations, and—most prosaic of all— published materials excavated from the Library of Congress,[15] dealt with the potential significance of everything from the effects of bomb damage on civilian morale to changes in ladies' fashions. While struggling to define their task and to be heard within the organization, they assembled a minutely detailed picture of the social, economic, political, and cultural structure of totalitarianism, and of points of vulnerability and resistance within it.

In the second phase of their paramilitary sabbatical, beginning in January 1944, the Central Europeanists turned their attention to anticipated problems of the postwar era and launched an extensive research program designed to assist American officers in the military occupation and governance of a defeated Germany. If one can speak of an R&A "line," it

was to steer a middle course between the extremes of a punitive Mor-
genthauism and the call to rebuild Germany as rapidly as possible as a
bulwark against the Soviet Union. Whereas the OSS in general exercised
little influence on the actual conduct of the war, the Europeanists of
R&A did play a demonstrably significant role in preparing for the peace
that followed. In fact, it is another small footnote to history that it was
none other than Herbert Marcuse, notorious in his later incarnation as
chief theoretician of the New Left, who drafted the order that formally
abolished the Nazi Party.[16]

The end of the European war signaled the third phase of their work,
which entailed the preparation of materials relating to the prosecution
of Nazi war criminals. Franz Neumann, regarded by many as the foremost authority on National Socialism in the government, left for Europe,
where he served as expert consultant to the American War Crimes Staff.
Marcuse moved into his Washington post to coordinate a series of briefs
on the principal Nazi organizations involved in the commission of war
crimes, followed by a conceptually larger analysis of "Nazi Plans to
Dominate Germany and Europe," perhaps the first systematic attempt,
using official documentation, to grasp the meaning of what had transpired.

Political and Psychological Warfare: 1943

In his famous 1895 Introduction to the *Class Struggles in France,* Engels
characterized that work as "Marx's first attempt to explain a section of
contemporary history by means of his materialist conception."[17] Under
the circumstances of government service, it would be impossible to claim
that the wartime work of Neumann, Marcuse, and Kirchheimer constituted a similar attempt to apply the Critical Theory to the concrete tasks
of the war, but neither were the theoretical orientations of these Marxist
scholars fully displaced by their official duties. Despite energetic campaigns on the part of William Langer's office to produce straightforward
information papers, executed in accordance with the canons of an objective, value-free, and scrupulously apolitical social science, resonances
of the unorthodox Marxism of the Frankfurt School could be heard within
the Central European Section of the United States' first intelligence
agency.

Much of their work was in fact produced under conditions resembling
those of their prewar essays for the Institute's *Zeitschrift für Sozialfor-*

schung. Indeed, Section Chief Eugene N. Anderson, who had already served the Institute during the first years of its exile as part of an advisory committee of distinguished American scholars, wrote at the time that "the spirit of cooperation among members has been remarkably effective. Much credit in this respect is owing to Dr. Neumann and Dr. Marcuse, who both believe in and practice this approach to their work."[18] In a manner reminiscent of the prewar years of exile in Morningside Heights, each report was discussed candidly and critically within the Section. Once approved and edited, it was assigned a security classification and circulated to Langer's office, to the appropriate operational branches of OSS, and to designated individuals, offices, and agencies in the Departments of War and State.[19]

Moreover, Franz Neumann's monumental study of the National Socialist "Behemoth," completed shortly before he entered the government, informed much of the Section's ongoing research (which in turn filled in many of its omissions and contributed to the extensive appendix to the second edition that appeared in the summer of 1944).[20] The thesis Neumann had argued was that National Socialism confronted the world with a new political form, a monstrosity anticipated by Hobbes in his description of the dissolution of the seventeenth-century absolutist state—the "Leviathan" of ancient Semitric eschatology—into "a non-state, a chaos, a situation of lawlessness, disorder, and anarchy" which he likened to its mythical counterpart, the "Behemoth."[21]

Germany, too, he argued, was devolving from a totalitarian Leviathan into a political system that could no more be called a state than the intellectual anarchy of Nazi ideology could be called a political theory. In a legitimate state, political decisions can be represented as a compromise between the ruling and the ruled classes, which implies the existence of some universally binding authority. Under National Socialism, however, political decisions in Germany had been reduced to a web of compromises *within* a composite ruling class made up of the army high command, the ministerial bureaucracy and higher civil service, leading representatives of heavy industry, and the leadership of the Nazi Party which penetrated all of them. Although the bulk of Neumann's research was devoted to documenting the network of interdependencies that bound these groups to one another, to an ideology of racism, and to a strategy of imperialist war, it was the disappearance of any higher authority that gave the system the unique and historically unprecedented character that he stressed in his conclusion: "I venture to suggest that we are confronted with a form of society in which the ruling groups control the population directly, without the mediation of that rational though coercive apparatus hitherto known as the state."[22] A new political form required new and unprecedented forms of political warfare to combat it, and the task of the Section was to provide the research services that would make that strategy possible. Although they were constantly enjoined that "there is no future in R&A as a pressure group" and that "a rigid distinction must be maintained between political intelligence reports and policy recommendations," they strained against the limitations imposed by these bureaucratic realities. As Langer's deputy Carl Schorske would later concede, "All our staff were politicized, and they had their own irrepressible ideas which they worked into their job as reporters and analysts."[23]

By midsummer 1943, the Section had come to regard the defeat of Germany as certain and was focusing its research on points of political and psychological vulnerability that might shorten the war and hasten the beginning of democratic reconstruction. That the same presentiment of Allied victory prevailed among the ruling classes in Germany seemed proven by shifts in the internal propaganda line—from "*Blitzkrieg*" to "*Festung Europa*"—and by major reorganizations which had the effect of transferring control over the war economy and internal administration more fully to the Nazi Party: the new Speer Ministry patronized the big industrialists and enmeshed private entrepreneurs in a network of compulsory organizations; Himmler rewarded the Junker aristocracy with the territorial spoils of his Eastern program, while using the Gestapo to assure the Generals of absolute control over the home front. The clear implication was that the Party, the one group with no hope of salvaging anything from defeat, was moving aggressively to offset its growing isolation by ensuring the identification of the traditional ruling groups with the policies of the regime. To close off all political avenues of escape was not only to turn potential opponents into accessories, "It is tantamount to a Nazi declaration of determination to fight to the bitter end under the leadership of the Nazi Party."[24]

Among what the Central Europeanists, following Neumann's Marxist terminology, unabashedly called the "ruled classes," the situation was somewhat different. Indeed, reports of war weariness, unrest, and even open opposition suggested to some observers that the internal collapse that had signaled the end of the first World War might soon be repeated. Their own analysis resisted such a deduction, however, on the grounds that subjective feelings cannot be isolated from the whole organization of society and are a factor only in connection with the action (or inaction) they produce. The totalizing drive of Nazism, which atomized the public sphere and destroyed virtually all intermediary institutions of civil society, was designed to render the effects of individual feelings negligible—"to force the industrialist to produce, the worker to work, the soldier to fight, no matter how much they may hate the regime and desire an end to the war."[25] In a telling analogy, Marcuse observed that just as on a modern assembly line, where it is the conveyor belt that dictates the pace of production and not the morale of the worker, so in Nazi Germany the totalitarian machinery of society sweeps along the non-Nazi and the anti-Nazi alike: "It is like the factory system," he concluded, "except that the worker cannot quit."[26]

This theory of totalitarianism would have major ramifications for their assessment of German guilt after the close of the war, but it also had immediate implications for political warfare so long as the hostilities continued. Neumann, Marcuse, and Kirchheimer believed that Germany had been defeated in World War I as much by the ideas as by the armies of the democracies, but that the totalitarian organization of National Socialism differed too fundamentally from the military dictatorship of the last war for simple propaganda to have a comparable effect. The originality of their own procedure—reminiscent, perhaps, of the Institute's work on such collaborative projects as the 1936 *Studies on Authority and the Family*—was to situate collective psychological phenomena within the institutional contexts in which they operate. Thus, they argued repeatedly against the "democratic fallacy" that civilian morale could be made a decisive political factor through the ordinary methods of psychological warfare, for Hitler too had learned the lessons of 1918: " 'Morale,' according to the present writer [Neumann], is an inconsequential factor in the German situation and will continue to be so until military defeat smashes the elaborate system developed by Nazi-ism to control morale."[27]

From the beginning, then, the work of the Section was predicated on the invasion of Germany and the destruction of the Wehrmacht, but this ultimate criterion did not reduce them to a state of passive anticipation. For one thing, there was nothing in their overall appraisal that argued *against* tactics that would keep up the pressure on the Nazi control apparatus, and they displayed considerable ingenuity in devising unorthodox measures for use by the external propaganda branch of the Office of War Information. Marcuse, for instance, proposed a rumor campaign alleging the spread of infectious tuberculosis among factory workers, while Neumann found in a decree ordering the standardization of coffins "excellent material for overt operations, about as follows: 'The standardization of coffins is the logical sequence to the standardization of the German mind, nourished entirely on Nazi propaganda; and to the standardization of the underfed, badly housed, and badly clothed bodies.' "[28] That this austerity measure recalled to him the Jewish prohibition against the decoration of coffins only sweetened the irony.

The recurrently ironic tone of their weekly reports suggests that the German émigrés of the Central European Section may have derived some satisfaction from dreaming up such exercises in black propaganda, and their frequent reviews of so-called "Dachau jokes"—anti-Nazi humor that could land a German or Austrian in a concentration camp—suggests that they seized every opportunity to have the last laugh themselves. Their main business lay not in such tactical skirmishes, however, nor even in an overall political strategy, but in the evaluation of enemy intentions and capabilities.

The intransigence of the Nazi leadership in the face of impending catastrophe itself provided the greatest incentive to elements in German society looking for a way out. Conservative opponents who may have favored a compromise peace with the Western allies were paralyzed by their complicity and by their dependence upon the Party's power to suppress any popular revolutionary unheaval.[29] The subject population, for its part, had no way of translating its antagonism toward the war into effective political opposition to the regime. What remained was the political underground in Germany, particularly the scattered remnants of the Communist, Socialist, and Trade Union movements. Prisoner-of-war interrogations, announcements of trials and executions, and other sources indicated that atomized cells had survived the terroristic measures of the 1930s and were showing renewed signs of political activity following the invasion of Russia and the mounting strains of the war. Paradoxically, however, it was Allied political warfare more than any other factor that prevented the labor underground from linking the class solidarity felt by German workers to their identification with the national cause and from organizing it into an effective anti-Nazi opposition. The Section thus frequently found itself at odds with the American administration as well.

From the time of the Interallied Conference at Casablanca the American position had been expressed in what Roosevelt called "the simple formula of placing the objective of this war in terms of an unconditional surrender by Germany, Italy, and Japan." Everything was henceforth to be subordinated to the military command, for whom the retreat of the Wehrmacht before the advancing Red Army and the American landing in Italy meant that by the summer of 1943 Germany was caught in a tightening vise. In the Central European Section, however, the belief was emerging that the defeat of Nazism would come through the convergence not of two armies but of external military force and internal political resistance. Military defeat was never conceived as an end in itself, then, but as the means to the destruction of fascism and the reinstatement of democratic institutions by the German people themselves.

This argument was cast as an explicit rebuke to those Allied leaders who publicly claimed to be waging a war against such metaphysical anachronisms as "Prussian militarism" or, in Churchill's phrase, "the Teutonic urge for domination."[30] Such slogans betrayed a dangerously inadequate understanding of the redistribution of social and political power that was the essence of the Nazi revolution, for the Germany of World War II was not the regime of the Junker aristocrat but of Krupp and I. G. Farben. Indeed, as Neumann demonstrated in a series of profiles of leading war profiteers, only those Junkers survived who had made the successful transition from the semifeudal worldview of Prussianism to the technocratic ideology of the industrial superorganizations.[31] Displacement of the political dimension of the war would undermine any meaningful strategy of political warfare.

In the view of the Senior Analysts of the Central European Section, the American statements played neatly into the hands of the Nazi propagandists, who could threaten with great effect that defeat would submit the German people to economic devastation, national dismemberment, and the burden of collective guilt: "Even as it is, the record [of resistance] is a tribute to human endurance and courage, and the revelation of a great hope. Faced with the sharpened instruments of Terror, the underground needs, in addition to its own growing strength, a guidance and a support which offer some reward to the endurance and the courage, and give some substance to the hope."[32] The strategists of American political warfare, confident of the ultimate military superiority of the Allies, instead provided unintended incentives for the weary citizen to endure and the defeated soldier to fight on instead of proposing concrete measures by which they might still extricate themselves from their hopeless situation. The demand for unconditional surrender in fact resonated perfectly with Goebbels' slogan of "victory or annihilation," and thus, according to the R&A analysts, violated the "cardinal requirement" of psychological warfare: "What is wanted is a positive goal for Germany which will dispel this fear and encourage German soldiers and citizens alike to revolt against their Nazi leaders and bring the war to an end."[33]

This dissenting position was only complicated by the fact that their analysis coincided with the political strategy of the USSR, especially the Soviet-sponsored "Free Germany" manifesto," which Neumann described as nothing less than "a master stroke of psychological warfare."[34] Reflecting its origins in a coalition of anti-Nazis ranging from the German Officers Union to the exiled Communist Party, the manifesto sought to redirect German nationalism into a force for democratic revolution and social reconstruction. It argued that the Allies would not invade a democratic Germany from which Nazism had been uprooted, and thus only if the dictatorship were overthrown from within could defeat be avoided and national independence assured.[35]

The influence of their recommendations may have been further undermined by their observation that the small but politically experienced and tightly organized Communist underground in Germany was the only group with the potential to mobilize the "other Germany" into an effective anti-Nazi movement.[36] This position would make the Communist Party a strong contender for political leadership in the postwar era, but they argued that by funneling moral, political, and financial support to the wartime underground the Allies could enhance the likelihood of a Western orientation of a united, democratic, and socialist postwar Germany. This idea, "which has been insisted upon by the Central European Section again and again,"[37] not only reflected a different conception of political warfare than prevailed within the government but implied a fundamentally different set of war aims as well. It was the first of many political battles they would lose.

Military Occupation and Denazification: 1944

Members of the Central European Section were fond of citing a remark current among German prisoners: "Enjoy the rest of the war—the peace will be terrible." Like the POWs, they were preoccupied with the connection between military and political developments and knew that the nature of the collapse of the German armies would bear directly on the internal political life of Germany for decades afterward.

Assuming, as they did after the declarations of Moscow and Teheran, that the Allies would remain united, they saw no possibilities for dissident groups within the Nazi Party to break away and try to negotiate a separate peace, a view that was only confirmed by the conspiracy of July 20 and its bloody aftermath. In a rare R&A success story, the President had on his desk one week after the event Franz Neumann's analysis of the failed assassination attempt against Hitler. In his interpretation, the abortive coup had its roots in a latent antagonism between the Party and the conservative officers' corps, a conflict whose first manifestation was the Roehm Putsch of 1934. At that time the Party had purged itself in order to preserve the autonomy of the Army upon which it depended; a decade later their positions were reversed, as the Party prepared to purge the Army to preserve its own autonomy. After D-Day the German Army leadership had begun to confront the spectre of the annihilation of the field armies, and the announcement—on July 19—that control over the Home Army was to be transferred to Himmler and the SS appears to have forced the conspirators' hands. In the last analysis, "the retention of the generals' control over the Army is the key to the understanding of the plot," for therein lay their only hope of concluding a negotiated peace with the Western Allies. Referring with unconcealed bitterness to the self-destruction of the Weimar Republic, Neumann added, "The Army leadership cannot count again upon a Social Democratic leadership which would entrust demobilization and reorganization of the Army to the old Officers' Corps, encourage the establishment of a Free Corps, and protect the Reichswehr from parliamentary control. If the generals lose Army control this time, they will be unable to exert any influence upon domestic developments or foreign policy."[38] The conspiracy, although narrowly based, provided the Nazi leadership with an undreamed-of opportunity to liquidate all real and potential oppositional elements; and by reducing the Army to what became in effect a Party formation, it left them alone in the field, committed if necessary to turning Germany itself into a battleground.

The Nazis' determination to press their fight to the finish seemed to imply two broad possibilities: either the regime would be deposed by the Allies in the wake of an integral defeat on the major fronts, or the military situation and the domestic control apparatus would deteriorate to such a point that the government could be overthrown from within through some kind of popular uprising. For the German émigré Marxists, the prospect of the latter was certainly not the "spectre haunting Europe" it may have appeared elsewhere in the government, where the desirability of forestalling a revolutionary movement in Germany was simply assumed. "I cannot accept this point of view," countered Neumann in response to a memorandum prepared for the Joint Chiefs of Staff. "A revolutionary movement aiming at the eradication of Nazism may be highly desirable," an eventuality that the Allied armies should seek "neither to encourage nor to prevent."[39] In either case, however, the Central Europeanists believed that the Allies would find themselves confronted with a perplexing dilemma: "In order to make sure of their victory and to remove the German danger, they will have to march into Germany and occupy her, but in doing so, they will probably prevent the anti-Nazi reaction of the progressive forces then coming to its fulfillment, and thereby will prevent a solution of the German problem which would give a better guarantee of future peace than any peace treaty could provide."[40] This solemn warning that military occupation could freeze the existing social situation at the time of collapse seems somewhat academic, however, for it is doubtful that the maturation of "the progressive forces" was seen as the solution to "the German problem" much outside of the Central European Section.

Even within the R&A leadership, not to say within the American administration at large, there was little sympathy for the wishful thinking characteristic of many of the socialist émigrés. On one occasion Marcuse wrote a straightforward class analysis of "German Social Stratification" that was criticized for reducing people to statistical "automatons" whose attitudes and actions are determined by their socioeconomic position,[41] and another of his reports, on "The Social Democratic Party of Germany," became the center of an acrimonious controversy between the Section and the Projects Committee. Nominally, the issue was whether the report reflected "objectivity and maturity in political research,"[42] but such methodological tempests recurred too frequently for their political implications to be doubted.

Within the Section, however, political differences tended to disappear within a common program to such an extent that Neumann, Marcuse, and Kirchheimer, although Marxists and known as such, can in no way be considered to have constituted a minority faction. According to John Herz, who worked closely with Kirchheimer on legal and administrative problems, "all of us could agree on this:

> Whatever one's analysis of the situation, and whatever one's ultimate objectives or hopes for postwar Germany, we knew that one had to start from a minimum requirement, namely, to restore, or create, in Germany that liberal-democratic framework of government and society which (a) would do away with "feudal"-authoritarian features that had characterized Germany throughout modern history, and (b) would form the basis upon which anything more far-reaching could subsequently be realized.[43]

They were already poised, then, when the Research and Analysis Branch, in the person of Langer's special representative, Hajo Holborn, was asked by the War Department to outline the program for the American military occupation and denazification of postwar Germany. Accordingly, toward the end of 1943 Franz Neumann began to outline the work of the Section on what would prove to be the first stage in dismantling the Nazi control apparatus in Germany and Europe.[44]

Work for the Civil Affairs Division occupied almost the full energy of the Section through much of 1944 and included the preparation of several compendia of factual background information for anticipated use by American occupation authorities.[45] In thus documenting the extension of Nazi controls over Eastern and Western Europe, Neumann, Marcuse, and Kirchheimer came as close as they ever would to meeting the austere R&A standard of political reporting, which fell somewhere between positivist social science and military dispatch: "Strictly impartial, designed to inform rather than to persuade; they should avoid all recommendations, whether explicit or veiled."[46] Despite their nominal submission to the language, truth, and logic of the Projects Committee, one can detect traces of the theoretical principles that framed even their most "objectivistic" selection of data. Most suggestive is the characteristic focus on the dialectic of rationality and irrationality that had been thematic for the Frankfurt School's view of the modern world generally and of the National Socialist fusion of bureaucratic administration and terroristic violence in particular:

> The sober and methodical steps taken by the Nazis to build up their system of police controls were supplemented by methods of terrorism. The men who created the administrative machinery described above were the same individuals responsible for the machine-gunning of civilians packed into

cellars and even churches, for the use of gas chambers and crematories for the innocent victims of Nazi racial theories, and for the execution of hostages.[47]

Traces of a theoretical program, however, do not in themselves imply a practical course of action. This challenge was met in the other branch of their work for the War Department, which consisted of a series of Civil Affairs Guides designed to assist Military Government personnel in dealing with specific problems in the liberated areas.

The charge of the Guides was to build a bridge from the basic collections of purely factual background information they had compiled to direct statements of policy which they were not privileged to make— "They are designed to point the factual information toward the making and executing of plans by those civil affairs officers assigned to this work in the theaters of operation."[48] The bitter interagency battles that surrounded this seemingly modest task, however, evoke once again the political tensions experienced by radical intellectuals in exile, for the Guides expressed long-range aspirations for the reconstruction of Germany that were not in harmony with the immediate objectives of other agencies involved in the project. The Section's ongoing contestation of tendencies at work in the government, and its attempt to draft a consistent policy of denazification and democratic reconstruction, thus amounted to a sustained exercise in theoretical practice and practical criticism. It also represents the field in which the concrete influence of the theorists of the Institute for Social Research was greatest—and their disappointment most acute.

In their concrete recommendations, the Civil Affairs Guides embody what now appears to be an almost palpable tension between the immediate requirements of the American occupation authorities and the long-range objectives of the German émigré socialists. In their program for the eradication of Nazism and the revival of German political life, Neumann, Marcuse, and Kirchheimer always acknowledged that the first concern of the occupying forces would be physical security under the rule of law. They feared, however, that under the pressure of circumstances, denazification would be limited to the dismissal of visible Nazi officials, the repeal of obviously Nazi laws and ordinances, and the dismantling of agencies specifically created by the Nazis for subjugation and terror. Their own goal, by contrast, was the eradication of the aggressive tendencies that had thus found expression in the Nazi movement, and they believed that this deeper level of denazification had to be conceived as an internal process. They attempted to reconcile these potentially divergent priorities by arguing that the best guarantee of American security interests was the revival of the indigenous political forces—in the form of the reconstituted political parties and the democratic labor movement—that alone could eliminate not just the institutions of fascism but its roots in German society.

While in some respects a tactical tour de force, this ingenious synthesis of military and political objectives would prove more easily said than done. It was generally assumed that the end of the war would bring a widespread collapse of controls throughout Germany and that the strongest impulse operating on the side of the occupation authorities would be to restore order and repair the machinery of a functioning society. This would create a constant temptation to pursue what Kirchheimer called an "opportunistic" policy of placing immediate technical requirements ahead of more fundamental political considerations.[49] Although there was a consensus in the Section that the immediate goal of denazification must be a return to the liberal-democratic status quo before 1933, they were forced by the totalitarian logic of events to be wary of resurrecting prematurely the defenseless institutions of the Weimar era.

The most dangerous vulnerability of liberalism, as the Frankfurt School theory had argued, lay in its literal belief in the distinction between the political and the purely technical or instrumental, a belief that the Nazis had exploited ruthlessly. To apply this logic to the task of denazification would be to misunderstand utterly the thorough penetration of social life that was the essence of the Nazi revolution and to underestimate the radical measures needed to depoliticize it. The obverse of their contention that every act of dissent in a totalitarian society is necessarily a political act was expressed in Kirchheimer's warning that "any decision made for or against technical-administrative streamlining would at the same time be a political decision."[50] National Socialism had achieved the collapse of civil society into the state that Hegel—Nazi ideologists notwithstanding—had decried, and it was now the philosphically charged mission of Military Government to reverse this premature reconciliation.

In this historic task the self-destructive liberal ideal of unrestricted competition in the political marketplace was at best a "democratic luxury" that postfascist Germany could not afford. Arguing the case against what he would later call "repressive tolerance," Marcuse led off the series of Guides by recommending the close supervision of all nationalist and rightist organizations and an attitude of leniency toward politically motivated attacks against them: "To treat these equally with the anti-Nazi groupings (for example to grant them equal protection from interference by hostile parties) would be tantamount to perpetuating the greatest threat to the security of the occupying forces and to the restoration of a peaceful order."[51] Neumann concurred, and, in one of their most bitterly contested positions, urged that a centralized police force be created as quickly as possible in order to deal with criminality and terrorism of the public by remnants of the Nazi Party.[52]

The actual process of identifying and weeding out Nazi elements would be an immensely difficult and problematical one, the more so because genuine Nazis (and anti-Nazis) were to be found among all social and political groups, and "at the time of the Allied occupation of Germany, almost everybody who is not unmistakably identified with the Hitler regime by his position and activity will represent himself as a non-Nazi or anti-Nazi."[53] Following a loose set of criteria that corresponded to the complex dynamics of totalitarian integration, Marcuse and his colleagues calculated that as a first step some 220,000 Nazi officials would have to be arrested immediately in a sweeping purge of national, regional, and local government. National Socialism was more than a system of political rule, however; it was to them a four-headed "Behemoth" that had devoured the economic, administrative, and military functions of the state as well. Accordingly, they identified by name a further 1,800 business leaders who were considered to be "active Nazis" and who were to be taken into custody pending investigation of their political records.[54] Once the prisons had been filled, they recommended that the remainder be detained in the concentration camps the Nazis had constructed for their own political enemies.

Kirchheimer, in the legal and administrative Guides for which he was chiefly responsible, further developed the program for the simultaneous destruction of Nazi institutions and the release of the suppressed energies of the political opposition. Extrapolating from his prewar theoretical work, he argued that the politicization of civil institutions could only be undone through substantively political countermeasures. In practice this meant that considerations of political reliability must take precedence in replacing the thousands of functionaries who would be dismissed, and that "Military Government should not be overanxious with respect to the technical qualifications of the substitutes."[55] The massive dislocations this would cause were unavoidable and more or less regrettable.

The final step in the Section's strategy of linking Military Government to the left-wing opposition was taken by Neumann, who had come to specialize in the diminished status of labor under the Nazis. Its trade unions and political parties had been the first victims of the dictatorship, with the result that alone among the various economic groups in Germany—business, agriculture, the professions—the working class was deprived of any representative organization. Neumann predicted that in the chaotic period following invasion, the labor underground would surface and could provide rallying points for progressive anti-Nazi forces throughout the community. In such a situation, Military Government should do nothing to interfere with the political activities of the unions. To the contrary, he wrote, "The promise of freedom to organize constitutes the most complete repudiation of Nazism and the most direct

The Central European analyst Herbert Marcuse, "whose later revolutionary role was then indiscernible," ponders the dialectic from his desk in Washington.

and complete avowal of democratic principles. Trade-union organizations, if re-established on a democratic basis, are likely to provide effective support for the ocupation forces."[56] Marcuse had already offered what amounted to an assurance that Communist elements in the labor movement, under conditions of military occupation, would almost certainly confine themselves to a "minimum program," and that the Social Democrats would revive their traditional line of liberal-democratic reformism.[57]

To the German-born Senior Analysts, then, it seemed obvious that the immediate security interests of American Military Government were fully at one with the long-range political objectives of the socialist opposition that was bound to surface as the war thundered to a close: The Allied armies would break the power of Nazism on the front, and the labor movement would uproot it forever from German society. A few years later, when the program had been effectively scuttled and former Nazis once again occupied commanding positions in government and industry, R&A alumnus John Herz summed up this heroic fantasy in an article called "The Fiasco of Denazification."[58] He might well have subtitled it "A Critique of Utopian Socialism."

War Crimes: 1945

In a strict sense, the author of a finished Civil Affairs Guide was the R&A Branch per se, and a given document cannot be attributed literally to the individual who bore primary responsibility for initiating, executing, or supervising it. Once the criticisms of his immediate colleagues in the Central European Section had been incorporated, it had to survive the political and methodological scrutiny of a maze of intra- and extra-departmental committees. It is thus possible to trace in detail the process by which certain of the more controversial guides ascended from the infernal status of a "Draft—Not Yet Approved" through the Seven Circles of Purgatory (internal review, Foreign Economic Authority, Department of State, Army and Navy, Interagency Editorial Committee, CAD/Pentagon, reconciliation with Presidential policy directives) before being sanctified with an official War Department number and transmitted overseas to the Civil Affairs Training School in Shrivenham. Comparison of the initial and final stages of the process supports a typical memorandum submitted by Neumann, who was confident of his authority and did not like to lose: "The meeting was generally satisfactory. All controversial points were decided in favor of OSS."[59]

Nevertheless, even where it has been possible to work with the initial draft of a report assigned to Neumann, Marcuse, or Kirchheimer, their official posts make it impossible to assume that it has the same authorial basis as a signed article in the Institute's *Zeitschrift für Sozialforschung.* Indeed, the torrent of guidelines, directives, and, finally, pleas that issued forth from the office of the Chief is the best testimony to the difficulties experienced by the academic recruits in general, and the Germanic theoreticians in particular, in adapting their native idiom to the spare rhetoric of officialdom. "Sobriety is imperative," they were instructed. "All parading of erudition which might have been spared without inconvenience is odious." The authors of *Behemoth, Reason and Revolution,* and *Punishment and Social Structure* were referred to humbling manuals on *The Art of Writing Prose* and *The Quest for Literature* with which to extirpate the locutions of Hegel and Marx from their writing, and they were subjected to lectures on "The Problem of Objectivity in R&A Reporting." This campaign was more than a localized eruption of the trans-Atlantic *Methodenstreit,* the methodological controversy that has smoldered throughout the intellectual culture of the twentieth century, for the Research and Analysis Branch had learned that in order to survive, "it is of the utmost importance that our political intelligence reports should strive for the highest degree of objectivity." At no point could they appear to be trespassing on the territory of the more established agencies authorized to recommend, make, or implement policy, "no matter how strongly we may believe we are 'right.' "[60] Not all of the wartime work of the Senior Analysts bears the anonymous imprimatur of the Research and Analysis Branch, however. The archival remains of the OSS include materials that record in quite personal terms the determination of the German émigré socialists to pronounce judgment on their homeland.

In autumn 1944, in the aftermath of the failed plot against Hitler, Franz Neumann circulated among his colleagues the first of three drafts he would write on "The Treatment of Germany."[61] Although he seems still to have underestimated the Nazis and overestimated the Germans, the Nazis' persistence in the face of certain defeat was finally beginning to shake his confidence in the imminence of Germany's delayed revolution, and he now felt obliged to call for guarantees on the part of any postwar government that the social structure had been purged of its aggressive elements. He also stressed "the utmost importance" of a consistent overall policy toward Germany, as if to acknowledge that democratization might not be the spontaneous internal process he appears earlier to have expected. Above all, he was convinced of the need for the greatest haste, regardless of the immediate consequences to the German economy: If cooperation could be expected at all, it would be while anti-Nazi sentiments were high and the Americans might still be regarded as liberators rather than as a hostile occupying power.

The most striking feature of Neumann's draft, however, lay not in the prescience of his recommendations but in the "considerations of political morality" that he finally permitted himself to introduce explicitly into his official writings: "Germany as a political entity," he wrote, the German people as a whole, "must share the responsibility for Nazism and its train of aggressiveness and atrocities."[62] As the Allied armies converged on the Reich, this sentiment rose to prominence in the work of the Section, and they were soon provided with a practical outlet for it.

Shortly after Hitler's suicide, Supreme Court Justice Robert H. Jackson was named Chief U.S. Prosecutor of German war criminals; he immediately appointed General Donovan to the prosecution staff and thus acquired the services of the Research and Analysis Branch of the OSS. Neumann, who had been drawing up plans for the postwar reorganization of the German and Austrian Units of the Central European Section, revised his program, and soon a staff of about two dozen specialists was immersed in research for the American War Crimes staff.[63] Until escalating differences led Donovan to withdraw his support shortly after the opening of the Tribunal, the Central European Section worked closely with Telford Taylor and Benjamin Kaplan from the legal department of the Office of the Secretary of War. In the course of working out research guidelines for the impending trials, Kaplan was a frequent visitor to the Section, and it may have been in this period that the German legal scholars—Neumann, Kirchheimer, and Henry Kellerman—finally learned that as confident as they were of their practical expertise, if they were to have any serious advisory influence they must develop their ideas in direct, continuous collaboration with their potential clients and not simply fire them off in the form of reports to be edited, distilled, excerpted, and ignored.

The complex determination of guilt and responsibility had already proven to be a pivotal element in the theory of political warfare evolved by the Central European Section throughout 1943; indeed, only if the Germans could escape the taint of universal complicity was a program of political warfare possible at all. In order to encourage internal resistance, the analysts had urged American and British policy makers to distinguish among levels of complicity, while probing in their own work the moral implications of a society that had effectively abolished the private sphere of individual initiative and responsibility. At the end of that year Kirchheimer and John Herz favorably evaluated the "Statement on Atrocities" of the Moscow Tripartite Conference, which affirmed the principle of individual rather than collective guilt and thus helped undermine Robert Ley's cynical taunt that "the nation has burned its bridges."[64] And by September 1944, while pressing the Government to clarify its position on an international war crimes tribunal, the Section was already studying in earnest the basis of criminal responsibility and drawing up preliminary lists of Nazi leaders to be arrested and charged:[65]

Hinkel, Heinrich	Verbindungsführer des Reichsarbeitsführers in dem Generalgouvernement (Warsaw)
Hinteregger, Dr.	Landsrat in Radmannsdorf, Südkärnten (Austria)
Hitler, Adolf	Fürher und Reichskanzler, Oberstbefehlshaber der Wehrmacht
Hitschmann, Dr.	Assistant to Polizeipräsident in Reichenberg, Sudentengau . . .

Neumann had broken down the problem of war criminals into three categories: first and most straightforward, the problem of Germans who had violated internationally accepted conventions of warfare; second, the complex problem of Germans who had violated municipal law; and finally, the problem of Germans who had technically violated neither international rules of warfare nor German nor domestic law but who were held to be in positions of political responsibility: "These are the leaders in whom we are really interested," he admitted, but "it is here that the greatest difficulties are encountered. How is their responsibility to be established?"[66] In answering this question, he returned to his well-tested strategy of allowing the Nazis to do the work for him. Since the established principles of Anglo-American jurisprudence were (thankfully) inadequate to the practices of the Nazi Behemoth, he turned for guidance directly to the most prominent legal theorists to the Third Reich— E. R. Huber, Werner Best, Otto Koellreutter, Hans Frank—and to their conceptions of "material justice" in the leadership state.

National Socialism claimed to have replaced the "formalistic" legal protections of the Weimar Republic with a substantive system of justice whose basis was the "unwritten living law of the people." It was embodied in the Nazi *Führerprinzip,* the leadership principle that governed the legal theory and organizational practice of the Third Reich and whose political, economic, and military ramifications Neumann had traced in *Behemoth.* According to this conception, every institution and association was organized as a hierarchical *Führungsordnung,* an order of leadership in which authority is concentrated in a single figure. Exempt from restrictions other than "the spirit of National Socialism," the leader formulates policies whose execution becomes the responsibility of a technical apparatus of subordinate officials.

This interpenetration of formal and substantive, of the political and the technical, became emblematic of much of the Section's work on the problem of criminal responsibility in a totalitarian state:

> A system under which broad policies are devised at a certain level of leadership but where the execution of such policies takes place at lower levels . . . would seem to place responsibility for whatever happens in the fulfillment of such policies . . . upon the particular leaders who controlled such realms, whether or not they can be proved to have given any specific orders or even to have known of the particular methods used in carrying out the general policies.[67]

The National Socialist party presumed the effectiveness of its terror and propaganda apparatus in ensuring the compliance of followers at lower levels of the leadership pyramid and held leaders accountable for deviations from the programs. Ideology, in this instance, corresponded well enough to reality to indicate the lines of the political counterstrategy the Central Europeanists recommended: "In reversing these standards and in making the Nazi leaders responsible for what *we* consider as war crimes, they would indeed have to answer for what has actually been done in accordance with their own standards and policies."[68] Turning the tables of the law on the theorists and practitioners of violence, they used their own logic against them and gave them enough rope quite literally to hang themselves.

Once they had identified the criminals, they returned to the grim task of documenting their crimes. Since the collapse of the German armies, Neumann's legal and political expertise had been greatly in demand, and in mid-August he returned to Europe for the first time since his flight in 1936. His itinerary brought him first to London, where he was given a bracing sense of the gulf that had separated the theorists and policy analysts of R&A/Washington from the chaotic realities of the European Theater, and then to Paris, where the European operations of the R&A Branch had been centered since the autumn of 1944. Finally—traveling under heavy guard for fear that he would be recognized—he entered the American zone of occupied Germany and made for Wiesbaden, where an R&A Mission, set up in an abandoned champagne factory, had been functioning since the beginning of July.

In his absence, supervision of the overall work of the Central European Section passed to Marcuse who—when he was not (somewhat incongruously) lecturing on posthostilities policies at the Army/Air Force School of Applied Tactics in Orlando[69]—coordinated the Section's preparations for the opening of the International War Crimes Tribunal at Nuremberg. During that summer, while the fate of OSS was being decided elsewhere, he and his colleagues prepared briefs on Himmler and Goering, on Nazi organizations involved in the commission of war crimes, and on "Nazi Plans for Dominating Germany and Europe" (a nine-part series for the use of the War Crimes Staff). Most of the information contained in these reports has been confirmed and surpassed in the course of forty years of relentless postwar scholarship, but this does not diminish their relevance to the present study. The manner in which they pose the problems and frame their answers, the categories they apply, and the priorities they express reveal both the limitations and the achievements of the German émigré socialists of OSS.

The structure of their case against the Nazi Behemoth grew out of Neumann's claim that it was a tightly integrated system, a corporate state managed by an interlocking directorate of political, military, and economic leaders. The tactics of the 1920s were only the first act of a tragic drama that closed with total war; Party ideology and Party practice were mutually adjusting elements of a single mechanism; domestic terror and foreign aggression issued from the same mandate. In effect, the émigré socialists treated National Socialism as the negative realization of the Marxist eschatology that had permeated their prewar theoretical work: a social totality that transcends the alienation of inner and outer, public and private, civil society and the state.

As determined as they were to establish the political dimensions of the indictment, the OSS analysts rejected in advance the charge that the impending trials would have the purely ideological function of parading the victory of the Allied armies in judicial robes. Nor were they distracted by the legal maneuvers required to judge a professedly revolutionary regime by norms it had openly repudiated: as Kirchheimer demonstrated, notwithstanding a sizeable body of extraordinary legislation that would have to be selectively rescinded, with few exceptions "the substantive rules of criminal law, including those pertaining to murder, were never revoked under the Nazi regime, even though they were never enforced when politically inconvenient."[70] Stripped of Nazi interpretation, a body of technical laws remained—innocent in their statutory or decretal form even where they had been vicious in their interpretation—in which the Nazis currently under indictment could find no legal support.

In general, the Central European analysts recommended that "the Jackson boys" pursue the strategy of deflecting all such legal protocols back onto the regime itself, to which end they concentrated on documenting the self-incrimination of the Nazi leadership. This was a straightforward, even tedious task, for the Nazi leaders openly and repeatedly acknowledged that in pursuit of the sovereign goal of "land and soil for the nourishment of our people," any means, legal or illegal, military or terroristic, was justified. Tracing the interdependency of Party ideology and Party practice over a 25-year period, the Central Europeanists prepared what was probably the most exhaustive documentation then available of the common roots of internal terror and aggressive expansion.

Of all the manifold levels of Nazi criminality, none was more horrifying or more resistant to rational analysis than the criminal conspiracy to exterminate the European Jews. Although they had reported regularly on incidences of official violence and terrorism, on mass deportations, and on the network of Nazi concentration camps, their papers prior to their work on the Nuremberg indictments yield no unambiguous evidence that they had grasped these as elements of a systematic policy of genocide. In their dual capacities as researchers for the prosecution and as philosophical guardians of the heritage of Western rationalism, they now set out to render intelligible this single, indivisible crime: "It is the purpose of the Prosecution to demonstate the existence of a common plan or enterprise of the German Government, the Nazi Party, and the German military, industrial, and financial leaders to achieve world domination by war. The destruction of the Jewish people as a whole, although an end in itself, was at the same time linked to and closely tied up with this aim of world conquest."[71] This précis was written by Irving Dwork, the Section's expert on Nazi policy toward the Jews, but apart from some chilling reflections on the implications of the Nazi extermination program for "the future of the Jewish people and of mankind," the draft bears the indelible stamp of Neumann's influence. The brief was in fact an elaboration of the so-called spearhead theory of anti-Semitism that Neumann had worked out some two years before and which appears to have served the Section as a feeble beacon against the blackness of fascist irrationalism. It argued that "measures against the Jews are always the 'spearhead' for general oppression," the "domestic testing-ground for universal terrorist methods directed against all those groups and institutions that are not fully subservient to the Nazi system."[72]

To the Frankfurt School analysts the systematic slaughter of some 5,700,000 noncombattant Jewish civilians—the Section's postwar estimate—was unintelliglble unless reducible to some pragmatic design, however sick, however evil. In pursuit of such a rationale, they argued that National Socialism, which had allegedly abolished the class struggle, needed an enemy whose very existence could serve to integrate the antagonistic groups within society. The Jews alone could fulfill this requirement, for reasons which they attempted to enumerate:[73]

(1) The Jew was the weakest enemy of Nazism; the attack on him therefore was the most promising and the least risky one.

(2) The Jew was the one enemy against whom the Nazis could hope to unite otherwise divergent masses of supporters.

(3) The elimination of the Jew, as a competitor, would be most profitable to the petty bourgeoisie which furnished the largest mass support for the Nazi movement.

(4) The Jew was found in all countries; Nazi anti-Semitism was therefore a convenient means for mobilizing potential Nazi allies in foreign countries . . .

(5) The ubiquity of the Jew as arch-enemy provided the Nazis with a justification for carrying the struggle for power beyond the frontiers of the Reich.

The most striking feature of this narrowly instrumental analysis may be precisely what is absent from it. Although we have seen the former Frankfurt School theorists turn with almost dogmatic consistency to the

Nazis themselves for clues as to the meanings of their actions, they seem unwilling to have taken the Nazis' professed hatred of the Jews literally and to have confronted the frightful implications of its deep resonance within German society. Did their insistence upon seeing the Nazi genocide of the Jews as explicable only in terms of something outside of itself serve them as a last, desperate attempt to salvage something from the shipwreck of Western rationality, or was it perhaps occasioned by a Marxist's lingering allegiance to the German working class? In a report on the "Current Status of Anti-Semitism in Germany," Neumann weighed the claim that German anti-Semitism was created and manipulated solely by the Nazi Party as a vehicle for the elimination of small business against the contention that it is deeply rooted in the hearts of the German people, but evaded the issue in favor of an analysis of the sectors of German society that objectively benefited from anti-Semitism. The enigma remained just as it had been planted by the author of *Behemoth* himself: "The writer's personal conviction," Neumann had ventured, "paradoxical as it may seem, is that the German people are the least Anti-Semitic of all."[74]

War and Peace

The Office of Strategic Services was disbanded by Presidential Order as of October 1, 1945. The reasons for its dissolution are complex, but the conspicuous cadre of German émigré socialists cannot have augured well for its survival. Secret Intelligence (SI) and Counterespionage (X-2) became the Strategic Services Unit of the War Department, and the R&A Branch was transferred to the Department of State as the Interim Research and Intelligence Service (IRIS). Neumann left the Department of State for the Department of Government at Columbia University in 1947, and the direction of the Central Europe Desk of the new Office of Intelligence Research passed successively to Marcuse and Kirchheimer, who, unable to find permanent academic positions, languished there where they "floated in limbo, distrusted by State Department professionals and seldom listened to."[75] Chilled by the glacial drift of the government into the policies and politics of the Cold War, they watched helplessly as the CIA arose, phoenix-like, out of the ashes of the manifestly antifascist Office of Strategic Services.

Franz Neumann's accidental death in September 1954 came at a point that found him wavering, in the estimation of a younger protégé, "between Marxism and liberal democracy,"[76] and we can do no more than speculate about the possible shape of his career as the lessons of the 1940s were gradually assimilated into his thinking. The battles he waged during the last years of his life, however, and a few unfinished essays from the year of his death give some indication of the problems that were preoccupying him.

By the time he left the government, Neumann had largely reconciled himself to the failure of his interlude as a public servant. Indeed, the German generals who, on July 20, had gambled on the affinities between their own anti-Soviet conservatism and the political objectives of the Western Powers now seemed to him closer to the mark than the R&A theoreticians who bet on the latent anti-Nazism of the German people. "It is astounding," he reflected, "that apart from isolated Anti-Fascist Committees, there was no great surge of anti-Nazi sentiment, no spontaneous revulsion, no demonstration of a will to proceed at any cost."[77] Though he had grown outspoken in his condemnation of the coercive socialist impositions applied in the Soviet sector, he especially criticized the Americans for committing the opposite error of failing to effect the social and economic changes that alone could ensure the survival of democratic institutions—clearly an untenable position to hold in the State Department in the first years of the Cold War. Democracy, after the lesson of Weimar, could never again be confused with the outward forms of parliamentary assemblies and the ostensible rule of law. A few weeks before his death he delivered an address in Bonn on the political conditions of free scientific inquiry in which he exhumed the warning of John Stuart Mill that threats to freedom may come as much from society as from the state; and in a set of fragmentary "Notes on the Theory of Dictatorship" he decried the absence of a systematic study of "the destruction of the line between state and society and the total politicization of society" that was the defining feature of the dictatorships of the twentieth century. At the end of his life he had begun to probe the irreducible substratum of repression that resides in psychic and political life, and the conditions in which it may assume its neurotic-destructive character. It is significant that his final public statements were on the theme of "Anxiety and Politics."[78]

Otto Kirchheimer experienced the same premonitions over the emerging shape of postwar German society. Already by the end of August he had written to Felix Gilbert and John Herz in Wiesbaden that their preliminary reports "confirmed our thesis . . . to the effect that 'de-centralization,' as provided by the Potsdam Declaration, really amounts to centralization on a regional level."[79] And even some two years later, in a memorandum he drafted for the American Jewish Labor Council on the persistence of anti-Semitism in Germany, he conceded that while much of the German population was impressed by the revelations concerning the deeds of the Hitler regime with regard to the Jews, "it is obvious that parts of Nazi ideology are still surviving, especially anti-Semitism among the peasantry and the middle classes."[80]

Along with this practical disillusionment, Kirchheimer shared with his Frankfurt School colleagues a theoretical concern with the shifting boundaries between state and civil society. This was particularly evident in Otto Kirchheimer's postwar scholarship, above all in his magnum opus of 1961, *Political Justice*. The title refers not to the quest of traditional political theory for a just social order but to the use of legal procedure for political ends—the "politicization of justice," as it were. Some of his most penetrating argumentation concerns the contributions and limitations of the Nuremberg litigation for the understanding of this process: "It defined the realm where politics ends or, rather, is transformed into the concerns of the human condition, the survival of mankind in both its universality and diversity."[81] Kirchheimer, too, came away from the OSS convinced that the encroachment of the political was the prevailing tendency of the modern era and that this was an inescapable and dangerous fact that legal theory and practice must henceforth recognize.

Herbert Marcuse, finally, offers the most obvious case of a radical intellectual who was determined that his theory keep abreast of the practice of the twentieth century. *One-Dimensional Man* (1964), the book that catapulted him from a professorial chair at Brandeis University to a decade of international celebrity, is more than a critique of the affluent, technological society; it is, in a sense, the study of dictatorship that Neumann had called for, but in its liberal rather than fascist form—"comfortable, smooth, reasonable, democratic":

> By virtue of the way it has organized its technological base, contemporary industrial society tends to be totalitarian. For "totalitarian" is not only a terroristic political coordination of society, but also a non-terroristic economic-technical coordination which operates through the manipulation of needs by vested interests . . . Not only a specific form of government or party rule makes for totalitarianism, but also a specific system of production

and distribution which may well be compatible with a "pluralism" of parties, newspapers, "countervailing powers," etc.[82]

Not only is the experience of the war evident in Marcuse's subsequent career—that can surely be said for most of his generation—but also the specific vantage point from which he observed it. From his desks in the Office of Strategic Services and the Department of State, Marcuse had reported in detail on the extension of political controls into all spheres of life and on reemergence in the immediate postwar years of the very forces that had precipitated that cataclysm. Against this background, his notorious formulation of 1965 deserves to be reconsidered: "Society cannot be indiscriminate where the pacification of existence, where freedom and happiness themselves are at stake: here certain things cannot be said, certain ideas cannot be expressed, certain policies cannot be proposed, certain behavior cannot be permitted without making tolerance an instrument for the continuation of servitude."[83] Not some alleged penchant for Stalinist authoritarianism lay at the root of the essay for which he was most fiercely condemned, but his direct experience of the "repressive tolerance" of the Weimar Republic toward the antidemocratic forces that would destroy it, a tolerance extended anew by the postwar occupation authorities.

· · ·

Although the famous demand for "the unity of theory and practice" pervades the rhetoric of Marxism, perhaps no other of its guiding axioms—except that of Revolution—has proven as unclear, ambiguous, or uncertain. Among the principal contributors to what is known as Western Marxism, the theorists of the Frankfurt School have probably received the harshest criticism for having weakened the critical, reciprocal link between intellectual and political labor, between a critical theory and a transformative political practice. Max Horkheimer even seemed to legitimize this rupture when he observed, as the clouds of war were already gathering, that "the kind of thinking which is most topical, which has the deepest grasp of the historical situation, and is most pregnant with the future, must at cetain times isolate its subject and throw him back on himself."[84] And Theodor Adorno, acknowledging that the sphere of private individuality, indeed, the "mutilated" consciousness of the intellectual, may become the locus of the displaced forces of social liberation, asserted that "if critical theory lingers there, it is not only with a bad conscience."[85] Overwhelmed by the seeming omnipotence of a fascist ruling class and the disarming of the radical opposition, the "dialectic of enlightenment," it is alleged, led them into a dialectic of defeat.[86]

The wartime experience of the "activist" wing of the Frankfurt Institut für Sozialforschung, however, represented by Franz Neumann, Otto Kirchheimer, and—in his own idiosyncratic way—Herbert Marcuse, seems to offer a corrective to any attempt to extrapolate from the premises of the Critical Theory to a politics of resignation. Their record in the Office of Strategic Services is mixed, and their own disappointment, frustration, and ultimate cynicism is the best deterrent to our temptation to romanticize this episode as the dreamed-of unity of theory and practice. To the contrary, had they compromised themselves intellectually or politically, their impact on the war and the peace might well have been greater.

But if we cannot speak of a sell-out, it is even less appropriate to speak of a cell, "boring from within." In this respect the federal agents who harassed Otto Kirchheimer during the McCarthy era were cut from the cloth as the ultra-leftists who would later use the OSS connection to defame Marcuse as an undercover agent out to destroy the New Left.[87] Perhaps it is most plausible to see them as a brake on tendencies already discernible in the embryonic intelligence establishment, but beyond that, metaphor must inevitably trail off into metaphysics. It can be stated with certainty, however, that in the Central European Section—"the pride and despair" of R&A, as an internal history confessed[88]—three Marxist intellectuals found more than simply a temporary refuge in a time of need. They produced there a creditable body of informed analytical work in an honorable attempt to realize the practical imperatives of a critical theory under the most challenging of circumstances.

· THREE ·

Historians Making History

The historian has only to write down and evaluate the course of events, and not take part in determining them. But times of great crisis lead him beyond this mission.

Friedrich Meinecke, *Die deutsche Katastrophe*

Early in 1946, while the ruined German cities still smoldered and suspected Nazis still filled the prisons and concentration camps they had built for their own political enemies, Friedrich Meinecke published his reflections on *Die deutsche Katastrophe*—the German catastrophe. The book is cast as a hymn of praise to Goethe and the *Goethezeit*, to an idealized "golden age" of free individuality nourished by a universalizing national community, and records the progressive fading of that ideal in the "blood-and-iron age" of Bismarck and the silver age of imperial liberalism, until it died a horribly tarnished death at the hands of the Nazis. It closes with his famous "wishful picture" of the *Goethegemeinde*, "Goethe Communities" that would spring up across the landscape of the shattered country to rekindle the creative fire of German *Kultur*.

The reception of Meinecke's effort to resuscitate the cultural values symbolized by Goethe varied according to the national experiences of its audience. In Germany the response was generally appreciative, at least partly in deference to his commanding stature in historical scholarship. Elsewhere, particularly among the recent victims of what he himself had counterposed as German "Machiavellism," the book was criticized as conceptually misconceived, denounced as an apologia, or dismissed as the pathetic daydream of a disillusioned old man.[1] Two historians bridged these communities, however, and stood in a special relation to Meinecke and to his attempt to decipher the irrational hieroglyph of "*Staatsrason*." Hajo Holborn and Felix Gilbert were trained by Meinecke himself in prewar Berlin but spent the war years in what would become a permanent American exile. History and biography conspired to impart to them a unique orientation toward "the German catastrophe."[2]

The two protégés met in the early twenties in the archives of the German Foreign Office—to which Felix Gilbert would return, under dramatically different circumstances in 1945—and their careers remained intertwined until Holborn's death in 1969. In connection with his work on the history of the Weimar constitution, Holborn had become increasingly associated with the leadership of the Social Democratic Party in Germany and was forced into emigration when his brilliant academic prospects faded after the Nazi seizure of power. Gilbert, who voted socialist and was descended on his mother's side from an illustrious Jewish family that dated back to Moses Mendelsohn, had also identified himself with the fortunes of Weimar and followed Holborn to America three years later, in 1936.[3] Upon learning that his most promising students had found a haven, Meinecke wrote to Holborn at Yale, "I trust that you will have the vital force to master the internal and external demands of your new existence, and that the root and branch of German scholarship that you transplant there will bear fruit."[4] With the coming of the war, the two protégés would rise to these "internal and external demands," though not, perhaps, in the manner their revered *Doktorvater* had intended. Indeed, they suspended their historical studies altogether to enter directly into the historical process.

The German Catastrophe

Whereas the iconoclastic Frankfurt School intellectuals cultivated a critical distance from the main currents of American life—"their own alienation-effect," in the Brechtian words of a friendly contemporary—Holborn and Gilbert worked assiduously to acclimate themselves to their new environment. Conscious of a certain Prussophobia among the old guard at Yale, Holborn avoided political discussion and astonished his graduate students with his punctilious command of English. Gilbert, precariously installed as assistant to Edward Earle at the Institute for Advanced Study, turned his training in the Meinecke tradition of intellectual historiography to the ideological roots of American isolationism.[5]

The impress of a century-old tradition of German historiography proved ineradicable, however, and marked the work they did both as academic scholars in the prewar Ivy League and as civil servants in the wartime OSS. They were trained in a period of intellectual ferment at Berlin University, when the Rankean tradition that had inspired the philosophical faculty since the reforms of Humboldt had come under scrutiny and was ceding some of its sovereignty to the ascendent social sciences. The historical profession in particular, once a progressive force allied with nationalism and liberalism against imperial autocracy, had been transformed into a conservative defender of the bourgeois state it had helped bring into existence. Historical research narrowed to an exclusive focus on the national state in its political and diplomatic aspect, and with few exceptions neither the claims of the social forces liberated by the breakdown of the Bismarckian Reich, nor the theories and methods most attuned to their significance, were admitted.

Although neither Gilbert nor Holborn would ever challenge the fundamental precepts of the "critical method" upon which Leopold von Ranke had founded the modern study of history—rigorous objectivity, the critical examination of original documents, the banishing of philosophical predispositions from the territory of the historian, the assumption that the past is a unified field and history a unified process—other influences penetrated the veil of Prussian orthodoxy during those years to illuminate their studies. Friedrich Meinecke, only then coming to be recognized as the outstanding historical scholar of the era, was unquestionably the decisive influence on both of them. Though himself steeped in the Rankean tradition that stressed the primacy of the nation state, Meinecke imparted to his students a larger view derived from his own lifelong search for a center from which to grasp the political and the cultural as simultaneous dimensions of history.[6]

Meinecke's principal accomplishment had been to survey the contours of intellectual culture and thus to expose the force of ideas in history. Equipped with this map, his students would survey rather different terrains, Holborn emphasizing the political and Gilbert increasingly the cultural field of historical practice. But they would share nevertheless more than just their lifelong friendship. In specialized studies that wavered, significantly, between the political turbulence of the sixteenth and of the twentieth centuries as well as in their historiographical essays on Herodotus and Thucydides, Machiavelli and Guicciardini, Ranke and Burchkhardt, both Holborn and Gilbert explored the mediation of politcal and cultural values that was taken as the heuristic task of the historian and the practical imperative of the citizen. Through the study of history and of historiography they sought neither to submit to the political status quo nor rise to some sphere of timeless values above it, but to use the very embeddedness of the historian as an instrument of critical research.

How little they must have anticipated that history itself would enable them to realize this high ambition. Holborn, widely respected for his encyclopedic knowledge of modern Germany, was among the first of the European émigrés to be drawn into the Research and Analysis Branch, to which he was recruited by his Yale colleague Sherman Kent, Chief of the Europe–Africa Division. Already influential as a political advisor, in spring 1943 Holborn was named one of three special representatives of Branch Chief William Langer, with responsibility for liaison between OSS and the military. Although Holborn was anxious to draw his old friend into the orbit of the burgeoning intelligence community then taking shape in Washington, Gilbert had on his own attracted the attention of Edward Earle, who was then dividing his attentions between his academic responsibilities at the Institute for Advanced Study in Princeton and the select Board of Analysts that directed the activities of the Branch. There followed interviews with Franz Neumann and other members of the Central European Section, and it was not long before a letter arrived from the office of Division Chief Kent: "Dear Mr Gilbert: On the off chance that you would be interested in a position in this office . . ."[7]

The rest, one may say in deference to their profession, is History. Although Holborn spent the remainder of the war shuttling back and forth between R&A headquarters and the Pentagon, while Gilbert moved from Washington first to the OSS Mission to Great Britain and then to its outpost in occupied Germany, the wartime careers of the two Meinecke students continued to intersect at vital points. Together they would describe a radical departure from the peculiarly German institution of *Gelehrtenpolitik*, of the engaged scholar. The academic elite had emerged into the twentieth century as a great ideological defender of the existing order, a role typified by Meinecke who now, to his credit, withdrew in the face of the fascist dictatorship "from the world of politics into the realm of ideas."[8] His two students found this tragic legacy to be profoundly instructive and were able to forge a very different link between "political power and academic responsibility."

R&A/Washington: 1943

In March 1943, Felix Gilbert took his place alongside Franz Neumann, Herbert Marcuse, and a dozen other political analysts in the Central European Section of R&A/Washington. Up to that time the main labor of the Section had been the production of a thousand-page *Handbook of Nazi Germany* prepared at the request of the Office of War Information but never published, and the *Strategic Survey of Greater Germany*, a collection of primary intelligence data intended to redress the pitiful dearth of basic information about the governments, populations, politcal parties, and natural and industrial resources of the enemy and occupied countries. When the young French historian David Pinkney consulted the Army Intelligence Corp's own handbook as part of his first assignment in the Western European Section, he was appalled by the misstatements, ommissions, and the general "thinness and dubious reliability" of American strategic intelligence for France,[9] and the situation for Germany was not much better. For much of 1942 the humanist scholars and social scientists of the Research and Analysis Branch labored to fill the void of current intelligence that would enable military authorities to deal most effectively with foreign resources.

OSS did not always make the most efficient use of its own ample resources, however. Gordon Craig, already an authority on recent European diplomacy, was chagrined to find himself assigned to a desk in the Africa Section, where he tried to navigate the unfamiliar literature on waterways in the Congo basin before leaving for a more suitable post in the State Department. Paul Zinner, rather than evaluating political developments in his native Czechoslovakia, was apprenticed to the art historian Richard Krautheimer, for whom he labored over Swiss newspapers with a dictionary and his high school German. Felix Gilbert himself, in this early transitional period, was given responsibility for political reporting on Hungary, an assignment that depended heavily on the expertise of his two assistants, Leslie Tihany and Robert von Neumann.[10] Only in midsummer, when Franz Neumann's directing influence over the Central European Section came to be felt, did he ease himself more fully into the mainstream of its work on Germany.

One of the conditions of the metamorphosis of academic scholars into intelligence analysts was that a collective identity descended over ideas and reports that in calmer times would have born more clearly the stamp of an individual author. This was particularly the case among the independent-minded Central European specialists, who gathered at least once a week for general meetings in which all views were aired. Before long, an assorted group evolved the added ritual of dining together in a local restaurant and then returning to someone's home for several more hours of private discussion. Felix Gilbert and Hajo Holborn were regular members of this Wednesday evening "seminar," as were Neumann, Marcuse, and Kirchheimer. American participants included Section Chief Eugene Anderson, whom Gilbert had first met in the company of Eckert Kehr at Meinecke's home in Berlin, and Harold Deutsch, who since April had been Chief of the Political Subdivision to which the Central European Section belonged. With Neumann restraining the fantastic flights of Marcuse, and the Americans musing over the eccentricities of their European counterparts, they debated the prospects of the German opposition, problems of military occupation, and the possible contours of postwar German reconstruction.[11]

The tasks of research and analysis thus proceeded in an atmosphere of intensity and a spirit of collegiality, disrespectful of the disciplinary allegiances of the university. Gilbert co-authored papers with philosophers and political scientists, exchanged services with economists and geographers, and thought nothing of an ad hoc collaboration with colleagues in the West European or Balkan Sections to produce an urgent memorandum or report. Most of his thinking, as expressed in reports prepared with Marcuse, Neumann, or the philosopher of history Hans Meyerhoff, concerned the internal cohension of the Nazi state and the interrelation between the German domestic situation and the battle fronts. Holborn, in this period, served in a much more independent position as a general consultant in German affairs, in which capacity he marshaled the weight of five centuries of German history to argue against strategies that detached military from social and political considerations.[12] As historians with an extraordinarily detailed and multifaceted knowledge of modern Germany, they helped to derive from these studies the set of theses on political warfare against a totalitarian regime for which the Central European Section came to be admired throughout the agency.

The fundamental tenet guiding the Section's work was that National Socialism was maintained by a mutual dependency between elements of the German ruling class, and that as long as the system of totalitarian controls continued to function effectively, no successful internal uprising against the regime could be expected. Only when the obvious hopelessness of the military situation finally discredited the Nazi determination for a fight to the finish did it appear that elements of the Army leadership, the weakest link in the totalitarian chain of command, might become the spearhead of a movement to terminate the war and depose the Nazi regime. "Just how this process will develop cannot, of course, be stated with scientific precision," Gilbert warned in a paper he and Marcuse submitted at the end of 1943. "We will attempt to outline that course of events which, after careful consideration of all factors involved, seems the most likely."[13]

Much of the preceding autumn had in fact been spent manipulating a series of variables and extrapolating from them a set of possible scenarios for the conclusion of the war. Would the allied nations remain united, or would political tensions finally split the Soviet Union from the Western democracies? Should the alliance collapse, would the Nazis resort to a camouflage shadow government in the hope of concluding a separate, compromise peace? What would be the consequences for the German labor movement? the response of the conservative anti-Nazi elite? There are not many occasions when professional historians are licensed to engage in conjectural exercises of this sort, but the tasks of wartime intelligence had extended their mandate to include the future as well as the past. Without models, precedents, or even the framework of a clear formulation of American policy, they had to proceed with a judicious admixture of close empirical research and disciplined extrapolation if they were to help military and diplomatic policy makers to anticipate developments rather than simply respond to them, and to do so on the basis of a sophisticated understanding of their significance.

In September 1943 these seemed to Gilbert and his friends to be among the most significant factors affecting the termination of the war and the destruction of the Nazi regime, although they acknowledged that "there is, of course, always present the possibility of a revolution in Germany regardless of the unity or disunity of the United Nations."[14] By the following month, however, the joint affirmation of the Allies at Moscow seemed to narrow the range of likely possibilities. There are several indications from the projects in which Gilbert participated during this period that he anticipated that the Nazi government would be overthrown in an internal coup d'état once the military situation had deteriorated beyond recovery but while the German armies were still basically intact and well outside of the German frontiers. Although this projection was not to be realized, the chain of reasoning he followed in reaching it is revealing of the style of thinking that prevailed in his group and of the nature of the intelligence services he and his co-workers hoped to provide.

A conjunction of military reversals, including the loss of the Rumanian oil supply, concentrated air attacks against the industrial centers of the eastern Reich, and the invasion of Western Europe, would, they estimated, be sufficient to materialize a movement for the overthrow of the Nazi regime. From the premises of Neumann's *Behemoth*—"a kind of bible for people working on Nazi Germany," as Gilbert readily admitted[15]—it was agreed that there was almost no likelihood that this would take the form of a popular uprising. To the contrary, a deteriorating military situation would only intensify the terroristic measures against all elements of the potential opposition. Localized and uncoordinated actions could be expected (food riots, work stoppages, spontaneous demonstrations), but the totality of the Nazi control apparatus was such that the regime could not be overthrown except by an organized force strong enough to contest that of the Nazis themselves. Only the Army High Command had at its disposal such a force and the political incentive to mobilize it in the interest of its own survival. Recalling that "a high degree of sober calculation has always been the strength as well as the weakness of the Prussian officer," the historian predicted that the commanders of several frontline divisions would strike at a point where they felt virtually guaranteed that the unity of the Nazi leadership would break under the weight of their coordinated assault, releasing the political support of the civilian population: "Large portions of the German and foreign workers will also support the rebellion," they concluded, "and will paralyze the Nazi regime on the local level by strikes, sabotage, and acts of individual terror."[16] That the attempted putsch of July 1944 would actually originate close to the headquarters of the High Command rather than among officers at the front lines, that it would be rapidly and ruthlessly crushed by the SS, and that it would find no deep resonance within the population at large were irrelevant, for the task of political intelligence was not to predict the future but to explain in advance the meaning of every likely contingency.

Accordingly, Gilbert's group focused upon the sort of German government with which the Western allies and Russia would have to deal in the event that the Nazi leadership were overthrown. In the situation they forecasted, it seemed probable that the unity of the Nazi leadership would finally be broken and that American military authorities would be obliged to deal with a bureaucratically colorless government of conservative elites. It might include either remnants of the "National Bolshevik" wing of the Nazi Party or of the conservative wing represented by Goering, and representatives of German labor, either reformist or revolutionary, might be drawn in; loyalists from the official Party formations (SS, SA) could be expected to put off their uniforms and attempt to exert their influence through underground channels. With the same patience he had used in his prewar scholarship to decipher the Machiavellian intrigues that lay beneath the gilded surface of the Florentine Renaissance, Felix Gilbert attempted, now in an anticipatory mode, to decipher the meaning of any such "National Peace Front" and uncover "the *real* forces behind this government."[17]

In this intellectual quest to anticipate the nature of the German collapse, the careers of the two Meinecke students once again converged. The Civil Affairs Division of the War Department (G-5), under the direction of General John W. Hilldring, had an especially practical interest in the conditions likely to prevail in Germany at the end of the war; its responsibility was to design the policies for the occupation and administration of the defeated territories. Since the middle of 1943 Hilldring had been searching in vain for a federal agency that could undertake a detailed study of the Nazified laws and institutions that would have to be dismantled. Finally, "in a spirit of desperation,"[18] he was about to subcontract the project privately to what remained of the History Department at Harvard (after the OSS had depleted its ranks) when Hajo Holborn, acting in his capacity as Langer's special representative to the Pentagon, proposed that the Research and Analysis Branch was uniquely fitted to undertake the task. Hilldring had sought an agency that could render assistance in the decidedly unhistorical task of "anticpatory thinking" about problems of military governance in countries to be liberated and about situations that may develop as a result of allied conquest; Holborn was able to persuade him that the key to the future lay in the past. "Nobody can make such predictions with absolute confidence," he cautioned, "but those who have studied the past and the present of the countries to be occupied and have explored the economic and social problems emanating from the present war should be in a position to define a good many of the questions likely to arise."[19]

Under Holborn's guidance, this project would grow from its original objective of assisting in the preparation for Military Government to the production of nearly one hundred handbooks and guides that, in the absence of anything else, would in many cases acquire the de facto status of field directives. These Civil Affairs studies, whose production became the main activity of the Europe–Africa Division for some 6–8 months, were designed to cover every aspect of life in the occupied and liberated territories of Europe. Once the general program had been developed, it fell to Holborn to coax the individual Guides through an interagency

Editorial Committee representing, in addition to OSS and CAD, the Foreign Economic Administration and the Departments of the Army, Navy, and State. Holborn had felt that neither the American military nor the civilian heads of government had a deep understanding of the relationship between the politics of war and the politics of peace and offered his services with noble but unrealistic aspirations. His postwar book on *American Military Government* (1947) gives no indication of the trials and tribulations of the historian who descends from reflection upon the historical process to active participation in it.[20]

Precisely because his assignment was to straddle the fence that separated the civilian OSS from the military, Holborn bore much of the brunt of this dislocation. During the early stages of the Civil Affairs Program he was repeatedly commended for the skill and acumen with which he negotiated the overall dimensions of the job. Despite deep reservations about the policy of unconditional surrender which he shared with most of the German-born analysts—and to which the Guides had to be geared—Holborn believed strongly in their internal worth.[21] No amount of diplomacy or personal initiative, however, could overcome the fact that while the military situation remained in flux, the administration temporized in articulating clearly what the fundamental U.S. policy toward Germany and the liberated areas was to be. Indeed, as late as February 1944, well after preparations for the program had gotten under way, there was still no official statement that the United States planned to occupy Germany and institute military government there, and even then the OSS program was subject to the changing terms of the ongoing debate over war aims and the conditions of peace. Research for the Civil Affairs Guides thus proceeded in a strange sort of vacuum, with no way of reconciling them to an overall policy framework nor any basis for resolving the conflicting views held by participating groups. His fellow historians tended to give Holborn the benefit of the doubt in this demoralizing situation, lamenting that there was no space under these circumstances in which such qualities of leadership as he possessed might be exercised. The economists involved in the project were less generous, however, pointing out that quite apart from the lack of basic policy, "the program labored under the further disability of being under the direction of Hajo Holborn who did excellent work in the promotional phases but proved incapable of coping with many of the later problems of the enterprise."[22] The difficulties alluded to in this memorandum refer to the procedure involved in the clearance of the individual Guides: each of them had to run a gauntlet of intra- and extra-agency review that severely tried the resources of the upstart intelligence agency and the community of engaged scholars who staffed it.

In his campaign to clear the OSS documents, Holborn was weighed down not only by this welter of petty jurisdictional disputes but also by more fundamental political issues regarding the diagnosis of German fascism and the prescription for eradicating it from postwar German society. The Foreign Economic Administration challenged their basic position that the German people and not Military Government should take responsibility for introducing democratic insititutions into Germany. The State Department's representative, in a spiriit of Olympian impartiality, objected to their recommendation that special provisions be made for the problems of Jews in postwar Europe as among other religious groups. And the Army and Navy insisted upon the subordination of everything to reestablishing conditions favorable to the security requirements of the occupying troops.[23]

In the course of the interagency warfare that plagued the whole of the CAD program and the interminable post hoc adjustments to changing foreign policy objectives, a set of general propositions emerged and came to constitute something like an OSS "line" on the functions of Military Government. Roughly stated, the perspective that can be derived from the hundred or so papers and the reams of minutes and memoranda that attended them was that Military Government could not realistically hope to play a messianic role and must avoid the temptation to cast itself as a positive force in postwar German politics. It was to be conceived rather as a limited instrument of short duration, committed in the wake-of-battle period to bare operational functions. Its responsibilities after this initial phase were to be limited to the dismantling of the German military establishment, the dissolution of the Nazi Party, replacement of Nazi personnel and apprehension of war criminals, and the removal of obstacles to the emergence of democratic institutions. "Otherwise," wrote Carl Schorske in his notes on an R&A planning session, "MG should try to do nothing positive."

> The real function of MG is to confine itself to seeing that non-Nazi forces in German society are given the right to emerge as they please. There should be no attempt to prevent a force from emerging unless it springs from Nazi ideology. What we want is a reputable Germany which can take its place in the world of democratic nations, a Germany which will be neither a British nor a Russian sphere of influence.[24]

How did Hajo Holborn and Felix Gilbert—Meinecke's representatives in America—adapt their historical skills to this closely delimited task?

·   ·   ·

The contribution of the Research and Analysis Branch to the Civil Affairs program was ultimately to consist of three related research projects, overseen by Holborn and other senior officials and transmitted by him to the War Department. Although they worked indpendently, Gilbert participated in all phases of it, and the course of his own contribution affords us a particular insight into the intellectual dynamics of the agency.

In mid-1943 the Central European Section of R&A inaugurated a series of monographs on "German Military Government over Europe" for the Provost Marshall General's office, which examined in austerely factual fashion the institutions created by the Nazis for the subjugation and exploitation of conquered territories. Gilbert contributed to the description of this control apparatus as it operated in Yugoslavia; the classicist Moses Hadas, more fittingly, perhaps, was selected to write the report on Greece.

The second large-scale project was the so-called *Civil Affairs Handbook on Germany* which ran to about two thousand pages and sought to provide Military Government planners (and, in their later incarnation as "Army Service Forces Manuals," field officers themselves) with basic compilations of factual material on everything from the Nazi Party to the Christian churches. The introductory handbook on the "Background to the Nazi Regime" was actually a brilliantly condensed narrative history of Germany from the early Middle Ages, carried by Gilbert himself through to the end of the nineteenth century and brought to completion by his colleagues after his departure for Europe.

This exercise may have done more to keep the author's historical skills sharpened than "to create the conditions which will make it possible for civilian agencies to function effectively"—the nominal charge of the Handbooks.[25] In executing it Gilbert traced the uniquely centrifugal tendencies that had marked Germany from the decline of Roman imperial authority to the eras of Bismarck and Hitler: regional particularism and an irreducible variety of political forms; religious schism, intellectual divergence, and cultural chauvinism; the contrast between the feudal cast of the east-Eibian social structure and the accelerating prominence of the Burgher class in the economically developed west and south. Against the actual disintegration of Germany as a political unit over the course of the preceding millennium, the maintenance of a unifying political bond had by the nineteenth century become a mere fiction: "In German terms, the national state of 1871 did not and could not solve the problem of the relations between 'state' and *'volk.'* "[26] This legacy of unresolved conflict pointed almost inexorably toward the conservative modernization and aggressive nationalism that thrust Germany into world politics in the nineteenth century and into World War in the twentieth.

The thesis of German deviation from the general pattern of European nation-building that Gilbert set out in his abbreviated "history of modern Germany" has become standard, due in no small measure to its extended elaboration in the magnum opus by that title which Holborn published in the postwar decades. The familiarity of this interpretation among academic historians, however, should not distract us from the essential point to be made about Gilbert's wartime exposition, a point so obvious that it is easily overlooked: Felix Gilbert evidently believed that it was necessary for Civil Affairs Officers to know that the roots of the Third Reich lay in the First, and to appreciate Nazism as the catastrophic dénoument of five centuries of German history. Beneath his Civil Service classification beat the heart of a professor.

The attempt to impart a historical education to CAOs who would be preoccupied with the restoration of public order and public utilities is illustrative of the challenges that confronted the displaced scholars of OSS, and of the leverage they still hoped to apply. As heirs to a tradition of German historiography with its roots in Meinecke, Burckhardt, and Ranke, neither Gilbert nor Holborn could conceive of Nazism except in terms of the political and cultural processes through which it had arisen and in defiance of which it could not be fully destroyed. "The biggest problem in the training of CAOs," lamented Professor Holborn as if referring to one of his PhD candidates, "has been to get them beyond the mere collection of facts and general information to an understanding of the political aims of CA operations."[27] With conscious deliberation the historians were resisting what would become the overwhelming temptation to secure the stability of the system through quick technical solutions to problems they perceived as intrinsically and essentially political.

Where they failed to contain the academic and political content of their prose within acceptable levels the process was in any case completed by others. Gilbert's draft manuscript was stripped of its historical allusiveness and vigorously purged of references to modern Germany as "the state of the owning classes."[28] Even in the severely edited form in which it was finally released, it may well have been implicated in the sweeping assessment made by a senior Civil Affairs Officer who, once the program actually got under way in 1945, complained that the OSS studies "contented themselves with glittering generalities" rather than addressing the critical exigencies of the moment.[29]

Gilbert's encapsulated history also included a number of excursions into the intellectual history of Germany, a fact not surprising for a student of the foremost advocate of the force of ideas in history. The coercive imposition of centralized state control over regional discrepancies, which he had shown to be the fateful achievement of the Bismarckian era in other spheres, served in the organization of cultural and intellectual life to constrain the development of tendencies that threatened the ruling system. The Weimar Republic had released the divergent tendencies of German intellectual culture, and it was this climate of free experimentation, of which he was himself a beneficiary, that Gilbert hoped to restore through his final contribution to the Civil Affairs Program—and to the work of R&A/Washington. The third project of the Research and Analysis Branch for the War Department was the program of Civil Affairs Guides for Germany, which differed from the Handbooks in permitting a limited measure of analysis and policy recommendations. From late winter 1943 until his departure for England, Gilbert worked with art historian Richard Krautheimer to develop a body of substantive recommendations for dismantling the Nazi organization of Germany elementary, secondary, and higher education and restoring to them the autonomy they had nominally won during the liberal era.

The two exiled academicians were exceptionally well-qualified to survey the recent, tragic history of German education and to offer a realistic assessment of the prospects of restoring at least the foundations of its prelapsarian greatness. Gilbert's humanistic credentials have already been shown to have been in order; Richard Krautheimer, one of the outstanding representatives of a tradition of art historical scholarship acclaimed for its catholicity and indifference to disciplinary boundaries, would rank among the most influential of the émigré humanist educators in America.[30] R&A approached two of the most accomplished products of the German educational system itself and confronted them with the challenge of re-educating the German educators.

The recommendations generated by Gilbert and Krautheimer were tailored to the R&A position on denazification generally, namely, that it must be carried out by German anti-Nazi groups themselves. The Civil

Affairs program, according to this conception, must eliminate all obstacles to the emergence of democratic institutions without signaling to anti-Nazi groups that foreign interference in German's cultural life was intended, much less that postwar German society should be refashioned in the image of the American New Deal. The schools and universities of Germany presented a particular challenge even to this limited set of objectives because they were among the institutions most thoroughly penetrated by Nazi ideas and personnel.

In the field of education—as in other spheres of German life—National Socialism had inherited a tradition of centralization and state control, only partially democratized during the brief interval of Weimar. Primary and secondary schools, art academies and technical institutes, and the universities were state institutions whose official status lent great prestige to all intellectual activities but especially to the traditional fields of humanistic learning, which had no direct political implications. There were long-range dangers inherent in perpetuating this system, but these were balanced by the immediate threats to social order that would result from closing the schools and universities until their staff, curricula, and regulations could be thoroughly investigated. The difficulties were complicated by the wartime damage to schools, the shortage of suitable instructional materials, and the partial disintegration of German society likely to attend the termination of hostilities. It fell heavily upon Gilbert and Krautheimer to strike the delicate balance that would ensure that the demilitarization of German education would be more enduring in 1945 than it had been in 1919.

At the primary and secondary level they recommended first that Military Government undertake emergency measures to get the schools going and keep the children and youth occupied. Second, Military Government should be prepared to assume direct control of functions exercised by the Reich Ministry of Education and conduct an immediate purge of leading officials at this and the regional level. Finally, MG should supervise the appointment of politically reliable local authorities who would undertake the actual running of the schools and begin investigation of all members of the teaching profession. Certain coercive measures would undoubtedly have to be taken in order to eliminate the Nazi slant from regular subjects: race biology from the natural sciences, Pan-German geopolitics from history and geography, premilitary training from gymnastics; even arithmetic and geometry handbooks would have to be scrutinized. At the same time, "MG should not institute or participate in . . . any gesture resembling the one-time Nazi act of burning books";[31] precisely in the interest of substantive and lasting reform, MG could not simply try to co-opt the existing system as the Nazis themselves had done when they turned it to their own political ends in 1933. Something akin to the restoration of the pre-Nazi system—with its peculiar overlay of democratic on reactionary, bourgeois on feudal, elements—was the point of departure, nor was it an inconsiderable one in view of the magnitude of the task.

The challenge posed by the universities was somewhat different. Felix Gilbert, educated in Berlin during the politically charged years of Weimar, suffered no illusions about the extent of the nazification of his generation, of the reactionary tradition of the German professoriate even under the Republic, or of the potential dangers of a mass of disillusioned, unemployed youth returning once again from the fronts as they had at the end of the first World War. Gilbert anticipated that even in those universities where the Nazi *Führerprinzip* may have been overthrown in the period of disintegration, "the anti-Nazi label of some new groups might frequently hide the same aggressive nationalism and militarism which were at the root of Nazi doctrine."[32] Accordingly, the Civil Affairs Guide to the denazification of the German universities drafted by Gilbert and Krautheimer advocated the extreme measure of suspending all teaching and other activities during the period necessary for the dismissal of active Nazis from the faculties and student bodies and the abrogation of all Nazi regulations and admission requirements. Political meetings should be permitted—albeit under the supervision of MG—because, as Gilbert accurately predicted, it would be in such forums that the reorganization of the universities could be debated by anti-Nazi groups within the German academic community itself. The responsiblity for cleansing the universities would, as in other spheres of life, be assigned to the Germans themselves, but to the victors was reserved the right of sanctioning the results: "Only after all the most urgent tasks of eradicating Nazism have been completed to the satisfaction of Military Government can the full reopening of the universities be considered."[33]

·   ·   ·

A certain development and recapitulation had taken place during this period of transition from academic office to government officer. On the one hand, it is striking to observe that the two tendencies the historians had brought with them from their apprenticeship with Meinecke continued to play themselves out in their respective careers. Holborn—"this quiet and deliberate North German," as Gilbert described his friend[34]— immersed himself in the military and diplomatic affairs that had always been the stock of the "Prussian School" of political history, while Gilbert, with his "softer" southern disposition, focused his attention primarily upon cultural matters, above all education and the revival of intellectual life.

Their academic training in Berlin may have fitted them at an even deeper level for their wartime duties of research and analysis, however. The intellectual climate in which they were trained in the 1920s, like that in which they worked in the 1940s, was dominated by the bitter methodological controversy between "the old and the new trends in German historical scholarship," as Karl Lamprecht had entitled his opening salvo in the assault upon traditional political history by the new social sciences. In both contexts, two competing rhetorics advanced claims to the mantle of rigorous science: the Rankean tradition affirmed the uniqueness of the historical past and sought to grasp every event "wie es eigentlich gewesen," through an approach that was structured, richly textured, and manifestly interpretive; the ascendent social sciences, represented in Washington by the Projects Committee of R&A, invoked regularity over individuality and causality over sequence and demanded a methodology that approximated pure factual reportage and that displaced the subject entirely from the text. Both in Berlin in the years following World War I and again in Washington twenty years later, Gilbert and Holborn eschewed either of these radical alternatives and groped instead for a conceptual apparatus that would bring into a tactical alliance the warring factions of "abstractness of generalization and the concreteness of aesthetic description."[35]

R&A/London: 1944

The political—as distinct from the methodological—significance of Gilbert's detailed studies becomes clear when they are inserted into the context of the ongoing debate over the fate of postwar Germany. The belated attention to this problem, which had come to exercise the President and his Cabinet only from the Moscow and Teheran conferences onward, was the bane of Holborn's existence for much of 1944. Throughout that summer, at weekly planning meetings of senior R&A officials which he chaired, Holborn was able to do little more than report on the continued vacillation of the interministerial European Advisory Commission (EAC), the Combined Civil Affairs Committee (CCAC) of the British and American Chiefs of Staff, the tripartite Allied Control Council (ACC), and various other bureaucratic acronyms that hoped to stamp their initials upon Germany and upon history: "With the major political problems still unsettled," he mused in mid-August, "we can hardly hope to produce anything of value."[36]

Against the fusion and confusion of military and political, wartime and postwar, objectives operating at higher levels of government, Holborn could only encourage the continued, methodical labors of the the R&A researchers. Their basic position, however,—that denazification measures should be put into effect even at the expense of efficiency and that democratic reconstruction was the responsibility of the German people and not the occupying armies—was finding its way increasingly into the official SHAEF *Handbook for Military Government* being prepared at the Civil Affairs Training School in Shrivenham. The so-called SHAEF Bible was still in an unfinished form when, in August, Treasury Secretary Henry Morgenthau saw it and reacted violently: interpreting it as an opportunistic scheme for the rehabilitation of the German economy, he prevailed upon Roosevelt to repudiate it and countered with his own "Suggested Post-Surrender Program for Germany," which called for a severe policy of demilitarization, deindustrialization, and partition.

"It is probably correct to say," Holborn later remarked with evident pride, "that much of the thinking that Secretary Morgenthau objected to originated with the OSS."[37] Far from being inspired by feelings of compassion toward the defeated Reich or political maneuvering vis-á-vis the Soviet Union, however, the R&A position was grounded in a historically minded analysis of the conditions most favorable to an enduring European peace. Preeminent among these was a Germany that had not only been purged of its fascist and miltarist superstructure but one in which the *internal* process of democratization could finally begin. Even when the famous JCS 1067, the "Combined Directives on the Military Governance of Germany," was finally issued to General Eisenhower, Holborn could observe with some irony that the unintended effect of Morgenthau's assault was to leave R&A's Civil Affairs Guides as the main corpus of thought on the problems of denazification, democratization, and postwar reconstruction. When late in the year the dust had finally settled around the Morgenthau affair, Holborn began to shift his attentions to the Far East and to the new Civil Affairs Center for the Pacific Theater. The occupation of Japan and the postwar imperial ambitions of the British came increasingly to preoccupy him, but in his retreat from the European Theater he left too few documentary traces for us to follow.[38]

• • •

During those tumultuous months, Holborn's old compatriot kept his own attention fixed squarely on the European Theater. In February 1944, over strenuous objections that his services were still required in the Central European Section, Felix Gilbert shipped out aboard the *Queen Elizabeth* to the OSS Mission in Great Britain. The tide had by this time turned decisively in favor of the Allies, and, like any good historian, he wanted to get as close to his sources as possible. Repeated attempts to lure Holborn to London were rebuffed on the grounds of his central role in the Civil Affairs Guide campaign and the experience that "men sent overseas are men lost to the work of R&A."[39]

At the London Outpost, Gilbert joined another stellar community of scholars in the displaced faculty seminar that was the R&A Branch: the historians Crane Brinton, Perry Miller, Leonard Krieger, and Arthur Schlesinger, Jr.; the sociologists Edward Shils and Morris Janowitz; and a battalion of economists, including Charles Kindleberger, Paul Sweezy, Walt W. Rostow, and Chandler Morse, who, as the newly appointed Branch Chief, directed the activities of research and analysis. From their vantage point on Brook Street, the problems of war and peace on the Continent acquired a much more immediate character than they had from OSS headquarters or even from Holborn's niche at the Pentagon, and Gilbert recalled that "although we were not always of the same opinion we were a rather closely knit group and we considered the Washington office as somewhat unrealistic."[40]

Just as the influence of the American military grew steadily in the European Theater as preparations for the Normandy invasion got under way, so the stature of the OSS rose in the estimation both of the American Joint Chiefs of Staff and the older, more established European agencies. The British Special Operations Executive (SOE) and Military Intelligence (MI-5 and MI-6) in particular—heirs to a 500-year tradition of espionage and counterintelligence—watched the OSS base in London grow from an undisciplined assortment of American entrepreneurs to an increasingly professional shadow-warfare organization of some 2,000 people and 14 branches with which it regularly cooperated. The London Outpost of Langer's Research and Analysis Branch, having resigned itself to its mandatory status as a research organization barred from critical evaluation or direct policy recommendations, developed a wide reputation for efficiency, productivity, and the technical excellence of its reports.

The OSS Mission to Great Britain recreated on its own scale the main braches of OSS/Washington, some of which came in time to overshadow those of the parent organization. The Special Operations Branch (SO), as close as OSS got to realizing the cloak-and-dagger fantasies of General Donovan, conducted commando operations throughout northern, western, and central Europe; Morale Operations (MO) waged "black" propaganda campaigns to strengthen pro-Allied sentiment in France and weaken German morale; William Casey's Secret Intelligence unit (SI), with officers posted in the U.S. embassy and in regular contact with a variety of governments-in-exile in London, secured first-hand information that was the basis of much of the work of the R&A scholars.

The Research and Analysis Branch had itself grown from two professionals and a pair of secretaries dispatched to London in April 1942 to a well-staffed and functionally variegated organization. Under the guidance of Allan Evans and Deputy Chief Crane Brinton, its responsibilities expanded from primarily liaison work with the object of procuring intelligence materials for Washington to the evaluation of bombing targets, research for the Civil Affairs program, preparation of materials in support of the Allied invasion of North Africa, and the servicing of requests for intelligence from a spectrum of British and American agencies. At times the need to establish their worth as a serious trading partner in the intelligence marketplace stretched their resources rather thinly—as Brinton mused, "I have no doubt the high point of my career in intelligence work came when I was called upon to answer a telephone request for the plural of 'epiglottis.' "[41] When Gilbert arrived in February 1944, the work of R&A/London was acclaimed for its erudition and, occasionally, for its value as well.

Although Felix Gilbert would officially be designed Chief of the German–Austrian Section of R&A/London, the unspoken reservations of the OSS executive about allowing German-born personnel to hold positions of authority spared him the most thankless administrative responsibilities. The integrated work program of the London Outpost from March 1944 onward served to channel his work in more productive directions, and he came to be widely admired among his colleagues for the historian's meticulous attention to detail, his personal congeniality, and his uncanny ability to compose polished reports at the typewriter. At the broadest level, the priorities of R&A/London, like those of the Office of Strategic Services generally, began at about that time to experience "a shift in major emphasis, so far as Europe is concerned, from studies for military plans to those of post-hostilities, primarily military government and civil affairs."[42] In turning from problems of war to anticipated problems of the peace, their work naturally shifted from a military to a predominantly political idiom.

This transition may have been most clearly expressed in Gilbert's analysis of the perceived disagreement between the American and English positions of Civil Affairs as they developed over the summer of 1944. The main points of contention—whether to retain or immediately dismantle the National Socialist welfare organizations, the extent of the denazification of Nazi economic ministries, whether maintenance of central agencies or even a central government would be an obstacle to the rebuilding of political life from below—in fact revolved around the more basic issue of the relative priorities of denazification and the establishment of a smoothly functioning administration in the initial period of occupation. The question for Gilbert was thus essentially misconceived for, as he wrote in a long letter back to Hajo Holborn in Washington, "it was not so much a dispute between the English and the Americam point of view but a dispute between those who looked upon Civil Affairs from a political point of view and those who looked upon them from a military point of view." Insofar as political differences between the future occupying powers remained, they referred ultimately to the relative dispositions of the Allied nations at the end of the war and to their maneuvering for position in its final hours; Gilbert did not find the English position, which envisaged the survival of a conservative, centralized Germany of some strength and power, to be wholly innocent. "This is definitely a question of interpretation," he advised his old comrade, but he believed that "the English have a very clear realization of the changes in the power constellation which the war has brought about." "They know that they will be on the defensive in the postwar world," he added, "and want to keep up as many defence positions as possible: From that point of view their inclination towards maintaining of central agencies in Germany seems to me not by chance."[43]

Gilbert's own work, then, for the remainder of 1944, reflected the advance of the Second Front. As chief political analyst for the Central European affairs he continued, as he had in Washington, to write weekly political analyses of events as they unfolded inside Germany and, secondarily, Hungary and Czechoslovakia. These reports, designed to inform military commanders about the situation in Germany, were transmitted back to Washington, where they may have been incorporated into larger and more general studies; but the scholar also remarked, "from a didactic point of view'" that such interdisciplinary exercises were important for the authors as well, for they form "an activity in which all members of the group cooperate (and) which prevents their going off into different directions and becoming mere technical specialists."[44] In such time as remained he published political analyses in the *European Political Report*, an R&A intelligence digest started by Paul Sweezy and edited successively by Gilbert and the energetic young Arthur Schlesinger, Jr., for distribution throughout the intelligence community in London, and also evaluated—often critically—material generated by the SI Branch and by Allen Dulles, who since November 1942 had been single-handedly operating a clandestine station out of neutral Switzerland.

In general, however, the London Branch was involved in tasks of a smaller and more practical nature than Gilbert had grappled with in Washington. He responded to specific intelligence requests for the continental operations of the Office of War Information and of other American (and British) agencies. He conducted interviews with German prisoners-of-war who were often able—wittingly or otherwise—to yield important clues on such matters as the effects of Allied bombardment on civilian morale. And he was responsible for maintaining regular contacts with the welter of German émigré groups in London. The specific projects he worked on, particularly after the Normandy invasion in June and the failed assassination attempt in July, corresponded to the changing priorities of the final months of the war and preparations for the close of hostilities in Europe.

Although Gilbert, along with most of the German-born scholars of the R&A Branch, felt that neither the idea of a divided nor of a "pastoralized" Germany had any credibility, he did recognize that the exigencies of defeat would require an indeterminate period of multinational military administration. With a fellow officer from the Geographic Section he helped prepare for the European Advisory Commission a plan for the zonal administration of Berlin, and in so doing made one of his enduring contributions to German history: "I pointed to the Grunewald and Dahlem area on the map and jokingly said, 'This is where my relations had houses; this ought to be the American section.'[45] The lines they drew have stood ever since.

Finally, Gilbert worked throughout much of the year on revising the denazification lists that had been prepared by his colleagues in the Central European Section in Washington. By his estimation, the criteria they had employed would have implied not only the virtual suspension of many public services but the arrest and detention of some 1.5 million persons in Germany, a task he viewed as hopelessly unrealistic in terms of the limited personnel available to Military Government, as well as inconsistent with its limited objectives. His revisions were motivated by a sense of the likely realities of the postwar situation and not by any feelings of compassion for the perpetrators and their accomplices (much less by any doubts about the necessity of a thorough-going process of denazification). Indeed, Gilbert was highly skeptical of plans for the impending trials of Nazi war criminals; as he began to project his thinking beyond the exigencies of the moment, he came increasingly to hope that the Germans themselves would rise up against their Nazi leaders and treat them as summarily as the Italians would soon treat Mussolini, rather than subject them to long judicial proceedings.

Gilbert's last piece of prewar scholarship had been an implied critique of the fifteenth-century humanist catalogue of ideal princely virtues in terms of the radical political realism of Machiavelli. In concluding that it would be better if the leading Nazis were expeditiously killed and a new start made, perhaps he was now recalling the Machiavellian injunction that "when he takes possession of a state, the new Prince must determine all the injuries that he will need to inflict, and much then inflict them once and for all. In that way way he will not have to renew them every day, and will be able to set the minds of the people at rest."[46]

R&A/Germany: 1945

In the last months of the war, while teams of specially trained OSS commandos were "piercing the Reich" from the skies,[47] the famous "Chairborne Division," as the Research and Analysis Branch was affectionately known, began hauling its typewriters and filing cabinets stealthily across Europe, a safe distance behind the advancing armies. In August 1944, within days of liberation, an OSS Outpost had been set up in Paris, with Harold Deutsch as Chief of R&A, and it immediately began siphoning off talent from London. Arriving scholars were not always able to suppress their personal reactions to the state of the European Theater as they found it. Of the older generation, Crane Brinton reported on his travels through France in late August with a nihilistic sense of eternal recurrence as he was reminded of the ravaged countryside "as I saw it in 1919."[48] Younger men such as Saul K. Padover (now well known for his tireless postwar Marx scholarship) found that Paris "seemed to have gone off its hinges," and basked in the tumultuous welcome given the American liberators.[49] But Viennese-born Lorenz Eitner, who would rise to prominence for his studies on the origins of the French *avant-garde*, heard in the violent reaction to an exhibition of nonobjectivist painting resonances of other, more disturbing cultural manifestations "that reminded me somewhat of the German tirades against *Kulturbolschevismus*. There seems to have started here, unfortunately, a cry for 'healthy' art."[50]

As soon as the "picture of complete unreality and bewilderment" had begun to clear, Gilbert himself settled into a demanding schedule of work. In addition to the regular tasks of field reporting, he began to work closely with the U.S. Group Control Council, which had requested from him background information on the German General Staff and recommendations as to what should be done with German officers. At the other end of the political spectrum, he reviewed the various "Antifa" groups that were spontaneously forming across Germany and to help determine the MG policy toward them.[51]

Paris, however, as important a center as it was for the acquisition of political intelligence from SI and from people arriving directly from enemy territorists, was a restless way-station for the Germanists of R&A. "The whole stay," Gilbert remarked casually of those extraordinary months, "though interesting and useful, was always of a somewhat transitional nature."[52] Indeed, one of the main activities of the Paris office from the beginning of 1945 was to prepare for the long-awaited R&A penetration of Germany itself. The previous September, General Walter Bedell Smith had written to the Joint Chiefs of Staff that OSS had "a group of trained experts who could be of great assistance to the U.S. Group Control Council and the Commanding General," and recommended that an OSS Mission be established in Germany under the directionof SHAEF "as soon as circumstances permitted."[53] In early April, an advance party under Col. Alfred D. Reutersham ventured forward from Luxembourg to locate a suitable headquarters, and by the middle of May a fully staffed OSS Mission was functioning out of an abandoned Henkell Trocken champagne factory on the outskirts of Wiesbaden. Harold Deutsch transferred his office from Paris to become Chief of the new R&A Branch with the young Lt. Col. H. Stuart Hughes, who had distinguished himself as head of R&A operations in the Mediterranean Theater, as his deputy. Chief of Political Analysis was Felix Gilbert, returning to a Germany as transformed by the events of the preceding decade as he was himself.[54]

The chaos and confusion that prevailed in the period of surrender astonished even Gilbert, who had spent much of the previous year trying to modify the extravagant plans of his superiors in Washington. Nevertheless, even amid this extreme disorganization a number of tasks required immediate and constant attention if opportunities were not permanently to be lost. While conditions in the American zone were still being secured, the various branches of OSS began preparing interpretive studies of political, economic, and social developments. And with an eye to future history, OSS was charged to assist in obtaining records and documentary material on every phase of the German war effort.

The Research and Analysis Branch in particular was responsible for developing an efficient program of field reporting involving observation and analysis, interview and interrogation, and—as usual—the servicing of spot intelligence requests from various client agencies and from R&A/Washington. To determine how best to discharge these manifold duties, the R&A executive—Deutsch, Hughes, and Gilbert—held a series of meetings at the end of June to outline a program of "Field Intelligence Studies" which would be described as "the real job of R&A/Germany during the next few months. They should be our *spécialité de maison*."[55] Gilbert and his staff—which included Franklin Ford, Leonard Krieger, Perry Miller, and Hans Meyerhoff—immediately began to work out the details of a comprehensive survey of the region immediately surrounding Wiesbaden that would cover everything from the spectrum of political thinking and church opinion to trade union activities, community organization, and the composition and operation of the local chambers of commerce.

Even with a relatively clear set of priorities, however, the general paralysis of German society constrained their activities in ways that the impatient Europeanists in Washington little understood. In the first of his weekly reports from Germany, Gilbert advised his colleagues to forget about questions regarding "the attitude of the German people" or the outlines of "a general pattern," for the forseeable future; the breakdown of communications and the absence of centralized authority themselves frustrated any attempt to generalize on more than a local scale. Furthermore, he protested,

> I believe that you do not quite realize the conditions under which the field reporting takes place. You cannot take a car and drive around the country wherever you want to go. You need orders specifying the purpose of your trip. You need clearance on nearly every level from the army group down to local MG, and this is a very time-consuming process. You must justify your presence before the local MG, as it is in his hands to give you permission to interview people and on whom you are dependent for food and shelter. The non-fraternization law limits your possibilities of investigating in places where you are not accredited.

They may very well have been America's first *secret* agents, but "we are not entirely *free* agents."[56]

The historians Edgar Johnson (left), Felix Gilbert, John Clive, and Carl Schorske bundled up against the chill of the Cold War: Wiesbaden, Autumn 1945.

When restrictions eased and a measure of physical security returned, Gilbert and his assistants began to move first around the American zone and then to venture ever further afield. By the end of June he was angling (unsuccessfully) for permission to interrogate industrialist Fritz Thyssen and the deposed Minister Hjalmar Schlacht, and managed at least a short conversation with Pastor Martin Niemöller, one of the most outspoken victims of the regime they had served. He had already made good use of his training as a diplomatic historian when at the end of April he and Krieger drove across Germany to survey the archives of the Foreign Office after their discovery in a castle near Meisdorf in the Harz Mountains. Again in August he was attached to the DeWitt Poole Mission to assist State Department personnel in interviewing German diplomats about Russo-German relations in the period prior to the invasion. As a traditional historian, however, committed to the primacy of the documentary record, "my enthusiasm for interviewing these German diplomats was limited."[57] Indeed, in the last months of his government service, during which he came increasingly to recognize the extent to which he had severed his ties to his native Germany, Gilbert's sublimated academic identity began to return in full force and to enter more conspicuously than ever into the political reporting he undertook.

Ever the vigilant scholar—as well as R&A's leading expert on the German universities—Felix Gilbert seized the opportunity to investigate the first stirrings of life within the German academic community and the reopening of the liberal universities in his native Baden. Accompanied again by Leonard Krieger, he made first for Freiburg and then in mid-July for Heidelberg University, where he attended political meetings, interviewed Martin Heidegger, Karl Jaspers, and other leading professors to have survived the Hitler regime, and in general monitored the academic debate over the politics of denazification and the philosophy of higher education in a postfascist era. Auditing the process from a position above the fray, the displaced Professor Gilbert was profoundly unimpressed.

The reports Gilbert and his assistants produced—subtly sarcastic, explicitly judgmental, and loaded, at last, with a most unprofessional freight of adverbs and adjectives—demonstrated how the divergent prewar traditions of the two universities had sealed their respective fates during the Nazi era and now constrained their recovery from it. The Freiburg faculty, "conservative in its political, and traditional in its scholarly outlook," had weathered the storm for the very reason that once its Jews and Republicans had been dismissed, "the Nazis had no ideological cause to attack it."[58] Typical in this respect was the philosopher Heidegger, whom Gilbert met in a lengthy interview with matters other than the existential ontology on the agenda. Unaware that this uniformed American intelligence officer might indeed have read his *Sein und Zeit* and know of his quest for the ultimate ground of being, the disgraced philosopher obsequiously agreed to every contradictory proposition put before him: "My impression about his personal attitude (I don't mean his philosophy) was very negative."[59]

Heidelberg, however, precisely because of its reputation for modernist experimentation and as the spiritual home of modern sociological theory in Germany, had attracted the intellectual leaders of German political liberalism and fell therefore under the mailed fist of the Nazi Ministry of Education. During the summer of the liberation, debate over reconstruction rapidly polarized between two generational factions among the professoriate: a returning older generation—led by Karl Jaspers and Alfred Weber—whose political records were unsullied but who had for that very reason been excluded from university life for more than a decade and whose sole reference point was the status quo before 1933; and a group of younger instructors, led by Alexander Mitscherlich, who had endured the intellectual sterility of the Nazi years and saw no possibility of returning to pre-Hitler conditions which they held partially responsible for it.

Whereas the older professors clamored for a formal constitution that would guarantee the future independence of the university and insulate it from outside interference, the younger group, Gilbert reported, "views the University's degeneration as part of the general degeneration of German life," a process that can only be reversed by dealing realistically with the social transformations wrought by a decade of fascism, war, and occupation. Jaspers, who had been elevated virtually by default into the position of University Senator, struggled valiantly to reconcile the two opposing factions with a call for a new system of values based on the union of scientific truth and liberal humanism, but Gilbert left his interview with the courageous *Existenz*-philosopher doubtful that "the present harmony of abstract thinking" could survive the manifestly political process of working out the intellectual content of this desired philosophical unity.[60]

More than the substantive void that surrounded the call for "a new order of values," Gilbert was appalled by the failure of the German academic community to inquire into those features of its own organization that had made it vulnerable to fasicst politicization, and its tendency to fall back upon its tradition of insularity over and against the outer world. The refugee scholar, schooled for a decade in the vastly more democratic structure of the American university and the wartime company of a team of progressive scholars-in-arms, finally discarded the mantle of dispassionate objectivity that had been conferred upon him by the Research and Analysis Branch. In a final blast against his former colleagues and countrymen, he charged that their failure to commit themselves to a genuinely new departure was symptomatic of a disease prevalent in wide sections of the middle class in all fields, namely,

> a certain hesitancy to acknowledge the necessity of fundamental changes, deriving from the bourgeoisie's share in the responsibility for the rise of Nazism, as well as from the undermining of the bourgeoisie's economic base which has resulted from the war. Thus, instead of seeking a new relationship to the social forces outside the bourgeois world, the tendency becomes one of attempting to justify an elite position by withdrawing from political and social discussion and assuming the traditional privileged role of a selected intellectual upper class.[61]

The grand tradition of German scholarship, already weakened during the Republican years by its resistance to the invigorating stimulus of new theories and methods, now seemed to him to be mired in an organization that was stiff, illiberal, and structurally disposed to reaction. The question of its recovery, of the possibility of reclaiming an almost legendary heritage of scholarly imagination, was quite literally "academic," for Gilbert's career as an intelligence officer was rapidly drawing to a close and his own plans for a return to a life of teaching and research did not include the community from which he had been physically and intellectually banished.

Beyond History

On September 20, 1945, the Office of Strategic Services suddenly vanished from the face of the earth, although its orphaned Outpost in Germany would linger on for another three months under the letterhead Strategic Services Unit of the War Department. Morale plunged—along with budget and staff—in anticipation of the inevitable, but also in the face of the mounting evidence that even for historians, *plus ça change*, *plus c'est la même chose.* The record of miscalculation, lost opportunities, and outright blunders, together with the piercing chill of winter and the Cold War, lent a somber finality to the last report of the Research and Analysis Branch, dated December 20, 1945. On that very day Felix Gilbert boarded an aircraft carrier and sailed once again from Germany to America, this time for good.

From their base in suburban Biebrich, the political analysts of R&A had traveled throughout Germany during the preceding summer and autumn and had observed at close range the betrayal of the best plans that Holborn had helped to design and Gilbert to oversee. In the first week of October, by which time the Potsdam agreements had ratified the zonal administration and the division of Berlin, Gilbert and Leonard Krieger traveled into the British zone to attend the historic national conference of the Social Democratic Party, its first legal gathering in Germany in a dozen years. Having surfaced from concentration camps, hiding places, and foreign exile, delegates from all four of the occupation zones and from the party Executive still in London responded to a call from Secretary Karl Schumacher to gather in a rural hamlet near Hanover where—under a gigantic likeness of Marx—they hoped to reaffirm and renew the socialist organization. Franklin Ford's warning to "tread carefully since R&A is thought of in some quarters as caring for little besides SPD and trade union connections"[62] seems not to have damped the optimism of the R&A delegation making its way to the undamaged Bahnhof Hotel in picturesque Wennigsen.

Such hopes as the OSS observers may have had for the SPD faded as rapidly as did the festive atmosphere of the conference, which by the second day had degenerated into a near shouting-match that divided the party along east–west lines in a manner that mirrored the hardening partition of the nation itself. Reminiscent of the schismatic twenties, the western-oriented "majority socialists" behind Schumacher disavowed the Marxian revolutionary tradition and issued an appeal to all classes on a nondescript platform of bourgeois political democracy. They were promptly challenged by an "independent" left-wing contingent from Berlin, led by Otto Grotewohl and Gustav Dahrendorf, who held fast to the tradition of working-class militancy and radical social transformation. Of Schumacher, Gilbert's report concluded that "the 'newness' in his Socialist approach consists merely in abandoning the old Socialist theory and adopting a new line consistent with old Social Democratic practice, rather than setting up new goals for action," whereas it was the radical

Berliners who alone perceived the social revolution that was merely being held in check by the occupation and "who really appreciate its meaning."[63] Despite the obvious partiality of the report, he felt that the SPD as a whole had missed a rare opportunity to turn a common face to the future. Referring to the unrelenting process by which the party, the nation, and ultimately the whole of postwar Europe were polarizing into two mutually hostile blocs, he noted with disappointment that the SPD had once again fulfilled its historic role of squandering every opportunity that was presented to it.

Gilbert would pursue his private conversations with Dahrendorf and other leaders of the radical Social Democratic minority later that month while he and Franklin Ford were gathering material on the political scene in Berlin. The two dismal reports they prepared, referring with rhetorical prescience to "the wall between East and West," invoked a metaphor whose foundations were already being cemented into place by the emergent superpowers.[64] Thus he came to the same pessimistic conclusions that had been drawn by Holborn back in Washington. Never particularly sanguine about the prospects of continued cooperation of the Western Allies and the Soviet Union, and given that such liberal elements as existed among the Germans prior to the Hitler era will have been "completely pulverized," Holborn had early on anticipated a protracted and difficult period of occupation.[65]

· · ·

Less significant for history, perhaps, than for historiography was another series of meetings held during those weeks. Earlier that summer Gilbert had already paid a visit to Friedrich Meinecke in Göttingen, where the elderly historian had spent the last months of the war, and now amid the ruins of Berlin he resumed an examination of the force of ideas in history that had been suspended for a decade. This is, to be sure, not a perfectly literal characterization of discussions that ranged widely and in fact avoided the issues weighing most heavily upon each of them: "I certainly didn't talk to him about *The German Catastrophe*," he recalled, "because I (and I believe also Holborn) thought this a rather touching and moving book but strangely remote from the political sphere."[66] Perhaps this reticence in the face of Meinecke's helpless gesture was born of a filial piety toward the honored *Doktorvater*. More suggestive, however, is the consideration that Hajo Holborn and Felix Gilbert had just witnessed "the political collapse of Europe" and the beginning of "the end of the European era."[67] But they had not observed it from the sidelines, and they could no longer be content with the inspired abstractions of academic discourse.

When Peter Gay sought a concise description of the artists and intellectuals who constituted the culture of Weimar and who carried its universal spirit with them into exile, he could do no better than to borrow from Franz Schoenberner the suggestive image of "the insider as outsider." The wartime experience of Hajo Holborn and Felix Gilbert, however, refugee academicians in the heart of America's first central intelligence agency, suggests just the reverse, that of the *out*sider as *in*sider. It should not be surprising, then, that as much as their historical training shaped their contribution to the work of R&A, their three-year sabbatical with the Office of Strategic Services left its mark on their subsequent academic careers. There is, indeed, convincing evidence to this effect.

At the most obvious level, the two academicians gained an insight into the functioning of real governments and the unvarnished process by which the decisions later studied by historians are actually made. This education in contemporary *Realpolitik* was deepened by their close wartime collaboration with two generations of the American historical profession. Established historical practitioners such as William Langer, Crane Brinton, and Perry Miller—whom Gilbert later credited with having written "the first serious, scholarly work which claimed to be an 'intellectual history' "[68]—challenged their European cast of mind as much as did the Undersecretaries and Colonels of the Departments of State and War. Many of the younger scholars have, in their turn, confirmed Franklin Ford's affirmation that his wartime association with thinkers such as Gilbert and Holborn "shaped my future as a historian, giving me almost unheard-of opportunity to pursue European historical study with the guidance of sophisticated émigré scholars."[69] Nor was the legacy of the OSS always so intangible: shortly after their return to civilian scholarship, Gilbert was leaving a small dinner party when Gordon Craig remarked in passing that they should really find some way "to put down something of our experience." Gilbert paused at the door, removed his coat, and the two retired to a private room where they hammered out the details of *The Diplomats*, the influential anthology that is so much a collective memoir of the Research and Analysis Branch that it has been called "an OSS operation *in mufti*."[70]

Second, the interest in modern political history that had led a shadow existence in the prewar scholarship of Holborn and Gilbert now rose assertively to the surface. Their subsequent careers would waver between the sixteenth century and the twentieth, as if by their proximity the traumatic events of the Second World War demanded continued appeasement. Less accomplished scholars might have found their intellectual energies dissipated by such competing claims, but the unwonted intrusion of modernity enabled Gilbert and Holborn to make pioneering contributions to the historiography both of the Renaissance and Reformation and of the contemporary world.

There is, finally, a deeper, "metahistorical" level at which the R&A episode left a permament impression on the émigré historians, more suggestive, perhaps, than the books they would write or the lasting professional alliances they had forged. Felix Gilbert and Hajo Holborn brought to the United States the inheritance of a century-old tradition of German historiography that had shifted uncertainly between poles represented by the figures of Leopold von Ranke and his errant disciple Jacob Burckhardt, and whose greatest twentieth-century exponent was their own teacher, Meinecke. In 1948, in his final public reckoning with his science and his art, Meinecke succinctly captured the ambivalence that history itself had imparted to this legacy and that he still hoped to transmit: "Since my student days," he declared, "Ranke has been my guiding star, my pole star. Only later for me did Burckhardt begin to shed his luminescence."[71]

The polarity of these pole stars cannot be reduced to a simplistic opposition of political history and cultural history, nor can the "signal importance" of the intellectual relationship between Ranke and Burckhardt be overestimated:[72] the same Ranke who stressed the centrality of politics and wrote that nation-states are "ideas of God" understood full well that *all* fields of history are "always conjoined and mutually conditioning";[73] and the state of Burckhardt's Renaissance may have been a "work of art," but it was a state nonetheless. Rather, for Meinecke, these two guiding stars illuminated the past from different angles and disclosed it in its different aspects. Ranke evaluated historical particularity through the primacy of the political, whereas Burckhardt, conversely, viewed the larger process of political development from the standpoint of human individuality and the specificity of the cultural formations it creates. Meinecke refused to dichotomize, much less oppose, these perspectives, and his own troubled journey from the statist conceptions of 1907, to the post-World War I writings in which "he threw the tension (between cultural and political values) into bold relief,"[74] to the cultural universalism of the 1930s and 40s testifies to his lifelong attempt to find in history the spiritual link between authority and freedom, development and individuality, politics and culture.

"Whoever wishes to travel down one of these roads must always follow the other road with his eyes," the elderly Meinecke instructed, and it is almost as if, as the clarity of his own vision was failing him, he had sent his two must trusted scouts down each of these two paths, both still shrouded in the darkness of "the sunless side of world history."[75] Hajo Holborn, who described himself as standing fully in the tradition of his fellow Berliner, Leopold von Ranke, would pursue the political essence of history, while Felix Gilbert immersed himself ever more deeply in the theory and practice of cultural history that Jacob Burckhardt had mapped from nineteenth-century Basel. It is significant that whereas Holborn would be honored by the West German government for his contributions to its political reconstruction and rapprochement, Gilbert had resolved already in the first months of the occupation that he had not the slightest intention of returning to Germany, nor the feeling that he wanted anything further to do with German politics. For a political Rankean, "all ages are equal under God," products of unique and unrepeatable conditions, and even the Nazi state must fall and be supplanted by a new political form; the forboding cultural pessimism planted by Burckhardt, however, lay in his conviction that the roots of cultural decline are deep and irreversible.

Despite their departures from a common terrain, the continued friendship of Meinecke's two protégés symbolizes the fact that each remained loyal to his master's injunction to "follow the other road road with his eyes." Holborn's political histories were enveloped by a deep meditation on the philosophical underpinnings of history and historiography, whereas Gilbert confessed that had his wartime experience in the OSS not tempered his intellectual and cultural inclinations, "I would have become even more *geistesgeschichtlicher* than I already am." Both of them turned the relation between "political power and academic responsibility" into central themes of their work.[76]

· · ·

We are ready, now, to recall the naive and sentimental image with which Meinecke had closed his reflections on *The German Catastrophe*: "To the Goethe Communities," he mused in 1946, "would fall the task of conveying into the hearts of listeners . . . the most vital evidences of the great German spirit."[77] The dream that sustained Meinecke throughout the fascist era may have been less of a fantasy than his two foremost students supposed, for they could not themselves have seen that the real community of the spirit lay not in Meinecke's "wishful picture" of the future but had gone into exile and taken up arms in its own defense. Holborn and Gilbert themselves, though mired in bureaucracy and frustrated by politics, had mobilized their historical training and applied it concretely to the exigencies of history, while passing on the legacy of Germany's shattered universities to a receptive group of young American scholars who would leave the OSS to redirect fundamentally the course of postwar scholarship. Is it too much to suppose that some small part of the ecumenical spirit that Meinecke had hoped to shelter during the long night of fascism had survived in robust form in the Office of Strategic Services?

The Political Economy
of Intelligence

*The fact that this intellectual process related directly to
violent acts of war gave to it, at the time, extraordinary
point and vitality.*

Walt W. Rostow, *OSS War Diary*

The dismal science was also mobilized and sent to the front; but, unlike
philosophy, history, and the more "humanistic" of the social sciences,
economics was already a battle-hardened discipline. Professional economists had first ventured into the government during World War I, where
they were put to work identifying potentially crippling bottlenecks in the
territorially limited, structurally intradependent, and relatively nonre-
dundant national economics of imperial Europe. In the interwar decades
a new generation of economists had entered the field, motivated in part
by the intellectual challenge of resuscitating the international economic
order, and many would begin their careers not in academic positions but
in one of another of the federal agencies that flourished during the
Roosevelt administration. In 1938 an outcast academician—Lauchlin
Currie—was admitted to the White House as the first economic advisor
to the President, and the onset of the Second World War accelerated
the mutual dependency of economic theory and government policy even
further.[1] At the dawn of the industrial era Adam Smith had explained
why a market-driven economy did not need economists to look after it;
the Keynesian revolution, which reached the shores of the United States
just as the collapse of a century-and-a-half of economic expansion was
calling into question the neoclassical equilibrium theory, demonstrated
that it did.

The economists recruited to the Research and Analysis Branch thus
tended as a class to be more experienced in the ways of the world than
their more humanistic counterparts, and the greater immediacy of the
concepts with which they worked gained them a somewhat more re-
spectful hearing in the councils of war. They were, moreover, a restive

lot, confident of the scientific foundations on which their own work rested and impatient with colleagues whom they regarded as mere fact-finders and whose approach they dismissed literary, journalistic, or preoccupied with irrelevant historical detail. The "total" war to which they had been conscripted was also an interdisciplinary war, however, and in time the attitude of the economists softened and they came to admit political, historical, and even psychological categories into their scrupulously quantitiative domain. It is this expansion of economic horizons and the recovery of the dual legacy of classical political economy—which was "to combine rigorous intellectuality with immense moral authority"[2]—that has defined their own distinctive challenge to the field.

Economic Autarky

The discipline of economics was in a state of continuous intellectual ferment in the 1930s, impelled both by internal theoretical developments and the external challenges of a world in depression. One of the main pillars of the emergent symbiosis of economic theory and public policy that characterized the era was the body of microeconomic thought developed principally at Harvard, the chief exponent of which was Edward S. Mason. After an early flirtation with the economics of European socialism, Mason's interests had shifted to the relations between government and business; he virtually launched the field of industrial organization with the hypothesis that the performance of individual firms is a function less of the idiosyncratic gifts or limitations of management than of the structure of the market in which they operate.[3] The analytical procedure implied by this formulation began with the identification of the largest possible number of environmental variables affecting a particular class of firms: the framework of law, transportation infrastructure, size and number of competitors, and so on. It is difficult to imagine a research methodology more suited to a program of economic warfare than the analysis of factors that may strengthen and, ipso facto, impair the functioning of an integrated industrial system.

In the summer of 1941, at the urging of his old friends Bill Langer and Phinney Baxter, Mason moved over from a wartime assignment in the Office of Production Management to begin laying the economic infrastructure of what would become the new OSS. From the Division of Research and Statistics of the Federal Reserve Board (FRB) he brought

Emile Despres to serve as Chief of what was initially called the Economic Group; Despres in turn recruited from the International Section of the FRB his close colleague Chandler Morse, who, as Assistant Chief, completed the triumvirate of economic administrators of the Research and Analysis Branch.

From his lofty vantage point at Harvard, Edward Mason was in a particularly favorable position to survey the professional landscape. The most promising of a younger generation of trained economists passed before him, and he was able quite literally to have his pick of the new crop. Wilfred Malenbaum was enlisted as the outstanding young specialist in agricultural economics, Donald Wheeler was one of the three Rhodes scholars brought in to study labor questions, and Walt W. Rostow was brought down from Yale to serve as Mason's personal assistant. During the first year the division simply grew without structure as successive recruitment campaigns against the graduate schools and federal agencies strung along the eastern corridor netted an impressive pool of talent. By the time the old COI had metamorphosed into OSS, Charles Kindleberger and Harold Barnett were analyzing the military supply situation in enemy countries, the statistician Walter Levy, conjured out of the refugee population, was monitoring oil intelligence, and a few more young Harvard instructors had arrived to work on problems of economic integration (Moses Abramowitz), industrial resources (Sidney Alexander and Carl Kaysen), and monopolies and cartels (the specialty of Joseph Schumpeter's radical protégé Paul M. Sweezy). Two Russian-born economists, the Marxist Paul Baran and Wassily Leontief, who would later win the Nobel Prize for the theory of input–output analysis already applied in R&A, were formally attached to the USSR Subdivision, as was the youthful Abram Bergson. Many of these economists entered R&A with substantial records of publication or public service already behind them, and Mason always suspected that this race of bold young Olympians was destined to eclipse the Titans of his own generation who had trained them. "The idea was apparently to grab as many 'bright people' as possible and turn them loose to figure out something constructive to do," recalled one of the elders of the Branch; "They wanted brash and brilliant operators who could carve out a working territory for themselves in the welter of rival agencies."[4] Not surprisingly, virtually all of them would rise to prominence in the postwar world of economic thought.

According to the original conception of the Coordinator of Information,

four more-or-less autonomous functional divisions were to work independently on economic, geographical, psychological (political), and regional aspects of the war. This oddly conceived plan created a situation
in which economists evaluating Russian rail facilities worked in splendid
isolation from historians and sociologists able to read Russian documents.
It was well-suited to the economists, however, who then comprised the
vanguard of a discipline barreling down the high road toward an axio-
matically based, hypotheticodeductive hard science immune to distrac-
tions arising out of social institutions, customs, values, and history. Even
the economic geographers of the Europe–Africa Division were looked
upon askance for their tendency to profane their immaculate statistical
conceptions with footnotes about regional distribution patterns. Coor-

Emile Despres, Chief of the Economic Subdivision: "There was a bit of the operator
in them, and they knew their way around."

dination was never comfortably achieved, and by dissipating the intellectual ferment of the group the arrangement seems almost to have been calculated to vitiate the capacity of R&A to carry out truly interdisciplinary research and analysis.

A state of what may be called economic autarky thus prevailed in the months when the Economic Group was being assembled in Washington: just as they were physically sequestered in their own quarters, the economists were intellectually removed from the political and ideological analyses being carried out elsewhere in the Branch and often suspicious of it. By temperament and training the economists were disposed toward studies that emphasized analytical, mathematical, and statistical skills rather than regional knowledge or specialized library work. Fascism, no less than liberalism, ultimately reduced to choices among economic alternatives, and the analysts of R&A felt assured that their ad hoc methods of economic forecasting could lead them to a rigorous assessment of enemy capabilities, from which they could deduce their military intentions. It was, therefore, an arrangement that was largely congenial to the economists, who flaunted their refusal to find common ground with the techniques of disciplines they regarded as scientifically suspect.

During this period the first recruits to the Economic Group tested their skills by preparing briefs for Donovan and the Board of Analysts on a variety of topical problems, and by December they were ready to issue the results of their first substantial foray into the field of economic intelligence, a comprehensive survey of *The German Economic and Military Position*.[5] This report provided some of the most detailed basic documentation then available, but its weaknesses derived precisely from the exaggerated division of intellectual labor according to which the Branch functioned. The economists operated under the reasonable premise that the German economy had been fully mobilized by 1941 and was operating at full capacity—an assumption now known to have been false.[6] Had they been forced into a closer alliance with the political analysts of R&A, they might well have recognized that the confidence of the Nazis in a swift and devastating campaign permitted them to leave significant reserves of capital stock in the civilian economy. The early OSS estimates were continually embarrassed by the German capacity to draw upon food supplies and industrial materials long after they were supposed to have been depleted, to move factories to double-shifts, and to replace specialized equipment damaged in bombing raids with general-purpose machine tools without severe reductions in plant efficiency.

Still, the interest rate was high among the economists, there was full employment of intellectual resources, productivity in the group was soaring, and the market for their products was expanding due to the expert salesmanship of Edward Mason. The hot-house effect of throwing together nearly fifty highly trained and supremely self-assured young economists was bound to produce work marked by discipline, resourcefulness, and imagination. No problem was too daunting in the halcyon days of 1941 and 1942, and in a swaggering spirit of methodological imperialism they took the entire globe into their jurisdiction: "We have taken over Europe," boasted a junior officer of the economics brigade; "We are moving in on the Far East and we will shortly get going on the USSR."[7] In March, despite their own acknowledgment that "the possible sources of inaccuracy are too numerous to list," they turned out a 200-page report on the German supply problem on the Russian front that correctly predicted that the single rail line and the long trek from the railhead would create logistical difficulties for von Paulus' army.[8] In August, when Donovan passed along the word that North Africa had been confirmed as the site of the first Allied landing, they threw themselves into a frenzy of uninterrupted labor and in a matter of weeks produced encyclopedic reports on the economic significance of Morocco, Algeria, and Tunisia that proved their worth in the planning of Operation TORCH. A rumor circulated throughout the Branch—not without foundation— that the economists habitually refused assignments they did not regard as intellectually stimulating.

The famous reorganization of January 1943, which initiated the traumatic process of integrating the work of the economists into the larger research program of the Branch, signaled not only an administrative rationalization, then, but a radical departure from the traditional practice of the field as such. In November the Economic Group, whose ranks had by this time grown to about seventy professionals, was finally moved into the Annex Building at 23rd Street and E and placed under the same roof with the historians, sociologists, and geographers of the new Europe–Africa Division, a move that was recognized as "symbolic" for it was the first time that the Economic Group was really integrated into the structure of the division and of the Research and Analysis Branch. Langer ought to have been decorated for his courage in assaulting the disciplinary fortifications behind which his scholars had immured themselves, and his historical ego was several times wounded-in-action. The economists first declared that they would not serve with political scientists or historians, and they relented only under the weight of "long-drawn debates and endless argumentation," not to mention a judicious admixture of bribery, cajolery, and outright threats.[9]

Since its emergence as an indigenous mode of theoretical discourse, American economics has been characterized by a progressive detachment from the other social sciences in the direction of an abstract, mathematicized, and hypothetical world of pure reason: moral zeal, historical perspective, a sense of institutional context, a view of the social totality, and other traces of its English and German ancestry gradually emigrated to more "qualitiative" disciplines or were systematically expelled.[10] In this respect the early organization of the Research and Analysis Branch simply reflected the conventionalized academic hierarchy that gave birth to it, and for the economists to accept the humbling status of epistemological parity with the other social sciences represented a dramatic challenge to the intellectual history of the discipline. The process of integration was a difficult one, grudgingly accepted by the unreconstructed economists, imperfectly realized, and marked by at least one attempted mutiny which Langer barely quelled: "They were a brilliant and effective group," he later conceded, "one of the most energetic and alert units in the branch and a great credit to the agency. But no one could describe them as cooperative or even entirely loyal."[11] After the spring of 1943, however, an intellectual *modus vivendi* came to be achieved between the economists and their humanistic brethren, the invigorating consequences of which were felt long after they were demobilized and had returned to their academic posts.

The Economists' War

Behind the marshaling of these intellectual resources lay the belief that strategic planners must consider the basic pattern of the enemy economies, have access to current information about points of potential friction in their military-industrial machinery, and be advised as to the significance of shifts in the allocation of resources between the civilian and military sectors. R&A aspired to fill this void by making available to the Joint Chiefs the services of a pool of professionals who would generate a continual stream of economic intelligence and were prepared to respond to ad hoc requests for spot estimates. Beyond these obvious tactical maneuvers in what their colleague Paul Samuelson called "the economists' war,"[12] a Grand Stretegy of sorts informed the work of the economic sections of R&A. This framework was elaborated in an early memorandum that Emile Despres prepared for then-Colonel Donovan toward the end of 1941. Although he described his observations as "personal and impressionistic" in character, the initial strategic evaluation of the chief of the Economics Division, barely two weeks before the United States entered the war, is clearly of some significance.

On the basis of his preliminary calculations, Despres estimated that even with the fullest concentration of productive resources, the requirements of a full-scale invasion of Europe exceeded the combined economic potentialities of the United States and the British Empire over the two-year period of preparation projected by military planners. He also elaborated this grim scenario: a series of territorial conquests could yield the Axis a chain of forward bases, access to a volume and diversity of resources that could sustain both their military and civilian requirements indefinitely, and control over the labor power of an immense subject population. If these conquests were followed by a breathing spell that enabled the Nazis to organize the areas under control into a coordinated administrative unit, they would have secured a virtually unassailable position. As a bare minimum it was essential that the Allies defend against further territorial gains—in the Caucasus, North Africa, and the Middle East. Checking the expansion of German power was merely the *sine qua non* of any preinvasion strategy, however, for on the grounds of relative economic capabilities alone, "the invasion of the Continent in 1943 can succeed only if German strength has in the meantime been considerably reduced."[13]

Despres described what was in effect a deadly race to bring American resources up to capacity while simultaneously reducing those of Germany to a level that favored an Allied invasion force. To achieve this primary condition, he outlined an offensive strategy that included a military program to establish salients from which to conduct continuous harassing operations, a political program to organize unrest and opposition in Germany and Nazi-occupied territories, and—closer to his own jurisdiction—an economic program centered around the air bombardment of carefully selected industrial targets. How to pay for the war was the problem being grappled with by the bold new generation of Keynesian economists in the Treasury Department, the Office of Price Administration, and the War Production Board; in OSS the problem was how to fight it.

On June 22, 1941, Germany and its allies invaded the Soviet Union, and by the end of the year had overrun nearly half a million square miles of European Russia. At the gates of Moscow they were driven to a halt by a combination of the Russian winter, the unexpectedly fierce resistance of the Red Army, and, it was assumed, lines of supply that were inadequate to the staggering requirements of a force of some 5,000,000 men. By the beginning of the new year a set of related questions confronted the emergent intelligence community. What were the precise factors that had combined to stop the German invasion some 500 miles inside the Soviet Union? When, where, and under what conditions would the German armies renew their offensive? Could the massive supply requirements of the "Theater of Operations" prove disruptive of German war production in the "Zone of the Interior" to such an extent as to affect the comparative advantage of the Western Allies?

The invasion of the Soviet Union prompted a massive research program, the first to which the whole of the accumulated intellectual resources of the Division were directed. The economists in particular set out to resolve some of these questions in a comprehensive analysis of "The German Supply Problem on the Eastern Front." The procedure whereby they reached their conclusions centered on an extended exercise in statistical inference which, given the slender base of empirical data they had on which to build, strikes the reader even today as a daring feat of logical reconstruction.

In their initial thrust into Soviet Russia, the Germans had captured a network of ten major rail lines upon which they depended to supply food, weapons, and all other forms of matériel to some 200 divisions. The basic problem of military supply, as an economist would formulate it, was to provide an average rate of delivery at least equal to the average rate of expenditure. From this perspective, the capabilities of the captured Russian railroads were a critical limiting factor in the renewal of the eastern campaign, and from the fragmentary data available the economists of R&A/Washington undertook to derive the capacities of the Russian rail transport system, on the one hand, and the objective supply requirements of the invading armies, on the other. Almost as an afterthought, as if to signal that this intricate thought-experiment had not been performed solely as an exercise in intellectual bravado, they confidently pronounced upon the earliest dates at which the spring offensive could resume.

Throughout the early months of 1942, while the surviving German divisions froze along the Russian front, Chandler Morse ordered his

Economics Division out into the Washington winter to collect information on an immense range of intra- and extrasystemic variables. From local railway officials they sought out technical information on the efficiency of locomotives at subzero temperatures and the conversion of Russian track to standard European gauge. They researched the daily forage requirements of the type of horses used by the German infantry (38 tons per division) and calculated the volume and weight of the dehydrated rations shipped to the troops. Extrapolating from United States Army ordnance specifications, they computed the daily tonnage of ammunition expended at seven different levels of combat intensity by infantry, Panzer, and motorized divisions, respectively. They averaged meteorological information over a period of years and built a massive edifice of statistical induction on the basis of hard data they were somehow able to secure for a particular 18-day period of the campaign. Once they had quantified all potentially significant factors in the German supply situation (at minimal and maximal levels), they attempted no less a task than to correlate the raw tonnage of supplies presumed to have been consumed along a 1,500-mile front by 200 divisions over a period of 167 days with the capacity of a road and rail system under conditions of heavy combat. This radical abstraction, which recalled the rarefied world of pure reason conjured by the classical political economists and which prefigured the spectral zone of econometric modeling that would haunt the postwar world, typified the intellectual appetite of the group and the daring methodologies they concocted to satisfy it.

The conclusions drawn from this extended logical exercise were of some consequence, if only because, by virtue of their departure from prevailing wisdom, they called attention to R&A and to the thoroughness of the work of which it was capable. The report concluded that the resistance of the Red Army was a more decisive factor in stalling the German advance than alleged difficulties of supply, which were generally not more than localized disruptions. To the contrary, on the basis of almost no firm empirical data they deduced that when supplemented by motor vehicles, German rail facilities had proven capable of delivering the 16,650,000 tons of supplies required during the last 5 ½ months of 1942, although they were strained to their limits and disruptions sometimes delayed or limited the scope of operations. Measuring hypothetical supply rquirements against estimated transport capacity, they came up with the reassuringly definitive conclusion that up to the present, at any rate, "our data do not indicate a general supply shortage."[14]

A second conclusion, of at least comparable significance, emerged out of the economists' attempt to determine the amount of rolling stock required by and available to the invading German armies. The evidence here was no less unsettling, for it illuminated for the first time the concrete implications of the enhanced economies of scale created by the occupation of Central Europe, and of the cushion of resources and labor power thus opened up to the Axis. Some 35,000 additional freight cars were estimated to be required to support every 200 km advance into enemy territory, but it was found that these could be diverted from the civilian economies of Axis-occupied territories without immediate consequence to German war production itself.

The final conclusion drawn by the authors of the report took the form of a prediction. Although rail facilities had proven barely adequate in the first six months of the invasion, the supply system operated successfully only by virtue of the enormous stores that had been amassed in advance. These had been seriously depleted in the course of the campaign; and although the relative conditon of the Soviet armies lay beyond their powers of prediction, in terms of absolute strength, at any rate, the conclusion is "almost inescapable" that the Germans would be much weaker when the Russian winter finally lifted its own siege.

Events would confirm the general accuracy of these conclusions, but beyond its substantive predictions this report commands our interest as the first extended application of the ad hoc methodologies devised in the group. As a rule, the Economics Division was not the scene of ideological rivalry among the Keynesians, classicists, and neo-Marxists who had entered the OSS from the turbulent academic universe of the 1930s, for the theoretical frameworks out of which they operated were mediated by the exigencies of war and the constraints of government service. This implausibly harmonious environment may be explicable—in retrospect, at any rate—by the fact of a common enemy but also by the nature of that enemy. The rise of economic science was broadly coterminous with the consolidation of the market society, and both political economy and its radical critique emerged very much in response to the dynamics of the market. The liberal provenance of the theories in which the economists had been trained thus proved to be a limiting condition in their applicability to the command economy of fascist Germany. Just as the political analysts of the Central European Section had insisted that the morale of the liberal individual was not a factor of consequence in the political sphere, so the Economic Subdivision recognized that the

German economy was not fundamentally determined by the market behavior of *Homo oeconomicus*. In the original "supply-side" regime, the only salient factor was Germany's capacity to produce, and the economists directed their common efforts to the analysis of these inputs—labor, capital goods, raw materials—and the ways in which they might be affected. Their specific research programs emerged out of collective brainstorming sessions and were pursued through intuitive methods that may only later have been formalized. Issues of capitalism, socialism, and democracy remained minor factional disturbances in comparison with the methodological class warfare that divided the economists from their less scientific colleagues. Indeed, it was ultimately neither a theory nor a formal methodology that bonded them so much as a common grounding in a scientific frame of mind.

Thus, the work of the Washington economists proceeded amid the dismal news of 1942. From railroads they moved on to a sophisticated estimate of German tank production. Using the well-known Gompertz growth curve, Harold Barnett observed that the 1935 figure upon which the Army's Military Intelligence Service (MIS) still relied corresponded only to the characteristic first phase of industrial expansion, marked by "slow development during the early years of the production program," a stage long since overtaken.[15] A short while thereafter they secured spectrographic analysis data on thirteen captured tires, from which they ventured a speculative reconstruction of the German synthetic rubber industry.[16] "However difficult these methods may be to apply," asserted the authors of an unusually defensive paper on "The German Anti-Friction Bearing Position," "we feel that they should be stated to clear our consciences of the burden of arbitrary assumptions."[17]

At the end of the year, encouraged by the Allied offensives in North Africa and the decimation of the German Sixth Army at Stalingrad, the economists turned their guns on the Luftwaffe. Someone plotted a graph in which he noticed that estimated losses of German aircraft over Russia consistently fell midway between Russian admissions of their own aircraft losses and German claims of Russian losses. From this ethereal calculus, which derived actualities from a completely spurious correlation between "German claims" and "Russian admissions," they produced "an OSS pattern of production, losses, and strength" that differed markedly from the detailed estimates generated by British intelligence. "It is perhaps rash to construct a hypothetical curve in the face of the tabulated production series published by the Air Ministry," they conceded, the moreso since they had frequently resorted to brazen linear interpolations and inspired guesswork, and recognized that more than one estimate "rests shakily upon a towering structure of assumptions."[18] They nonetheless dismissed the "bits and pieces method" characteristic of the more empirically minded British in favor of what was becoming an American specialty, "a deductive production curve constructed on statistical foundations which, unrelated to the mass of intelligence, both operational and engineering," seemed to fit the "cold reality" encountered by Allied fliers in the skies over the European theater. "This may sound a bit presumptuous," remarked Sidney Alexander in a slightly different context, "but modesty, false or otherwise, was never a failing of the economics division of OSS."[19]

Behind these imaginative reconstructions lay an increasingly coherent program of economic analysis and an evolving methodology which they tested against general theories of industrial growth and corrected with whatever fragments of raw data they were able to secure. The general considerations adumbrated by Despres in mid-1941 had developed over the course of the next eighteen months into an integrated program to establish a dynamic picture of the enemy economy. "By intuition rather than plan," reported Chandler Morse, "we focussed on what we perceived to be actual or potential areas of weakness that might endogenously become militarily significant or be given an exogenous military push in that direction."[20] By the end of the first year, once the basic pattern of the enemy economy had been established, this program was being pursued by five research units that had crystallized out of the original Economics Group. The Military Supply Section, directed first by Harold Barnett and then the more experienced Charles Kindleberger, followed the organization of the Axis armaments industries and constructed production curves of tanks, guns, airplanes, and munitions. The Industrial Resources Section, whose Chief was Sidney Alexander, contributed analyses of production trends, inventories, and military-industrial requirements of basic minerals, metals, and oil. Wilfred Malenbaum's Agriculture Section produced unorthodox estimates of production/consumption rates and concluded that the German food situation was not, as it had in the closing period of the First World War, likely to become a factor affecting the course of the war.

Under the direction of Donald Wheeler, the economists of the Labor Supply Section drew just the opposite picture: combat manpower, they accurately predicted, rather than oil or food, would prove to be the critical bottleneck in the German war economy. This demographic forecast was derived in part from one of their more imaginative exercises in intelligence. Svend Larsen, an economist of Danish origin, had become troubled by what he suspected were unreasonably high estimates of German battle casualties produced by the British Ministry of Economic Warfare (MEW) and accepted too readily by U.S. Army Intelligence. From his European experience he recalled the German practice of filing obituary notices of officers in local newspapers, giving rank, unit, and location of death, and from American experts he learned that there is a fairly stable correlation between battle casualities and military rank. The labor economists worked out a simple arithmetic formula, and OSS/Switzerland supplied them on a regular basis with some 57 local German newspapers through which they were able to monitor German battle casualities throughout the war with a high degree of accuracy.[21] Finally, Moses Abramowitz and the gifted young theorist Lloyd Metzler formed the core of the Economic Integration Section, whose job was to assemble aggregate figures from the discrete data produced throughout the Subdivision and feed them into an evolving statistical picture of the Axis economy.

As American forces entered the field of combat in the Mediterranean, access to hard intelligence increased, and the seat-of-the-pants techniques devised by the economists became more empirically secured and more conceptually refined. Sidney Alexander of the Industrial Resources Section in particular began, toward the beginning of 1943, to outline what he called "the science and technique of serial number analysis," locally known as the OSS "Numbers Racket."[22] As noted earlier, R&A had come to suspect that accepted figures of enemy production were resulting in a dangerously inaccurate picture of military and industrial strength, and Alexander became convinced that "a more scientific approach was required to the whole problem." It was known that every major item of military equipment carried markings that indicated, in addition to serial numbers, the place and date of manufacture, and some attempts had already been made to monitor changes in German aircraft manufacture and to compute German tank strength by the relatively primitive method of subtracting the lowest from the highest serial numbers of captured vehicles. In London, however, Alexander had managed to obtain from British military intelligence documents that suggested to him that numerical sequences were deliberately interrupted and that tanks were not uniformly deployed to the fronts by lot. By midsummer he had impressed Donovan himself with the argument that "the production, supply, and 'pipelines' of German military equipment was the subject most needing scientific investigation," and he secured permission to gather first-hand information from the battlefields of North Africa and Sicily. Flanked by an American driver and a captured Afrika Korps mechanic, he careened around the Tunisian desert in search of military hardware that had been captured, abandoned, or damaged beyond repair. The numerical data he collected were deposited with Richard Ruggles and a team of analysts in London, who deciphered them and quickly established that the volume of German tank production was indeed very much lower than had previously been believed but that the rate of production had been steadily increasing in spite of Allied efforts to disrupt it.[23] Information of this sort was of manifest strategic importance and, in the hands of the RAF and the Eighth Air Force, of great operational value as well.

With developments of this sort, the work of the Economics Division of R&A entered a new phase. As the Allied advance across the Mediterranean opened up the field of intelligence gathering, the "ideal essences, poetic or logical terms which thought may define and play with" became increasingly soiled with engine lubricants, tire treads, unexploded artillery shells, and other "terrible irruptive things."[24] Simultaneously, the economists began to win ground in their own campaign to be heard by the Joint Chiefs under whose nominal jurisdiction they labored. "Little regard was at first paid to the OSS estimates by these professional military men, who looked with mingled skepticism, contempt, and jealousy on the amateur authors, the method, and results,"[25] but their own persistence and the testimony of events slowly won for them a clientele.

Nor were the economists' reports merely read and added to the general store of background intelligence on enemy capablities. A major escalation in the program of economic warfare occurred when, back in Washington, Alexander's group was able to show that only two manufacturers were involved in the production of German tank engines and that gear boxes were assembled in only two specified plants. With this information the new science of serial-number analysis left the laboratory and ushered the Economic Division into the real world of target selection in the air war over Europe. Accordingly, the focus of its activities began to shift from Washington to the small squadron of economists that had been gathering in the R&A Outpost in London.

Operation OCTOPUS

Ever since Thales cornered the market in Ionian olive presses, speculative thinkers have recognized the strategic importance of oil, and the economists of OSS were no exception. Walter Levy, the first of the German émigrés to be brought into the Research and Analysis Branch, was recruited by Donovan himself on the strength of an analysis he had written for *Fortune* magazine of Germany's drive for self-sufficiency in oil, "the *sine qua non* of modern industry, modern warfare, modern transportation."[26] By fall 1943, this field of research had become such an integral part of the R&A work program that a separate Oil Section, under Levy's direction, was carved out of the organization. As the essential limiting factor on German's capacity to sustain a mechanized war, synthetic oil fueled the economists' drive into the European Theater of Operations, where they argued their case with such persistence that they were more than once accused of being more interested in truth than in winning.

A beachhead had been secured already at the end of 1941, when the Yale medievalist Allan Evans was despatched to London to represent the Coordinator of Information out of offices on the top floor of the U.S. Embassy. In a blaze of early activity he and the small staff that followed him opened channels with the British Ministry of Economic Warfare and the Political Warfare Executive, the Naval Intelligence Department at the Admiralty, and the interagency Joint Intelligence Committee. They were given access to Home Office officials and dignitaries of foreign governments-in-exile. They were allowed to spirit away from the School of Geography at Oxford a huge relief map of Japan left over from one of the world fairs, and even to supply Washington with a London telephone directory, "then an article as scarce as any secret document."[27] R&A/London opened officially on May 15 under the direction of Shepard Morgan, a well-connected investor and professor of government at Williams College, with the Europeanists Crane Brinton and Russell Dorr assigned to matters of political and economic liaison, respectively. The effusive welcome given the Americans throughout 1942 drowned out the incipient epistemological dissonances that would soon disrupt communication between these alien communities, intelligence and intellectual.

Toward the end of what was celebrated as "the American year," dissension between the Foreign Office and the Department of State over postwar political alliances, between the RAF and the Eighth Air force over their respective 'philosophies' of air power, and between Churchill and Roosevelt over the opening of the second front had emerged as points of Anglo–American friction. They paled, however, in comparison with the "incompatibilities in scholarly approach" that divided the rival British and American shadow warfare organizations. Indeed, long before any colonial subjects became restive, perceptive observers might well have discerned the decline of British imperial authority in debates over such vital matters as the proper footnoting of intelligence reports:

> British research tends to center around the authority; a British office will appoint the best man available to deal with a given subject and will then be prepared to accept his findings with relatively little question. American scholars, on the other hand, ingrained in the Ph.D. tradition, rely on no man's word but require every statement to be supported by reference to its sources.[28]

Clearly, if the world were to be made safe for democracy and "the Ph.D. tradition," the Research and Analysis Branch would have to be mobilized in its full interdisciplinary force and sent to the front. The economists were among the earliest scholarly recruits in the European Theater, and it was from their London headquarters that they led R&A across the threshhold from academic theory to military practice.

The background to this escalation of intelligence activity lay in a long-standing rivalry between the American and British air forces that came to a head during 1942. The doctrine of strategic bombing, as it had evolved in the decades following World War I, held that the military function of aircraft lay not in combat but in the systematic attack against the enemy's capacity to mobilize armies in the first place. RAF Bomber Command, ill-disposed toward humanitarian considerations in the wake of the Battle of Britain and ill-equipped for technical reasons to achieve accurate air strikes against specific targets, had translated this into a strategy of nighttime "area bombardment" designed to wreak maximum havoc on economic productivity and civilian morale and thus precipitate collapse and capitulation. The underlying strategic theory, such as it was, held that in what the Italian strategist Giulio Douhet had called "la guerra integrale" the "enemy" consists not only of narrowly defined military targets but of the entire structure of economiic and civil life that sustains them. As it was perceived by their American allies, the British position was to rely on the unsystematic use of air power alone to win the war by reducing Germany to internal chaos—"a hammer with no anvil," commented the laconic Charles Kindleberger, and Walt Rostow scoffed at their "dreams of causing a Wagnerian cataclysm" through such unscientific means.[29]

Long before the outbreak of the Second World War the American Army Air Corps had produced its own strategic concept, ratified at Casablanca and vigorously represented in the European theater by Colonel Richard D. Hughes, senior target planning officer for the U.S. Air Forces in Europe. This doctrine held that the most effective use of air power lay in high-altitude daylight bombing of industrial targets selected for their specific value to German military mobilization. Hughes claimed that such a program of "precision bombing" lay within the capabilities of the Flying Fortresses that had begun to arrive in England in the fall of 1942.[30] The strategy of precision bombing, however, rested upon two factors that lay outside the competence of military planners: a general theory of the complex interdependencies of the enemy economy, and detailed intelligence as to the location, organization, and layout of the specific targets of maximum vulnerability as identified by the theory. In pursuit of the intellectual resources upon which the untested doctrine of precision daylight bombing depended, Hughes prevailed upon Ambassador John G. Winant to assist him in securing a staff of experts whose training lay not in military but in the even more dismal science of economics. Into this field of battle marched an intrepid regiment of OSS economists, who constituted themselves as the Enemy Objectives Unit (EOU) in the Economic Warfare Division of the U.S. Embassy.[31]

In September 1942, Chandler Morse—"the man of affairs of the Despres-Morse team"—traveled to London with Walt Rostow and Roselene Honerkamp to set up operations in a bureaucratic netherworld between OSS/Washington, the American Embassy at Grosvenor Square, and the United States Strategic Air Force (USSTAF) headquartered at Wydewing. Following the customary interlude of jurisdictional sparring with the other American agencies involved in the air war, he obtained from Hughes a nominal charter in the form of a memorandum proposing an "American Study of Bombing Objectives" which specified only that the immediate requirement of the Eighth Air Force was an analysis of potential targets in terms of their importance to the German war effort.[32] On the basis of this broadly defined mandate Morse proceeded over the next few months to assemble a remarkable team of omnivorous young economists—Rostow, Charles Kindleberger, Carl Kaysen, Harold Barnett, and a dozen others—whose task was to digest all available economic intelligence and transform it into a rigorous science of air warfare.[33]

In the absence of more specific instructions, the EOU subjected the whole of German industry to the experimental methods it had been called upon to devise. As an intellectual limbering-up exercise, the economists first launched a series of reports on potential targets throughout German Europe in which they provided microscopically detailed intelligence about the location, function, and layout of particular industrial facilities, and indicated the precise points of maximum vulnerability in each of them. This exercise, which grew over the next eighteen months into a series of some 285 "Aiming Point Reports," forced them at the outset to define a theory, a research methodology, and a means of establishing an effective liaison with the Army Air Forces; it thus served to initiate them into the lethal mysteries of strategic planning.

The most distinguishing characteristic of these early papers, and that which would set the EOU apart from other intelligence agencies, was that they rested upon a foundation of empirical research that brought the economists about as close as wartime conditions permitted to the primary data of analysis. Chandler Morse's insistence that the scholarship of his post-graduate recruits be in no way derivative taxed their ingenuity as to the best way to familiarize themselves with the industrial terrain on which their battles would ultimately be waged. Within three weeks of his arrival Morse himself took the lead by touring the Imperial Hydrogenation Plant at Billingham, which operated on technical principles broadly similar to those of the German refineries at Leuna. While he inspected its generators, compressors, and injectors, researchers elsewhere made on-site studies of propeller forgings and ignition assemblies. Back in London, they pored over ground reports, transcripts of prisoner-of-war interrogations, and aerial photographs supplied by their incredulous rivals in the Ministry of Economic Warfare, who viewed the Americans' preoccupation with specific buildings and bridge spans as evidence of "undue optimism and even faint morbidity."[34] In the evenings they honed their analytical skills with invented exercises: "How many sheep are there in Bavaria?" "What is the most economical land route from Gdansk to Gibraltar?" Someone burst in and asked for a telephone number: "I don't know it," retorted Carl Kaysen, "but I can estimate it."

By mid-November they were able to produce their first complete report, which analyzed the Siemens Cable Works in Berlin in terms of the two "aiming points" most vulnerable to bomb damage and most costly to repair, and whose destruction was calculated to disrupt the entire manufacturing process for the greatest length of time.[35] Colonel Hughes, impressed by their knowledge of roofing materials and incendiary devices, and evidently aware of the new stage of stretegic if not scholarly thought represented by their research, authorized them to press on to ball bearings, rubber, and ultimately to the oil industry, which lubricated the entire Nazi war machine.

This was not a group that would be content to run errands for the Eighth Air Force, however, or simply to add to the pool of strategic information about designated sites in the German industrial system. As social scientists, they found the analysis of dozens, and ultimately hundreds, of potential targets significant only insofar as they could be situated within a rigorous analytical framework. Inspired as much by intellectual as by practical opportunities, the economists reasoned that if the destruction of a control room or a gas generator could cripple a particular plant, there must be an analytical formula that would predict its capacity to disrupt the industry of which it was a part and the war economy which it helped in some measure to sustain.

The documentary record of the EOU testified to a pronounced attitude of condescension toward the "romantic notions" that flourished within the British Air Ministry, toward its "vaguely defined" objectives and its failure to justify its target selection with a "formal rationale" derived from a solid analytical picture of the Axis economy. To fill this void, William Salant, a brilliant young economist who had grown restless measuring bridge spans and recording serial numbers, took the first shot at drafting a conceptual statement that would provide a quantitative basis for ranking potential targets in terms of their military value. In the last weeks of 1942 Salant circulated an internal memorandum on "The Selection of Industrial Bombing Targets" and thus initiated a discussion that would undergo successive stages of refinement throughout the duration of the European war.[36] His memorandum is remarkable for its insistent regression to first principles. In essence, Salant challenged his colleagues to move from the mere cataloguing of discrete targets to a concept of *target systems* derived from the functional interdependencies of a highly coupled industrial system.

The document, which laid the intellectual foundations not only for the

EOU "Party Line" but for a so-called Philosophy of Air Power that would survive well into the nuclear age, reduced the problematic of strategic bombing to three independent and exhaustive questions:

(1) Can you hit it, and at what cost?
(2) Can you damage it if you hit it?
(3) Will damage to the target hurt the enemy?

To resolve these questions quantitatively in terms of any potential target, he proposed that the problem be conceptualized as a simple set of ratios:

$$\frac{\text{impairment to enemy}}{\text{(physical damage)}} \times \frac{\text{(physical damage)}}{\text{(tonnage of bombs)}} \times \frac{\text{(tonnage of bombs)}}{\text{cost to us}}$$

$$= \frac{\text{impairment to enemy}}{\text{cost to us}}$$

This simplified formula—"How much harm can be inflicted on the enemy per unit cost to us?"—was clearly not the final word: it was necessary still to devise a consistent standard with which to quantify such variables as "physical damage." They also had to introduce a reliable temporal axis into the equation. Capital theory was invoked to measure the extent to which labor power could be substituted for missing inputs, and conceptual refinements were introduced to measure the "depth" to which a bombing raid penetrated the whole economy in terms of the time lag between damage to production facilities and actually experienced shortages at the battlefront, and to adjust for the "cushion" of resources upon which a mature industrial economy could draw (inventories, substitutions, the civilian sector) to take up the slack. From the British Photo-Intelligence Unit at Medmenham they learned the art of photographic interpretation that enabled them to correct their estimates with a continuing flow of damage-assessment data.

These practical and theoretical refinements were built into the second series of papers produced by the EOU group in London, the so-called "Target Potentiality Reports" they began to churn out in the spring of 1943. Prepared under the shadow of D-Day, these papers sought to determine how to use the air forces to maximize damage to German military resistance at the moment of invasion. The choices were between diminishing the inflow of armaments into the field by attacking them at the point of production or accelerating outflow through actual combat wastage. Economic, as distinct from narrowly tactical, reasoning produced different answers for different target systems, but it also enabled them to establish target priorities on a strictly quantitiative basis. The analytical procedure by which they came to focus in this period on German single-engine fighter aircraft is revealing of their collective thought process and merits a closer look.

The operative concepts were a pair of ratios: monthly production to total front-line strength, and, correspondingly, monthly wastage to total overall strength. By badgering the Air Ministry for estimates of production schedules and Air Force colonels for average rates of combat loss, the economists were able to generate a table of monthly production figures for the dispersed and decentralized German aircraft industry, as well as for other potential target systems: submarines, tanks, motor trucks, as well as such crucial factors in the production process as ball bearings, magnetos, and precision grinding wheels. On the basis of these figures it was easy to show that where monthly turnover was high and the pipeline was short (26 percent and 3 ½ months, respectively, for aircraft as compared with only about 7 percent and 8 months for submarines), maximum attrition would result from constricting the inflow of replacements by attacking production facilities rather than shooting them out of the sky. Conversely, where the time lag from the beginning of production to deployment was long and the rate of replacement low, the reduction of frontline strength would not be felt for too many months materially to affect the impending Allied landing. Once this temporal dimension was factored into the equation, "There is a strong *prima facie* case for concentrating our efforts on diminishing the *production* of quick-moving items like aircraft, and on increasing the *wastage* of durable ones like submarines."[37]

In February 1943, Charles Kindleberger relieved Morse in London, and under his management the Enemy Objectives Unit was brought up to full strength and its methods formalized. Shortly before his arrival the small staff of EOU had fought off an attempt to compromise its freedom of action when the Pentagon despatched a team of civilian experts to determine whether EOU should be returned to Washington and absorbed into Air Force Intelligence (A-2). When they saw that the operation was by this time functioning smoothly, that EOU economists had partially written the bombing directive approved by Roosevelt and Churchill at Casablanca, and that an effective program of collaboration had been achieved both with the kindred Research and Experiments Department of the Ministry of Home Security and with the Eighth Air Force, the Pentagon raiders returned home empty-handed. Under Kindleberger's direction the reputation of the unit would continue to rise in the estimation of both British and American agencies. A particular turning point in the fortunes of EOU came when they were able to demonstrate, through photographic analysis techniques, that the RAF was continuing to target—at significant loss of life—a Folke-Wulf plant in Bremen that had in fact been secretly moved to Marienburg: "Kindleberger doesn't miss a thing!" marveled one of his British counterparts.[38]

Kindleberger had come from the Military Supplies Division of R&A/ Washington, where he had been directing research into the German aircraft industry in particular, and he kept the Luftwaffe within his sights throughout the first year of his tenure in EOU. By February 1944, the Allied air forces had begun to assert their control of the skies over Europe and to vindicate the operational feasibility of daylight precision bombing. In strategic terms this meant that the complex and geographically dispersed oil industry could finally be elevated to the status of primary target system, for it could now be shown to lie clearly within reach of American heavy bombers.

Following up immediately on the successes of the Eighth and the Fifteenth Air Forces against targets within the German aircraft industry, Harold Barnett drafted on behalf of the Enemy Objectives Unit a plan for "The Use of Strategic Air Power after 1 March, 1944." In the original Casablanca Directive of January 1943, the Combined Chiefs of Staff had formulated a stragetic plan that established a system of primary targets but contained the qualification that the order of priority among them could be varied "according to developments in the strategical situation."[39] Operational considerations had undermined the economic case for oil in that American bombers had up to that point proven vulnerable to German fighter defenses and, moreover, the theory of economic warfare required that targets be struck with sufficient force, precision, and persistence to affect military capabilities. The imperceptible effects of the few spot raids that had been conducted against particular "important" targets— Ploiesti in the preceding August, for instance—had in this sense proven nothing, for to be *militarily* significant it was estimated that at least half of the production capability would have to be destroyed, and these raids followed up over a three-month period to prevent recovery.

Against this background Barnett began to formulate the case for oil as the economists saw it in the three months prior to the invasion: "Until the present it appeared that a target system of about 50 to 60 targets was beyond Air Force capabilities. In view of the substantial destruction of German fighter production and consequent lesser fighter opposition, this job may now be within USSTAF and RAF capabilities.[40] The undertaking proposed by the renegade economists was a large one, for it entailed the destruction of half of Germany's oil production facilities by D-Day. Operational obstacles to Germany's refineries and synthetic plants had been overcome by the addition of gasoline wing-tanks that enabled fighter planes to escort the long-range bombers; in terms of damage to tactical mobility, front-line delivery, and the morale of the German High Command, "no other target system holds such great promise for hastening Germany's defeat."

The morale of the economists fared less well during this campaign, when Eisenhower decided—between false alternatives, they felt—to secure the Normandy beachheads by targeting the French rail system instead.[41] It was at this point, when "the political battle for oil as a primary target system" seemed lost, that the EOU escalated its tactics and went underground to conduct "a running guerrilla battle" to increase the proportion of effort that was allocated to the oil war. Assured, ambitious, and alert to the intrinsic connection between intelligence and operations, the economists set about very deliberately to secure the routes from economic theory to military practice. From "the foxholes of Berkeley Square" they launched their own "Operation OCTOPUS" by which they descended into the inky waters of wartime London and quietly spread their tentacles into the various Allied planning staffs open to them. Kindleberger attached himself to the Allied Tactical Air Command, Carl Kaysen reappeared at the headquarters of the Allied Expeditionary Air Force, while Harold Barnett insinuated himself into Army Intelligence (G-2, SHAEF). Other members of this "pride of intellectual lions" prowled the corridors of British officialdom, including Walt Rostow, who had already been infiltrated into the Air Ministry to gain access to the top-secret decoding operation known as ULTRA.[42] Even if no real subterfuge was involved, it is telling that when the secret agents of the Research and Analysis Branch finally went underground, it was to be heard by their own commanders rather than to eavesdrop on the enemy.

Thus the Enemy Objectives Unit joined the two-front war that was being waged by so many of the other academic detachments of the Research and Analysis Branch—against the massed armies of the enemy, and against what they regarded as the intellectually misconceived policies of the Americans and their allies. Their mission was first to establish the credibility of applied economics within the tactical framework of the "rail plan" that Eisenhower had decided upon; once this had been demonstrated, they hoped to advance briskly along the strategic oil front. The first campaign, accordingly, was against the principal author of the rail plan, Professor Solly Zuckerman, whose prewar studies of dominance hierarchies in primates had led him, by a somewhat circuitous route, to a position of influence as scientific advisor to the warlords of the joint Allied Expeditionary Air Forces.

The duel between Zuckerman and Kindleberger—whom the former recalled as "an intensely serious and hostile young man"—could be analyzed in terms of what history demonstrates to have been the respective merits of their positions, but the record seems frankly incon-

Charles Kindleberger, "an intensely serious and hostile young man" (left, seated), with the Enemy Objectives Unit. Seated next to Kindleberger are Roselene Honerkamp and Irwin Nat Pincus; standing, left to right, are the economists William Salant, Walt W. Rostow, (?) Selko, and Edward Mayer.

clusive and is not, in any case, our principal concern. Nominally the controversy centered on the best means of disrupting the movement of German troops into Normandy while the Allied invasion forces secured their "lodgement," the candidates being the destruction of rolling stock in French and German marshaling yards and the surgical plan of bridge and line interdiction, sponsored, after exhaustive analysis, by EOU. More pertinent for the intellectual history of intelligence, however, are the levels of "structural conflict" on which this acrimonious debate was conducted: Zuckerman's native rhetoric of biological analogy versus that of statistical economics; the "abstract reasoning" and "presumed logical analysis" of the economists as against the "sound empirical basis" on which the eminent primatologist claimed to ground his position; the nature of the authorities to which each side appealed, and their radically divergent conceptions of what finally constitutes an acceptable proof.[43] Zuckerman argued that the disruption of the Italian rail system he had observed in 1943 could be extrapolated to the German-run railways of northern Europe, and he chided "the young Kindleberger" and his ilk, "supported by their equally academic and inexperienced staffs," for their resistence to the cold logic of the Baconian attitude. To economists, however, "delay, disruption, and disorganization" were hopelessly vague objectives to aim for, just as "cost" and "damage" were meaningless as isolated variables. The linguistic terms are clearly emblematic of the battle of world-views in which this proved to be a particularly evocative skirmish.

Although the issue was formally decided in favor of Zuckerman's rail plan, in a grand anticlimax whose details are a matter of military record, the EOU rail interdiction scheme was vindicated and quietly absorbed into the overall strategic plan, and in the closing months of the war the heavy bombers finally went after the German oil industry as a first priority. The morale of the economists had been severely tested in the months around D-Day, for it had been precisely on the high ground of scientific method that they had taken their stand against their historical and sociological brethren back in Washington, and it was on this very ground that they had been challenged. With their spirits and their credibility restored, the Octopus surfaced, and in midsummer the unit turned to an analysis of the tactical bombing program and a search for the means of hastening the collapse of the German capacity to resist. Walt Rostow was perfectly candid in acknowledging that "it was a conscious attempt to recapture the scientific spirit."[44]

From D-Day to V-Day

The last months of the war were exhilarating but frustrating for the economists. Fortress Europe had been breached and Germany was obviously beaten but, like a punch-drunk boxer, refused to fall down. In the meantime soldiers and civilians died, ancient cities crumbled, and the onimous constellation of postwar politics crystallized. The Runstedt counteroffensive in the Ardennes was viewed as the desperate gamble of a beaten but still formidable adversary, but also as evidence of the extraordinary resiliancy of Germany's industrial economy, and Allied intelligence experts searched in vain for the "key" that would permanently disable the German war machine. The Enemy Objectives Unit pressed for the continuing attack on German's battered oil targets, but came gradually to the conclusion that no key existed and that the war in Europe was destined to end " 'not with a bang but a whimper.' "[45]

Still the hyperintellectual squadron of EOU economists fought on to make the world safe for the scientific method. In interagency committees they unleashed against fifth columnists marching on the citadels of rigorous social science a devastating barrage of sarcasm. Undercover assumptions betrayed by the mystic language of "exerting pressure on the enemy," "inflicting damage," or "inducing general economic and military confusion" were exposed and paraded derisively within quotes in their reports. Rose Honerkamp routinely deleted sarcastic asides from Kindleberger's memoranda. To the bitter end the economists clung dogmatically to the doctrine that specific targets must be chosen with definite strategic ends in mind and that quantifiable standards must exist by which to measure results. They had in fact learned by this time "that one must, if anything, be overpure in arguing this and that the giving up of even a bit would lead to further and further inroads until we'd have a pure terror-transport-towns program."[46] Their own system of priorities was vindicated by every report of German tanks and trucks abandoned along the side of French roadways, undamaged but with their fuel tanks empty. Rostow labored in these final months to coordinate strategic and tactical, military and economic planning lest the war end inelegantly "in a blaze of mediocrity . . . without planning, without exploiting the intelligence, without thinking through our full capabilities."[47] Barnett monitored ordnance and military supplies, and Kaysen followed military transport problems but let it be known at the highest levels that "we were not a slot machine into which SHAEF/Air could put slugs and receive target lists in return."[48] By September EOU had more or less closed up shop as a target selection outfit, and the young scholars devoted increasing amounts of their energies to assisting in the planning, organization, and documentation of the postwar Strategic Bombing Survey.

Others, however, ventured closer to the front. William Salant had secured early reassignment to the Target Analysis Section of the Mediterranean Army Air Forces (MAAF) and thus became the first of the economic evangelists to preach the gospel of EOU in foreign lands. From the headquarters of the Fifteenth Air Force he and Phillip Coombs helped guide the air war against the Ploiesti refineries, which they followed in meticulous detail, poring over aerial photographs and ground reports, identifying the most vulnerable bottlenecks that emerged, and estimating the demands on repair facilities, valued, as always, at postraid prices. As the strategic value of the Rumanian oil fields declined after eight months of bombardment, they urged the advance of the oil front through Austria and Czechoslovakia and into Poland. Every potential target was thoroughly analyzed, including the small synthetic refinery at Polish Oswiecim, but there is no indication they were aware of the other facility in the town the Germans had renamed Auschwitz.[49]

Charles Kindleberger spent the last summer of the war attached to G-2 of the Twelfth Army Group in France and Luxembourg, working directly with General Bradley and feeling at last that he had found "a beautiful outlet for any ideas which may occur to me."[50] His general line of thinking was that tactical bombers should be used to maintain a line of road and rail interdiction that would force the German armies to detrain at ever greater distances from the front while continuing the strategic attack against oil to deny them the extra fuel the rail interdiction scheme would impose. The crossing of the Rhine rendered somewhat academic the distinction between strategic and tactical plans, but even then the polemics between partisans of opposing views did not abate: "I hope that you no less than I take satisfaction in academic controversy," he warned the Assistant Chief of Staff of British Army Intelligence in mid-April, "but let me warn you that I am an old hand at it, and have both raved and been raved against in the economic periodicals in the United States."[51]

· · ·

The spectacular aerial maneuvers of the Enemy Objectives Unit should not induce us to neglect the intelligence that remained on the ground among the economists of R&A/London and Washington in the last year of the war. Indeed, the problems grappled with there were at least as challenging in their intellectual content and much more so from the point of view of politics.

At the end of March 1944, Chandler Morse had returned to the European Theater to direct the entire research and analysis program of the London Outpost and to oversee a tenfold expansion of its professional staff. His fellow economists, true to form, had until then maintained closer ties to their professional counterparts in Washington than to the mere historians, sociologists, and political scientists with whom they shared office space in R&A/London. Before they could contribute to the integrated work program of the Branch Morse had to wean them "away from the analytical and statistical studies of which they had been so proud, and to interest them in the larger but vaguer and more subjective type of analysis which was familiar to the political staff."[52] Reassured by seeing one of their own at the helm, the economists relented somewhat and began to take account of the dynamic forces that would condition economic life in the posthostilities period, and thus the work of the political and economic analysts came finally to converge in London as it had in Washington.

The turn from a formalized conceptual apparatus, "so constructed as to transcend any particular set of social relations," to a contextually specific critique of *political* economy was intellectually congenial to those among the economists who had come to R&A with the conviction that "the legitimate purpose of abstraction in social science is never to get away from the real world but rather to isolate certain aspects of the real world for intensive investigation."[53] This, at any rate, was the formulation proposed by Paul Sweezy in defense of the Marxist position which he described as the attempt "to uncover the true interrelation between the economic and the non-economic factors in the totality of social existence." This methodological commitment, if not the radical political commitment it inspired, prepared him to play an influential role in discussions of American interests in the European settlement.

Sweezy had been transferred to London in December 1943 to coordinate research on economic policies in the period of occupation and to report on trends in British thinking about the postwar international economy.[54] He quickly came to see that the basic constellation of the Europe-to-come would be determined by the emergent rivalry between Britain and the USSR, and he undertook to interpret the "Marxian reasoning" of the Soviet leadership to his superiors in regard to the impending European settlement. The foremost consideration, he insisted, was not an innate aggressiveness in Soviet society but the inflexible requirement of military security. Resuming the argument on which he had concluded his 1942 *Theory of Capitalist Development,* Sweezy anticipated that the Russian position would be premised on the guarantee that Germany could not be used as a base in any future imperialist, anti-Soviet enterprise. "It must be remembered that they are Marxists," he advised, "and will not think of Britain and the United States as either benign or static entities whose political character will remain stable into the distant future":

> They will think of the U.S. as the most powerful capitalist country in the world, suffering from the contradictions of capitalism in their most acute form (over-accumulation, monopoly, class conflict, all of which are only veiled by wartime economic expansion), and with a relatively weak working-class movement. They will calculate that in another five, ten, or fifteen years a violent form of reaction may come to power in the U.S. [as it had in Germany] and set out to solve domestic problems through a world program of exploitation which would inevitably be accompanied by an anti-Bolshevik crusade.[55]

To aid his government in resolving the evident contradiction, Sweezy even ventured a means of escape from the impending impasse that promised to alleviate the concerns of the Russians without prejudice to the objective interests of the United States:

> My suggestion is that there is at least a possibility of a compromise satisfactory to both sides. This calls for a Germany which has been genuinely purged of its most vicious and reactionary elements and which is free to develop its domestic social structure in accordance with the desires of the mass of the German people . . . Secondly it calls for policies which will permit economic expansion and full employment, first of all in Europe but no less important in Britain and America. If we can really accomplish the latter, of course, the Russians can stop worrying about the threat of American reaction and imperialism.[56]

Since he did not believe that a capitalist society could achieve these objectives, Sweezy was in effect recommending that the United States commit itself to a socialist program of internal economic development as a solution to the impending polarization of the international system.

Regarded by his fellow economists as an amiable Stalinist, Sweezy was nonetheless fully integrated into the left-leaning staff, and his radical agenda found its way into a position paper prepared, "after considerable discussion," by the "Post-war Problems Committee" of R&A/London, a body that represented both the Political and Economic Subdivisions. The most ominous tendency in the emerging situation, as they saw it from close range in London, was the evident determination of the Conservative Party to preserve the status quo in Britain itself and to use the vestiges of colonial power to create "a sort of 20th-century Holy Alliance which would have the purpose of buttressing and protecting the existing structure of British society."[57] The success of this neoimperialist policy, they warned, would result in a Europe hung between two evenly matched camps, led by England and Russia, in which potential causes of conflict would never be lacking: *This is the situation most favorable to the outbreak of a new European war."*

The question that would confront American policy makers would be whether or not to provide the support without which British policy could not succeed, and R&A/London offered a highly ambiguous assurance as to the consequences for Europe of withholding it:

> In this case there would surely take place in Europe a marked shift in the locus of political power. It would be away from the hitherto ruling classes— the mobility, the large landlords, the great industrialists—which have supported or collaborated with Nazism and Fascism and which are already discredited in the eyes of the masses, and towards the workers and peasants who constitute the bulk of Europe's population and who have borne the brunt of resistance to Nazi and Fascist domination. This shift in power would not take the same form everywhere, but it would result in the aggregate in fundamental changes in property relationships and in the introduction on a large scale of socialist relations of production.[58]

This formulation, which anticipated the spontaneous formation of "something like a federation of European socialist states" into which Russia would itself gradually be drawn, seems as if it would be more persuasive to readers of the Marxist *Monthly Review* than to the American delegates to the European Advisory Commission. To the analysts of R&A/London, however, it seemed in 1945 to offer the best hope of preventing Soviet domination of the Continent and of forestalling another European war.

The OSS position that emerged from the months of discussion that followed did not take precisely the radical line proposed by Sweezy and the London economists. For one thing, Despres was now consulting for the Department of State on European Reconstruction and Finance and Mason sat on its Cartel Committee, and both knew that their patrons were somewhat less interested in OSS proposals for the socialist reconstruction of the United States than in its views on reparations, industrial disarmament, and the food situation west of the Oder. Even within the left-leaning administration of R&A the discussion of the postwar economic environment narrowed to a more immediately pragmatic range of problems. "Our true economic interests in Europe are of secondary importance," wrote Emile Despres in what would become the semioffical position of the OSS Economic Subdivision.[59] The major consideration was the security of the United States, and this depended upon defusing the potentially explosive relations between Britain and the USSR that had come to dominate thinking within R&A long before the Nazi war machine had ground to a halt. A strong and independent Germany could become the fulcrum of a future conflict between "Britain as a declining empire faced with the fact of rapidly expanding Russian strength," a conflict into which the United States would inevitably be drawn. A thoroughgoing policy of disarmament, demobilization, and denazification was the *sine qua non* of any permanent peace settlement, but the long-term strategy which Mason and Despres represented—unsuccessfully—to the State Department stressed tripartite cooperation in maintaining a weak but unified and economically viable Germany in which "large elements of socialism" would have to be tolerated.

We have lingered over this far-fetched scenario as evidence of "the road not taken" at a pivotal moment in world history, and perhaps to raise a monument to the political failure of the OSS. It was the first and last time in the history of American intelligence that such an unabashedly radical program could be stated, discussed at the highest levels, and incorporated into offical recommendations, but beyond that they could not go. We cannot afford the luxury of conjecture as to the course that history might have taken had the United States committed itself to the program outlined within the Research and Analysis Branch: the radical democratization of Germany; resistance to the conservative-imperialist tendencies among America's closest allies; the forging of a realistic accommodation with the new Soviet superpower. True, we have thus far been spared the renewal of global warfare that the scholars-in-arms of the Research and Analysis Branch predicted, but it is no less conjectural to deduce that this is because the wiser course was taken.

The History and Value of Economics

With the wisdom of historical hindsight, it appears that one of the most conspicuous features of the R&A episode was to thrust professionally trained economists into government service and indeed, into the forefront of military planning. "The 'Party Line,' " insisted Rostow as the European war was drawing to a close, "was a doctrine of warfare, not of economics or politics."[60] Perhaps, but it was a doctrine of warfare that only political economists would have thought of.

One factor in particular helps to explain why the Economic Subdivision was more successful than any other unit of R&A in bringing its theoretical labors to bear upon the course of the war. The economists, for reasons directly related to the nature of their profession and the period in which they were trained, were simply a more worldly lot than their colleagues who dwelt across the quadrangle in departments of history, philosophy, or sociology. Despres, Morse, and Kindleberger had all come to OSS from the Federal Reserve Board and, no less than Mason himself, were accomplished administrators who knew how to make their voices heard

One of the few political alliances that survived the war was struck between the radical political economists Paul Baran (left) and Paul Sweezy, shown here some years after the war in the New York offices of the *Monthly Review*.

among policy makers. They attracted about them an ambitious group of younger scholars, many of whom had also served apprenticeships beyond the walls of the university and who had been drawn into the field at a time of intellectual ferment that favored the aggressive and iconoclastic: "There was a bit of the operator in them," one alumnus later reflected, "and they knew their way around."[61]

For those neither trained nor particularly disposed to "sing of arms and men," it proves difficult to recapture the spirit of intellectual adventurism and ethical engagement that prevailed among the economists of the Research and Analysis Branch. Indeed, the delicately balanced accounting procedures, meticulous inventory controls, and finely tuned production schedules of a well-ordered firm, we might have supposed, would be so easily wrecked by a rain of 500-lb bombs that it hardly seems necessary to apply the methods of economic science to the job. In a sense, the challenge confronting the economists was to make just this case, and to convince their clients in the Departments of War and State of the marginal advantage to be gained by applying the refined methods of neoclassical analysis to the violent business of war. "Of course it is all a question of margins," the young Carl Kaysen assured them, "and therefore a little quiet thought by a well-trained EOU man is all that is needed to produce a clear statement of the problem."[62]

In this campaign the economists proved nearly as successful as the physicists in bringing their science to bear on the war. This was not solely because of the intrinsic intellectual elegance of their work, nor even because of the moral preference of pinpoint targeting to the all-out campaign of "de-housing" Germany's industrial working class advocated by Air Marshall Sir Arthur Harris of RAF Bomber Command.[63] Indeed, it was on economic grounds alone that they pointed out that easily replaced "low-skilled laborers" would be the most likely casualties of indiscriminate area bombing and that civilian morale was an insignificant factor in the totalitarian equation. Rather, it was simply the case that the war was a close thing, and behind the lifeless rhetoric of "gross wastage" and "acceptable losses" lay real human lives. To shorten the war by even a day, to impair the ability of the German generals to equip a regiment or transport it to a battlefield, justified recourse even to the armchair strategists of the Economic Subdivision. In any case, the tragic aspect of war is not that it reduces human beings to the status of abstract factors in a cost-benefit calculus; bourgeois economics had been doing that already for two centuries.

In fact, the rarefied ether of pure economic reason which the economists breathed did not survive the war unclouded. It was not the Germans who had invaded their mathematical empyrean, however, but the historians and philosophers against whom they originally defined themselves, but with whom—after years of guerilla warfare—they were finally drawn against their will into a tactical alliance. This, at any rate, is the explanation we derive from the points at which the alumni of the Economic Subdivision depart so strikingly from the larger contours of the discipline to which they gradually returned. We believe that in the interdisciplinary crucible of the Research and Analysis Branch, the economists—*qua* economists—learned about history and about values. This is a fairly radical proposition from which many of the economists might well dissent, and it would be reckless to insist upon it too narrowly. Still, it casts such a suggestive light on some remarkable intellectual affinities that I cannot resist pursuing a few notable trends in postwar economic thought.

· · ·

Edward Mason was already spending several days per week consulting for the State Department during the last months of the war and continued on to become Deputy Assistant Secretary with responsibility for postwar foreign trade policy and the settlement of war debts, and then chief economic advisor to the United States at the Moscow Conference in 1947. The global issues with which he had grappled at the helm of R&A rendered somewhat parochial his prewar interests in industrial organization and launched him into the field of international economic development and a career that would be studded with foreign honors, presidential appointments, and academic distinctions. The other members of the administrative triumvirate—Emile Despres and Chandler Morse—moved from public service to academic careers at Williams College and then Stanford and Cornell, respectively, both marked by what Morse described as "a certain catholicity of interest and a focus on economics as a *social* discipline comprehending history, sociology, and especially politics," rather than simply the problems of economic efficiency that dominate neoclassical economics today.[64]

Whereas the elders of the Economic Subdivision were already well-established in the profession, the academic careers of many of the younger economists were launched in the Research and Analysis Branch and followed spectacular trajectories. Having spent the war years helping to take the German economy apart, the prolific Kindleberger passed the early Marshall Plan days in the State Department as head of the Division of German and Austrian Economic Affairs (GA) helping to put it back together. In 1948 Kindleberger moved into an academic position in the iconoclastic Department of Economics at MIT, and although he would later remark that the "literary" diversion of economic history was "a splendid way to spend one's retirement," the reality is that already in the early 1950s he had made the decision not to fill the mathematical and statistical gaps in his training left by the war years, and a fascination with financial history and the history of economic thought has led a shadow existence in his writing and teaching ever since.[65]

A Marshallian perspective on "economics in the long view" applies *a fortiori* to Walt Whitman Rostow, his fellow campaigner in the wartime EOU and then deputy chief in the GA Division. It would be imprudent to suggest that Rostow was redirected by the war to the interrelated fields of economic history and economic development, for this program had been laid out already in his undergraduate years at Yale on the strength of "a kind of black-market economic theory seminar in 1933–1934": "I decided, aged seventeen, to devote my professional life to combining history with economic theory in two senses: using economic theory systematically both to illuminate economic history and to explore the complex interactions of the economy with the non-economic sectors of society."[66] There are two considerations that must be acknowledged, however. First, it is hardly trivial to observe that nothing in his intense wartime experience deterred or distracted Rostow from this program, nothing in the immersion of the economist in history that did not reinforce his sense of the debt of economics to history.

Second, we may concede that the economists who ventured or were otherwise lured into R&A were in some respects a self-selecting group, already predisposed to see the world in a more prismatic fashion and vulnerable to the intrusion of noneconomic and even nonacademic variables. Economic theory is a relatively easy business, for one may narrow the field of variables more or less at the discretion of one's editors. Rostow was not the only one to learn from OSS that applied economics differs in that *all* the relevant variables must be accounted for, whatever violence this does to the elegance of one's favorite model. Failure to meet the highest standards of academic integrity did not expose one to a caustic footnote in a rival journal; it meant that an American flier would be shot down in flames.

The same sorts of lessons were learned by other members of the Enemy Objectives Unit, even if they managed to free themselves from the misguided fascination with strategic air power that Rostow brought with him to the Johnson White House. Immediately upon the close of hostilities, Carl Kaysen was despatched to Germany to report on the effectiveness of the strategic bombing program he had helped design and to evaluate on the basis of his observations the capacity of Germany to pay reparations out of undamaged capital equipment and productive capacity.[67] He left the European theater for good in September and, after three days spent sampling the life of a State Department bureaucrat, fled back to the Ivy League to complete a PhD at Harvard and to begin there a distinguished academic career marked by a significantly greater receptivity to the other social sciences than is characteristic of the field. There is some irony here: in the OSS brash young economists such as Kaysen had elevated themselves to a scientific height uncontaminated by political, institutional, or other "qualitative" factors, and from which they pronounced with disfavor upon the pretensions of their lesser colleagues. By 1966, when he succeeded J. Robert Oppenheimer to a controversial directorship of the Institute for Advanced Study, his fall from scientific grace had been complete and this very receptivity was his undoing, for it laid him open to the Institute's physicists and mathematicians, for whom even economics hardly qualified as a science.[68]

The postwar career of another prominent member of the youthful team of R&A economists, Sidney Alexander, followed a broadly similar route. Discharged from active duty, he returned to an assistant professorship at Harvard armed with a realistic understanding of how governments do and do not work, a feeling for the practical mixture of theoretical and empirical research that lies at the heart of economics, and—the trademark of R&A—a supreme confidence that with a little discipline one could mind anyone else's business better than they could themselves. These traits marked his subsequent work in the public interest and his return to teaching at MIT in 1956. In addition, however, a certain substantive thread that can be detected in the work of many of the R&A economists stands out with particular thematic clarity in Alexander's influential postwar work, both as a citizen and as a scholar at the philosophical edge of the discipline. This is the conviction "that the rule against an economist's making value judgements professionally lacks legitimacy, that the exclusion from economics of normative judgments embodying human values is based only on an arbitrary definition of economics."[69] Although it was surely not his intention to do so, Alexander provided here a philosophical formulation of the principle that guided the practical engagement of the Economic Subdivision with its fascist adversary.

Paul Sweezy also departed from the academic mainstream, although in ways that might well have been predicted from the Marxist perception he held of "the present as history." Sweezy established himself in Germany during the first months of the occupation where, under the distant supervision of Berlin Chief Allen Dulles, he analyzed the political pro-

Carl Kaysen estimates the damage to the Cologne Cathedral.

grams of the Communist, Social Democratic, and trade union movements in the shattered capital. Sweezy's mounting hostility toward official U.S. policy was reflected in the reports he wrote during that summer: "My own impression is that there is a good deal more anti-fascist—I will not say 'democratic' because that remains to be seen—potential in German than the weakness of the underground has led us to believe. So far, however, I see no signs that MG has any plans or, for that matter, desire to harness this potential to its own purposes."[70] Neither the federal nor even the academic establishment offered a politically feasible environment for him in the wake of his experiences, and it was under these circumstances that he founded in 1949 the independent Marxist *Monthly Review,* which remained a lonely voice of American socialism until the emergence of the New Left.

This crucial period in world history is fraught with ideology and intrigue, but it is a fair generalization to say that the position argued by the OSS economists in the immediate postwar years was that to give precedence to the punishment of Germany or the political neutralization of the USSR would subvert the long-range security of Europe and the hope of a lasting accord with Russia on the main lines of a peaceful postwar settlement. In the delicate postwar balance, these objectives could best be achieved indirectly—"crabwise," as Kindleberger put it— by first laying the foundations for technical cooperation between east and west in economic matters.[71] Technical solutions were not ends in themselves; but grounded in concrete institutions and informed by an irreducible historical logic, they could become instruments for the advancement of qualitative political objectives.

We could continue along these lines, but the pattern would remain, albeit with significant variations and outright exceptions. Economics remained for this outstanding generation the quantitative discipline that it inherently is, but it never folded back upon itself into a mathematical solipsism devoid of historical determinations, political goals, and what Alexander called the need to introduce "meta-ethics, or the language of the normative" into its rhetorical arsenal.[72] They remained, in other words, political economists in the rich sense of that term intended by Adam Smith, their forebear who had held the chair not of economics but of Moral Philosophy at Glasgow, and who knew well that "statistics" was just what its name implied: the quantification of state power.

In December 1984 a contingent of aging OSS economists held a sort of 40-year reunion at the annual meeting of the American Economics

Association in Dallas. Charles Kindleberger, inheriting an AEA presidency that must at times have seemed reserved for graduates of the Research and Analysis Branch, had convened an extraordinary panel devoted to the proposition that economic history is "A Necessary though not Sufficient Condition for an Economist."[73] This was a fitting valedictory for his generation, for although some of the most prominent members of the profession participated in the discussion, it could not help but call attention to the "marginal" status of history—in the decidedly uneconomic sense of that term. Against the speculative excesses they had encountered in R&A they had insisted upon the most austere standards of analytical rigor and empirical precision. Once demobilized, however, they fought to defend the embeddedness of economic theory in a human world of history, politics, and morality. Armed with this dual legacy, they raised a challenge to the discipline that they did not shrink from accepting themselves. Its consequences can be discerned in the exceptional breadth of interests that marked the careers of this group, in the historical perspective that informs them, and in the disreputably literary sensibility they express. They enriched the profession, perhaps in spite of themselves, because they had learned to see beyond it.

FIVE

Social Science in One Country: The USSR Division

Despite the glamorized notions which have gathered about some of the activities of OSS, the work of R&A was a real research slugging match.

Philip Mosely, "The Growth of Russian Studies"

The historical importance of the Research and Analysis Branch, as should by now be evident, varies according to the standard that is applied to it. Some of the most intellectually challenging work done within the organization—the theoretical analysis of German fascism performed by the group around Franz Neumann—fell largely upon deaf ears. The practical labors of the target selection teams in London, by contrast, contributed materially to the prosecution of the war, although they did little to create a permanent body of theory. Elsewhere, as we shall see, the legacy of R&A was to redirect the intellectual priorities of a generation.

The work of the USSR Division suggests yet another model with which to evaluate the intellectual history of American intelligence. To a greater extent than any other group in R&A, the scholars who followed the course of the war as it bore upon the uneasy Soviet alliance dealt with problems that would survive into the postwar era and would preoccupy the American intelligence agency that was heir to OSS. More relevant to our own admittedly academic concerns, however, the substance and especially the collaborative methodologies practiced in the USSR Division constituted a research agenda that would literally define the field of postwar Sovietology. This in no way implies that the economists, sociologists, and historians who applied their skills to the Soviet Union conceived their task in the manner that permeated the academic and intelligence communities during the cold war, for in R&A the enemy was still German fascism; Soviet Russia was a vital if unstable ally. Indeed, if anything marked this group of scholars it was their aspiration to a posture of political neutrality and rigorous scholarly objectivity. The

Russian specialists of R&A recognized both the intellectual complexity and the political delicacy of the issues within which they were dealing, and they approached the Soviet experience with a framework as free as possible from prior allegiances. For the *apparachiks* of the USSR Division, the party line was rigorous social science.

Viewed internally, the history of Slavic studies within the OSS falls naturally into three phases. First was the period, rife with methodological and epistemological tensions, of the organization of the Division, the clarification of its mandate, and the recruitment of a professoriate with which to staff the various proposed sections. Second was a period of frustration—"the doldrums," as it would be recalled—in which the political, economic, and geographic subdivisions labored in an institutional vaccuum to compile a picture of the Russian military situation and in so doing to establish the value and credibility of their work. Finally, late in 1943, the shifting fortunes of the war caused the focus of the Division to shift from immediate Russian capabilities to the prospects for postwar reconstruction. By this time the Division's reports were eagerly sought out within the government and had earned it an authoritative voice in the formation of official opinion.

What Is To Be Done

On September 1, 1941, as the massed German armies advanced on Moscow and the world marked the second anniversary of the start of World War II, Geroid T. Robinson was summoned to Washington by William Langer. Robinson, the professor of Russian history at Columbia University, was responding to an unprecedented appeal. Little was known about the capacity of the Soviet Union to absorb the force of the German onslaught, but its ability to do so, and to tie up a major share of the German forces, was a factor of the utmost importance.

Nowhere was the lack of reliable information more acute than with respect to the closed society of Soviet Russia, but for no other theater was there a greater scarcity of qualified experts. For fifteen years, restrictions on travel had severely limited the access of foreigners to the Soviet Union. The number of foreign consulates in Soviet territory had been sharply reduced, and until the beginning of the war the only American representation was at the U.S. Embassy in Moscow. After the purges of 1937–38 it had become virtually impossible to obtain information from Soviet citizens either in the USSR or abroad. Within the academic community, scholarly contacts had come nearly to an end even before the war, as Soviet scientific journals discontinued the use of Western languages and the flow of publications from the USSR was radically constricted. The onset of war brought scholarly exchange almost to a halt.

Geroid Robinson, known to his colleagues as "one of the leading artisans in the modern field of Russian studies" and to his graduate students as a ruthless taskmaster, seemed best qualified to build a professional research staff that could operate within these constraints.[1] At its peak strength, in mid-1943, he would command a division of some sixty social scientists, flanked by three lieutenants who were equally well-known in the academic trenches: John A. Morrison, one of only two American geographers professionally concerned with the Soviet Union, came down from the University of Chicago to become Robinson's deputy and chief of the new Geographic Subdivision; Bernadotte Schmitt, founder of the *Journal of Modern History* and professor also at Chicago, would direct the Political Subdivision; Chief of the Economic Subdivision, after protracted negotiation, was Harvard's Wassily Leontief, the Russian émigré economist who would win the Nobel Prize for the theory of input-output analysis—a conceptual framework whose elements were first tested in R&A.[2] Even before the commissioning of this distinguished officers' corps, however, the new division was checked by the lack of a battle plan and a shortage of troops.

This was not, however, due to any shortage of volunteers: committed partisans ranging in hue from American Trotskyists to White Russian monarchists assailed the directorate with offers and applications, all of which were politely declined for fear that their presence would discredit the claims to objectivity on which the credibility of this division, more than any other, depended. Scholarly candidates were subjected to the same standards of political scrutiny. The appointment of Alex Inkeles, fresh from Philip Mosely's "super-intensive" Russian language course and recommended by him as "the best graduate student in six years" to have passed through the Sociology Department at Cornell, was delayed until his wife resigned her temporary clerical position with the Soviet Purchasing Commission. The political economist Paul A. Baran had regularly to defend against allegations that he was "an agent of the GPU." And John Scott, engaged to prepare a series of reports on the Ural industrial area, himself urged that the FBI be notified that his father was the "notorious Red," Scott Nearing, lest R&A be accused of being innocent dupes of the NKVD—or worse. From its inception the Division leaned over backward to avoid taking on personnel who could compromise its appearance of professionalism and impartiality, and at least one technical specialist, whom Robinson defended as "one of the most valuable men in this organization," had to be dismissed after being denounced for unspecified "communist connections."[3] The sensitivity of the directors extended even to what Nietzsche called "the Edenic impulse" of name-giving: the USSR Political Subdivision—unlike its Europe-Africa or Far Eastern counterparts—was initially known only as the "Special Intelligence Section," lest its mission, rather than its subject matter, be construed as "political." And at a meeting specially convened to discuss the official name of the entire operation, the "Soviet Union Division" was rejected for fear that in common usage it would be referred to as the "Soviet Division"—"an extremely unfortunate name for an American research organization," Robinson ruled.[4]

Nor were political considerations the only obstacles to assembling a research staff. Difficulties of an academic nature were felt even more acutely. The principal recruiting ground for the Research and Analysis Branch was, as we have seen, the American university establishment, but the importance of the USSR in world affairs had been insufficiently appreciated in academic life prior to the war. Indeed, according to an authoritative estimate, not more than a dozen American-trained scholars had equipped themselves during the prewar decades for research and teaching in their disciplines as applied to Russian studies.[5] The scholarship of the 1920s and 30s had been richly pluralistic in its approach to the Soviet Union in terms of both methodology and ideology, but the field of Slavic studies remained marginal and underdeveloped. Robinson, in one of his ritual appeals for more personnel, pointed out that many university teachers had actively discouraged their students from selecting research topics in Russian history, politics, or literature and that in consequence, "the number of competent American students of Russian affairs at the outbreak of the present war was deplorably limited."[6] The sudden emergence of the Soviet Union from a pariah nation to one on which the future of the Western powers depended thus placed an enormous burden upon the relatively small number of people possessed of the specialist knowledge, linguistic training, and research experience necessary to make effective use of Russian documentary and statistical material.

The unrelenting efforts of Robinson and Morrison, their appeals to William Langer, and the personal intervention of General Donovan himself enabled the Division gradually to build up an intellectual infantry of talented younger scholars. Barrington Moore, Jr., trained at Williams in Classics and adept at working with fragmentary sources, was brought over from the Justice Department, where he had been working impatiently as a propaganda analyst under Harold Lasswell. Another aspiring classicist, Robert C. Tucker, had been reading Aristotle with Werner Jaeger at Harvard when he was diverted "by his majesty Chance" into an intensive Russian language course and then into R&A. John Curtiss, author of the acclaimed *Church and State in Russia,* was asked to organize a Morale Section, to which was added the historian Alfred Levin, the psychologist Urie Bronfenbrenner, and the sociologist Alex Inkeles, who had first to be rescued from atop a telegraph pole in the Army Signal Corps at Shenango, Pennsylvania. Edward Mason, always more interested in intellectual acumen than political conformity, induced the Marxist economist Paul Baran to join OSS as a specialist on Soviet and Polish economic affairs; and Abram Bergson, fresh from a dissertation on the structure of Soviet wages and already the author of a classic treatise on welfare economics, was appointed chief of the Population and Manpower Section. To these younger scholars, who would become principal architects of the postwar field of Sovietology, was added a distinguished reserve army of consultants—including Cornell University's Philip Mosely, the country's leading authority on Balkan affairs, the pioneering Sovietologist John N. Hazard, and Vladimir Timoshenko of Stanford's Food Research Institute—who stood in the wings to take on special assignments or offer expert advice.[7]

By the time the troops had assembled in Washington, the OSS order-of-battle had evolved along lines indicated by politics, bureaucracy, and epistemology. Soviet affairs were initially subsumed within a larger East European research unit that had responsibility for European and Asiatic Russia together with the eight Baltic and Balkan states. That division of intellectual labor corresponded to an early stage in the history of R&A, however, one that Deputy Chief Morrison characterized as "the *Sturm und Drang* period, when the 'regionalists' and the 'functionalists' were eating largely of the apple of discord and there was much confusion in Zion."[8] With the growth of the organization and the emergence of expansionist tendencies among certain factions of the professoriate, the issue of how best to take hold of the world in all of its interdisciplinary complexity once more became acute. Economists, psychologists, and even geographers insisted that the scientific generality of their methods and the universal validity of their conclusions transcended national boundaries. Robinson, however, insisted with equal vehemence that the peculiarly "interlocked and integrated" character of Soviet society demanded a correspondingly coordinated research program. For a year he had been patiently recruiting the most interdisciplinary faculty—historians and sociologists as well as economists, psychologists, political scientists, and geographers—that could be found within the Research and Analysis Branch and battled fiercely against the epistemological Balkanization of his team. In the end he was successful in securing the foundations of what was literally the first "area-studies" program in the United States: research on Eastern Europe was transferred to the sprawling Europe-Africa Division and directed by Harvard's Robert Lee Wolff, and the new USSR Division came into its own as the only unit in R&A authorized to practice social science in one country.

The First Five-Year Plan

Referring to the planned invasion of Soviet Russia, Hitler swore to his generals that "when Barbarossa commences the world will hold its breath and make no comment," but he had not reckoned with the prolific scholars of the Research and Analysis Branch. While Edward Mason's economists were estimating the logistic requirements of the German invasion and Central European analysts were mapping the German pattern of occupation, the faculty of the USSR Division counterattacked along two fronts. In November 1941, as the first stage in a conscious strategy to win for themselves a clientele in the crowded intelligence market, the newly formed research unit undertook to determine the means of transferring Lend-Lease supplies to the beleaguered Soviet Union. The second problem, and the one that set the research agenda of the Division, concerned the Russian capability to absorb the German blow and thus continue to tie up a major share of German forces. The empirical base from which to make this assessment was shockingly slim, but the consequences for Europe either of a crushing defeat or a separate peace could be catastrophic.

The logistical challenges of transferring 17 million tons of food and military supplies to the Soviet Union occasioned the first series of reports prepared in the Division, overseen by the geographer Morrison and largely executed by Oliver Lissitzyn and the staff of his Regional Intelligence Section. These papers dealt with matters of a largely technical character: winter shipping in the Bering Sea, harbors and ice conditions in Kamchatka, east Siberian airfields, the condition of the North Afghan Road, and alternatives to the ports of Archangel and Murmansk should the Germans succeed in closing them. Although of great practical importance, these reports can no longer bear the weight of deep interpretation except as evidence of the creative research strategies devised to execute them. From the American office of the Lithuanian Automobile Club, for example, the professors secured an invaluable cache of up-to-date road maps. Officials of the Caterpillar Corporation helped them to estimate the efficiency of tractors as subzero temperatures. Constatin Nikiforoff of the Regional Intelligence Section was sent to Seattle to interview a deserter from a Soviet merchant ship reported to have first-hand information about Siberian port conditions. The absence or unreliability of basic data about the Soviet Union taxed their ingenuity, and Deputy Chief Morrison informed William Langer that because so little basic research had been done, "to secure factual information on the USSR in general requires at least *double* the number of man-hours of research that are necessary to obtain similar data for any other country."[9]

In contrast to these laborious but straightforward information papers, the series of so-called "capabilities studies" prepared during this period were conceived in a spirit of interdisciplinary scholarship virtually without precedent in the field of Russian studies, and they were executed with a freedom from ideological coloration that now seems remarkable: "To satisfy 'G. T. R.'," recalled one of his subordinates, "one had to be thorough, documented, objective and careful about one's conclusions."[10] Discrepancies with official Soviet claims were patiently corrected, but these rectifications were more characteristically grounded in a commitment to rigorous scholarship than in partisanship. Indeed, if the Russian people were truly enjoying the bountiful fruits of collectivization while repelling the German invaders, what need had they for the quantities of Lend-Lease grain their leaders were requesting? Ideological factors were acknowledged—as they had been by social scientists from Thucydides onward—to the extent that they exerted an influence upon the larger field of inquiry. Thus Marxian categories were routinely employed in the USSR Division insofar as Soviet leaders acted in conformance with them, and the shape of their work was in the last analysis determined by the integrated structure of Soviet society itself: "The major guiding principle in the work of the USSR Division," noted Morrison, "is that economic and political intelligence work on Russia must be integrated in the same high degree if such work is to produce an understanding of Russia that will be of value to American policy makers."[11] Armed with this realistic insight and disciplined by the party line of value-free social science, they ventured into the vast uncharted expanse that Churchill had at the beginning of the war described as "a riddle wrapped in a mystery inside an enigma."

Owing to the paucity of reliable data, it was actually easier for the R&A Branch to produce hard estimates of the aggressive potential of the German enemy than of the defensive capabilities of the Soviet ally. Census figures, which had allowed them to make precise calculations of German combat manpower, were for the Soviet Union sporadic, contradictory, and, after 1939, unavailable. Russian war matériel, Robinson observed, "is not measurable because of the lack of statistics, apart from the actual figures of American and Allied shipments to Russia."[12] Combat losses, the empirical relation of production to wastage, and other vital data seemed virtually incalculable. To a greater extent than other division chiefs, Geroid Robinson was frustrated by this situation, for he embodied an academic tradition that enjoins one from publishing until all the evidence is in. Accustomed to terrorizing his graduate students into complete mastery of their sources, Robinson suffered from the bad conscience of a traditional scholar forced to compromise his standards to the exigencies of the moment. The uncertainty with which he led his troops into a field of discourse that demanded a continual flow of estimates, predictions, conjectures, and more-or-less-informed guesses is evident in the qualifications and disclaimers that mark his earliest papers; they suggest that in no other theater of intelligence did academic scruple weigh so heavily.

Gradually, however, the scholars of the USSR Division began to amass a statistical base that was, if not flawless or complete, at least the best that could be found. From official figures published before 1938 they extrapolated forward to current population trends. From a list of awards published in *Isvestiya* they noted that the manager of the Stolinsk steel plant had received the Order of Lenin for raising production 14 percent above the quota set for 1942, which, when cross-referenced with a propaganda piece in *Industriya* on the tasks of industry during the present war, gave them a plausible estimate of steel-making capacity in the region. Agricultural economists noticed that their Soviet counterparts had quietly changed their accounting system from "barn yield" (which included losses on the threshing floor) to "biological yield," creating the impression of a sharp increase in grain production; they corrected their final estimates for the tonnage of stored reserves eaten by mice. "The status of the results is, frankly, somewhat obscure," Morrison conceded; "To date they have not been challenged but this may merely reflect the fact that no one else has been so audacious as to tackle the problem."[13]

As primitive as these methods appear by later standards, they testify to the statistical void that confronted the pioneering Sovietologists of R&A. It became increasingly clear, moreover, that the Library of Congress and the scant materials they received from abroad could not satisfy their academic appetite for facts and figures. During the crucial months of June and July 1943, during which the Red Army decisively reversed the German offensive in central Russia, OSS received from Soviet sources a paltry forty pages of mimeographed material whose value was "practically useless." *Pravda* and *Isvestiya* arrived six to eight weeks out of date when they arrived at all. Important periodicals—*The War and the Working Class, Under the Banner of Marxism*—reached them more often as rumors than as resources.

The cloud of unknowing that hung over the Soviet Union represented nothing less than "the chief failure of American intelligence," in the view of the Division Chief: "In my last monthly report I once more emphasized the immense importance of having in Moscow a representative who would collect newspapers, periodicals, and books systematically, and would forward them promptly."[14] This appeal was part of a campaign Robinson waged throughout the first phase of his tenure as Chief to open channels of information from the USSR. Averell Harriman rebuffed his request "to take one of our people to Moscow," despite promises that any such agent would act not as a spy but a scholar, would ask no awkward questions, and would pursue printed materials only. Lend-Lease officials declined to attach to their Moscow office any member of an organization regarded by some Soviet officials "as roughly equivalent to certain parts of their NKVD." General John R. Deane, head of the American Military Mission to the USSR and a personal friend of William Donovan, campaigned for a cooperative exchange between OSS and Soviet intelligence, but even with the belated endorsement of Ambassador Harriman his proposal was overwhelmed by opposition from the FBI, Army Intelligence, and finally the White House.[15]

In April 1944, by which time the unique services the Research and Analysis Branch was equipped to provide had come to be recognized, the USSR Division finally secured indirect representation in Moscow, but at the cost of one of its most valuable younger analysts. Robert Tucker of the Regional Intelligence Section was transferred to the Auxiliary Foreign Service and attached to the U.S. Embassy to monitor Soviet foreign policy as it was reflected in the official press and to send interpretive dispatches back to Washington where—when relations with the State Department were good—they were made available to R&A. Long before this, however, the Division had begun to supplement its narrowly circumscribed field of intelligence-gathering activities.

At the end of 1942, Robinson and Irving Rudd, the Russian-born, Harvard-trained statistician who directed the Industrial and Military Supplies Section, flew to London to explore the possibilities of cooperation with their British counterparts. As an opening they carried with them a series of reports that embodied R&A's assessment of the Soviet position, and in the course of working through the discrepancies with British estimates became aware of the greater resources available overseas. The two Americans remained in England through the spring of 1943, establishing contacts with academic scholars at Oxford and civil servants in London and laying the groundwork for a "Russian Mission" to the R&A Outpost. The first permanent representative, Thomas Hall, arrived in May; and although he found British estimates still to be colored by "wishful thinking," within a few months he had established contacts with nearly a dozen agencies willing to furnish information on the USSR which they had been compiling since before the OSS had been created. The cooperative spirit of the British intelligence establishment—composed in large measure of fellow scholars—was in marked contrast with the cold reception given the USSR Division by the War Department in Washington. At the very moment that Ensign Hall was availing himself of the files of the Ministry of Economic Warfare, Geroid Robinson was being told by the American Military Intelligence Service in Washington "that it is a War Department policy to prohibit our access to information possessed by the War Department on the U.S. (which we use for purposes of analogy) and on Russia."[16]

As information began to flow into R&A/Washington, a comprehensive picture of Russian capabilities began to take shape that was the distinctive contribution of the USSR Division during the first phase of its operation. Its general conclusions, however—both economic and political—departed so radically from conventional wisdom that even when they were able to move from basic research to current intelligence the scholars of R&A still found themselves ignored and isolated. That the German invasion had cut deeply into Russian productive capacities was obvious, but they argued that the structure of Soviet industry and agriculture was such as to deny to the Germans immediate benefits of the occupation. In the Ukraine and North Caucasus the Nazis inherited an agricultural base geared toward centralized, large-scale production, and a peasant population in which both patriotic and separatist tendencies coexisted. This placed them in the peculiar position of trying to maintain "a collective system of agriculture which they have condemned with the help of certain anti-collectivist peasants whose desires they have been afraid fully to satisfy." Unable either to operate the collectives at maximum productivity or to abolish them outright, "the Nazi agricultural system in Russia has been hanging in the air."[17] In industry, the occupation raised problems that were no less complex, for the destruction of equipment by the retreating Russian armies, the greater revolutionary spirit of the industrial working class, and a host of other factors conspired to prevent the outright appropriation by the Germans of a functioning economic infrastructure.

While the structure of Soviet society itself denied to the Germans the spoils of occupation, for the Russians the effects of the invasion were judged to be immediate and catastrophic: the loss of 40–50 percent of productive capacity in some industries, critical food shortages resulting from the occupation of the Russian "breadbasket," and a casualty rate that resisted computation. It was, however, a crisis the Nazis were unable fully to exploit. The winter of 1941–42 thus found Germany and Russia in a sort of standoff, with the Soviet economy battered but far from disabled. The diplomatic front was likewise suspended in a tense equilibrium by what Robinson called "the profound and long-standing suspicion of all non-Communist governments" on the part of the Soviet leadership, a suspicion reciprocated by many persons in official positions abroad.[18]

To break this deadlock in favor of the West, above all Stalin had to be convinced that it was to his advantage to stay in the war, and Robinson at one point took the unusual step of arguing for a major increase in supplies and equipment to be shipped to the USSR and for sending an Anglo-American expeditionary force to secure the northern supply route. This bold recommendation—his only personal trespass into the policy field—reflected the party line that prevailed within the USSR Division and to which even the cult of objectivity was subordinated: the necessity of maintaining the alliance, upon which the outcome of the war and the security of the postwar world depended. Robinson was even known to have opposed research proposals that might have exposed political strains between the Soviet Union and the Western Allies. A considerable share of the Division's intellectual resources were, accordingly, directed to the resolution of this basic question of whether Stalin would in fact remain in the war, or whether he could at some point decide that it was in the best interests of the Soviet Union to conclude a separate peace with Germany.

A two-year delay in the opening of the promised second front, Anglo-American uncertainty over Russia's territorial ambitions in eastern Europe, and a host of other factors contributed to the instability of the alliance and to a climate of mutual suspicion that supported unilateral actions. Reports of clandestine meetings between Soviet and German officials had already reached OSS from its overseas outpost in Stockholm. The problem was put to Morrison, who approached it in proto-Kremlinological fashion by attempting to step into "the logic of the situation" as perceived within the Soviet leadership itself: "In any realistic speculation as to whether Russia might negotiate a separate peace," he wrote in a controversial report in August 1943, "it is necessary to keep constantly in mind the cornerstone of Russian foreign policy: the security of Soviet territory and the Soviet state."[19] Whereas the hard-pressed Germans had a real incentive to strike a deal that would enable them to disengage from the eastern front, the Soviets, now on the offensive, would be concerned with two longer-range requirements: securing themselves against future outbreaks of German militarism and maintaining the ties with the West upon which their postwar reconstruction depended. Despite its superficial plausibility, Morrison argued on the eve of Stalin's overtures at Teheran, the internal "logic of the situation" indicated that a separate Russo-German peace would be seen as prejudicial to the long-term interests of the USSR and could be safely discounted as a possibility. The report, which could hardly be reconciled with the notion of an ideologically driven monolith, was killed by the Projects Committee before it ever left R&A.[20]

Conclusions such as these were often met with suspicion or indifference, as was much of the work produced in the USSR Division during its first two years. Ironically, as Hitler's own intelligence staff was warning him in August 1942 of the strength of the Soviet forces massing at

Stalingrad, the Research and Analysis Branch issued the first of its own favorable estimates of Russian capabilities—to a similarly hostile reception. Over the next year the analysts of R&A predicted that in terms of manpower, basic industries, military supplies, food, transport, and morale, "Russian strength is likely to remain high" and that "the Soviet Union may be expected to offer, in the summer of 1943, as strong or possibly even stronger resistance than it offered in the summer of 1942." The OSS projections tended in fact to err on the side of caution and to underestimate the recuperative powers of the Soviet economy, but they came closer to the truth than the pessimistic views that dominated official thinking in Washington. There was an elaborate speculative structure, admitted economist Abram Bergson in retrospect, "but on the whole we made out rather well."[21]

As the events of the war, military and diplomatic, confirmed the general accuracy of these estimates, the reports of the USSR Division came to earn a belated credibility. After months of neglect, the interagency Joint Intelligence Committee, the State Department, the Lend-Lease Administration, the War Production Board, the Federal Reserve Board, the Office of War Information, the Army Industrial College, and even the Surgeon General began to request from them specific studies and to solicit their expertise. In August 1943, in a rare invitation into the councils of *Weltpolitik,* Robinson accompanied the OSS delegation to the Québec Conference, where he presented a twelve-point protocol for American-Russian cooperation that earned high praise for the Division.[22] For some dispirited analysts this recognition came as too little, too late, and for others the costs of their hard-won credentials had been too high: Robinson thought nothing of exacting a ruthless 2,347 hours of overtime from his staff between April and July 1942, of driving his troops through the night to meet an early morning deadline, or of attempting to operate his Division by remote control from London. But the Stakhanovite regime of the USSR Division prevailed and slowly gained for them the respect of their academic colleagues in OSS and the patronage of the Departments of War and State.

Peaceful Coexistence

The regimen of central planning, ruthless productivity drives, and forced collectivization produced results that ushered in a new era of *mirnoe sosuchchestvovanie*—of "peaceful coexistence" with the other branches of OSS and of the U.S. government at large.[23] The shift in the fortunes of the USSR Division toward the beginning of 1944 corresponded also to a shift—indeed, to a "fundamental reorientation"—in the direction of its research program. Using fragmentary data and improvised social science methodologies, the Russian analysts of R&A had predicted that the Soviet Union could withstand the economic devastation of the German invasion and had the political determination to do so. This assessment set the agenda that would guide their research through the end of the war. Russia's economic capability and political resolve presaged the role of Soviet power in the postwar world, and the focus of the USSR Division shifted accordingly to problems of internal reconstruction and Soviet political intentions in Eastern Europe, the Balkans, and Germany. Here as well, however, the professors produced results that were notably out of step with the main lines of official thinking.

The entry of the Soviet Union into center stage was marked by the German retreat to the Polish and Rumanian frontiers, and on the diplomatic front by Stalin's successes at Teheran. This dramatic reversal confronted the United States with a challenge and an opportunity that was formulated in a position paper prepared by the USSR Political Subdivision in the closing months of 1943:

> Since recent military and political events have demonstrated that Russia has both the ability and the intention to make its power felt in the postwar period, the vital question becomes: Under what conditions and to what extent will the Soviet Union be willing to use this power cooperatively? . . . A deliberate mutual effort at cooperation would tend to stabilize Europe at a democratic level, while the continued pursuit of largely independent strategies and policies by the Western Allies would probably lead to the pursuit by the Soviet government of larger objectives.[24]

The various sections of the Political Subdivision, by this time under the direction of the Prussophobic Bernadotte Schmitt, approached this historic question in a series of reports that argued from premises not commonly associated with American intelligence on the Soviet Union.

A principal activity of John Curtiss' Morale Section—created in the period of concern over the possible collapse of Russian resistance—had been to monitor the Soviet press and theoretical organs of the Communist Party for indications as to the strength of the domestic front. In the last half of 1943, in the months following the dissolution of the Comintern, this tedious routine began to yield a pattern in Soviet propaganda that confirmed the broad ideological retreat from "world revolution" to "peaceful coexistence" that had been evident from the beginning of the war. There appeared in the Communist press a new tendency to differentiate between the "predatory imperialism" of Nazi Germany and the benignly democratic regimes of Britain and the United States. Soviet newspapers printed exhortations to patriotism and productivity rather than the spread of revolutionary propaganda abroad, and in domestic radio broadcasts the theme of internal development entirely displaced the struggle against international capitalism. These maneuvers did not mean that the Soviet leadership had abandoned Marxism-Leninism or that Stalin had become reconciled to a future of "capitalist encirclement," but they did indicate that "present-day Marxism has been oriented toward the winning of the war and cooperation with the Allied powers."[25] At about this time the unit changed its name, significantly, to the Internal Political Section.

A growing body of printed materials—ranging from official foreign policy declarations to domestic propaganda leaflets—signaled the willingness of the Soviet leadership to subordinate doctrinal consistency to the achievement of common goals even after the cessation of hostilities. In short, evidence was emerging to suggest that Western action (and inaction) had been a decisive factor in the formation of Soviet policy, and that the degree to which the Russians had committed themselves to common postwar goals, as one report put it, "has varied directly with the extent of the expected Allied contribution to the task, to be precise, of killing Germans."[26] The USSR, if these inferences were correct, could be viewed neither as an ideological monolith operating within an international vaccuum nor as a regime guided by purely opportunistic impulses. The breakdown of the alliance might still provoke a renewal of Soviet expansionism and of revolutionary activity throughout the world, but this eventuality would follow from the logic not of Marxian dialectics so much as Machiavellian *Realpolitik.* Behind the bellicose rhetoric of the Communist Party lay a veiled appeal for a world of stable, peaceful coexistence. The alliance of socialism and democracy in the defeat of Nazi Germany had created a unique historical opportunity that could not be expected to return.

Internal developments disclosed by the ongoing research program of the Division throughout 1944 provided increasingly strong support for an attitude of realism and rapprochement in dealing with the Soviet Union. As much as American public opinion may have looked forward to the demise of Bolshevism, neither communist nor noncommunist sources testified to unusual restiveness among the Soviet peoples themselves. To the contrary, both in industry and agriculture "the workers are apparently convinced that they have a direct stake in winning the war, and have given lavishly of their skill, energy, and health."[27] The weight of official propaganda, the threat of the secret police, and the severe penalties provided by the Stalin Constitution operated to neutralize opposition, but the Communist Party itself, however it may have been viewed abroad as the emblem of repression, had nonetheless succeeded in arousing the enthusiasm of the Russian masses "to an astonishing degree":

> It has led the people of the Soviet Union through a desperate struggle to the threshold of complete success . . . Although it may be argued that the people are not fighting for the Communist Party but rather for their homes and families, the Party has been the leader of the fight . . . Stalin, the personification of the Communist Party, seemingly has never enjoyed greater esteem.[28]

Divisive national sentiments had been diverted against the common enemy; the Red Army, the only institution within Soviet society capable of mounting an organized resistance, would emerge from the war as the agent of victory, fully identified with the regime and loyal to it.[29]

The domestic popularity of Stalin and the identification of the Communist Party with the national interest were not, to be sure, prominent themes in the American perception of Russia. Indeed, viewed retrospectively against the seamless discourse of Cold War Sovietology, this was a radical claim and one from which the faculty of the USSR Division would themselves in many instances retreat. Subsequent ideological developments, however, whether in government or academia, do not alter the fact that in R&A the outlines of global polarization were clearly discerned, and the analysts of the USSR Division in particular took the lead in arguing against measures that could destabilize the postwar world. They did so, moreover, on the basis of a considerably more disciplined and exhaustive analysis of the dynamics of Soviet society than had ever been attempted in the United States.

A central theme of Soviet wartime propaganda was that only by virtue of socialist industrialization, the forced collectivization of agriculture, and the iron leadership of the Communist Party had the peoples of the Soviet Union been able to marshall their national resources in defense of their homeland, and the USSR Division neither accepted nor dissented from this claim. This is surely not to say that the logic of the social sciences enabled the scholars of R&A to view with perfect equanimity the brutal record of Stalinism or to accept *prima facie* the official statements of Soviet authorities. In the austere conception of G. T. Robinson, however, the scholarship of the Research and Analysis Branch must focus upon the empirical balance of power as it was actually taking shape, the options that followed from it, and the points of potential friction that could occur within it. This was no academic exercise, even if academics seemed to be the most qualified to perform it, but "one of the most difficult problems that history had ever presented," and one that Robinson faced with stoic disregard for personal or political preferences. What mattered was that "after the defeat of Germany, the two strongest world powers will be the United States and the Soviet Union, with Britain as a weaker third" and that "for a considerable period, the general course of history will be determined largely by the relations between the two major powers."[30] Nothing could be more vital to the security of the postwar world than a framework of compromise and cooperation among the Great Powers, and Germany was certain to be the arena in which it would be most severely tested.

On the eve of the long-awaited opening of the second front in Europe, Geroid Robinson himself took the lead in laying out the basis of the three-power coalition that he hoped would survive the coming occupation and develop into a permanent international organization for collective security: "The program," he cabled his three representatives in London, "is based on our conviction that everything possible should be done to avoid a clash of interests between the British and the Americans on the one hand, and the Russians on the other."[31] The most effective step that the United States could take in this direction would be to secure at the highest level a framework of political agreement in respect to zones of occupation, the problem of reparations, and the character of the German government to which the three occupying powers would eventually be willing to surrender the country. "It will not be easy to develop a working compromise between an expanding and dynamic power (the Soviet Union), a developing but essentially satisfied power (the United States), and a power that shows symptoms of decline (the British Empire)," Robinson warned, and the burden of compromise could be expected to fall most heavily upon the West; given a maximum wisdom and energy on the part of the Western Allies, however, "the chances seem to be somewhat on the side of compromise and cooperation."[32]

Against the view that dominated official thinking in the State Department—that it would be unwise to attempt to solve postwar problems while hostilities were continuing—R&A took the position that an accord reached well in advance of the defeat of Germany was the absolute precondition of any future system of general security and three-power cooperation. In a lengthy memorandum to the London Outpost, the Chief belabored the theme that had become his central preoccupation during the closing months of the war:

> It is obvious that, in order to make serious friction less likely, the Three Powers should negotiate detailed *advance* agreements among themselves for the conduct of MG in Germany; these agreements should go into effect behind the separate battlefronts just as soon as any German territory is occupied; otherwise, irreconcilable differences may develop even before Russian and Anglo-American forces meet on German territory.[33]

If the character of the occupation were determined *de facto* by the positions of the contending armies at the time of the armistice rather than according to mutually agreed principles, the likelihood of a complete breakdown of the alliance would be dangerously high. The work program of the Division in the last months of the war reflected the parlous state of U.S.–Soviet relations as they were taking shape. Even the Civil Affairs Handbook on the USSR, researched by Alex Inkeles, Vera Dunham, and Margaret Miller, was geared to the accommodation of American and Russian interests in Germany. Designed for the use of Military Government personnel, it was to be "largely political in content, with a touch of Emily Post and Dale Carnegie . . . Essentially it would be a guide on how to get along with the Russians, how to avoid committing certain *faux pas,* and what to expect of persons trained under the Soviet system."[34] Most projects, however, were aimed at higher levels of diplomatic contact.

The paramount interest of the Russians in preventing a westward orientation on the part of a new Germany, it was assumed, would deter them from policies that could lead to conflict with the Western occupying powers. Although denazification could be expected to be thoroughgoing in the Soviet zone, Russia's interest in reparations would discourage agrarian, industrial, or financial reforms that could disable the German economy. Moreover, the assymmetry in the economies of the projected Eastern and Western zones argued against measures disruptive of the pattern of interzonal commerce that would have to be established in the initial period of occupation. Insofar as international conditions permitted, the Kremlin leadership would place economic recovery ahead of immediate political objectives and would subordinate its revolutionary aspirations to military security and the strengthening of Russia's national position. "At the conclusion of hostilities in Russia," stated a major report prepared in anticipation of the Yalta Conference, "Russia will have neither the resources nor, as far as economic factors are concerned, the inclination to embark on adventurist foreign policies which, in the opinion of Soviet leaders, might involve the USSR in a conflict or a critical armaments race with the Western powers."[35] It was not necessary to presume the beneficence of Stalin in order to draw such a picture, but only to evaluate the imputed interests of the Soviet regime itself.

Three years of close collaboration—orchestrated by the firm, guiding hand of G. T. Robinson—had drawn the scholars of the USSR Division toward this broad consensus. They had been impelled by the exigencies of war and the nature of their subject matter into an unprecedented degree of integration and coordination that was nowhere more pronounced than in the final stage of their research program. Late in the war the Research and Analysis Branch was commissioned by Assistant Secretary of State Dean Acheson and Donald Nelson of the War Production Board to chart the probable course of Russian economic reconstruction and to envisage the role of the United States in that process. This assignment—the one major study to which every section contributed—marks what is, from an intellectual point of view, the crowning achievement of the USSR Division. The interdisciplinary team was by this time functioning smoothly and, under the direction of the economists Wassily Leontief and Abram Bergson, produced a work of synthetic scholarship that is remarkable as much for what it attempts as for what it achieved.[36]

The starting point of their analysis was that Russia would have lost by the end of the war a staggering 25 percent of its productive capacity, distributed fairly evenly across all sectors of the economy, which the Soviet government would be under enormous pressure to restore at least to prewar levels.[37] The reconstruction of the socialist economy would presumably follow the same sequence of five-year plans by which it was originally built up; and, as in the 1930s, the balance between the competing choices of long-term capital reinvestment, military expenditure, and current consumption would be determined partly by internal conditions and partly by the international situation as it was perceived in Moscow. The Soviet strategy for reconstruction would reflect but would also to a considerable extent determine the character of the post-war era.

Using essentially the same procedures as those employed by Soviet planning authorities, the analysts of R&A took it upon themselves to determine the rate at which economic reconstruction could proceed. First the effective productive capacity was established for the leading sectors of the socialized economy for the years 1928–1940, using official Soviet statistics where they were available, interpolating across gaps in the data, and correcting them for fluctuations in the value of the ruble and variations in accounting techniques. These figures yielded a statistical picture of the pattern of Soviet prewar economic development up to the point of the German invasion. They next attempted to compute the magnitude of devastation which they reckoned had flung the Russian capital position back to the levels of 1937–38.

The field of national income estimates was one that the senior OSS economists dominated during the war and after—Leontief in the general terms of the input–output model and Bergson with special reference to the Soviet economy in particular. Using the Cobb–Douglas function, which expresses the stable relationship that exists between the magnitude of output and the amounts of labor and fixed capital applied in the process of production, the Kuznets index of industrial production, and other formal analytical tools of economic forecasting, they demonstrated that if the Soviet Union were able to take advantage of foreign credits, the period of capital reconstruction would be approximately three years from the end of hostilities. As striking as this estimate appeared to be, the really startling disclosure was that virtually the same rate of reconstruction could be achieved *without* the aid of foreign loans or reparations, entirely on the basis of domestic resources. Patterns of investment and allocation might differ, improvements in the standard of living deferred, and state controls tightened, but the difference in the rate of overall economic recovery would be at best a matter of months: with or without foreign assistance, "the 1940 national income is reattained by 1948 . . . A level of income corresponding to that projected for 1942 under the Third Five Year Plan, which was interrupted by the war, is reattained in 1950–51."[38]

Had they received due attention, the OSS calculations would have given pause both to liberal and to conservative policy makers in Washington who saw American trade credits as the ultimate weapon of foreign policy in the postwar world. It had been widely assumed that the Soviet economy had been so damaged by the war that Moscow would be long unable to pursue an aggressively independent foreign policy—"for generations," Walter Lippmann had predicted. The meticulous analysis carried out in the USSR Division, however, indicated that as an economic bargaining point the promise of American loans might carry some weight, but in the political sphere it could be wielded neither as a carrot nor a stick. Bergson and Division Chief Robinson brought their findings to the attention of the highest State Department officials to whom they were given access, but they were received with apparent indifference.

Their projection of the factors affecting Russian postwar reconstruction, with and without the benefit of foreign trade credits, had envisaged a favorable international political situation—"uncertain, but not tense"—in which Soviet military expenditures were reduced to their 1938 levels and demobilization returned a considerable labor force to industry and agriculture. An alternative scenario was noted in their report, which envisaged continuing tension in the international arena following the defeat of Germany and a consequently high level of military preparedness. Whether out of optimism or naiveté, this "marginal" possibility, which would in fact be frozen into place during the next two years, was dismissed virtually without analysis. The scholars of the USSR Division, on the basis of their intensive wartime drill, had developed the uncanny ability to think their way into the Kremlin: using Soviet data, statistical techniques, and ideological suppositions, they had undertaken nothing less than the speculative reconstruction of the Russian national economy from a distance of thousands of miles under the most challenging of conditions. They were less successful, it would seem, in penetrating the policy process in Washington, D.C., for even as the footnotes to R&A 2060 were being typed, decisions were being made that would unravel the intricate web of deductions on which they based their calculations and their hopes.[39]

The historiography of the Cold War is preoccupied with identification of "turning points" and "missed opportunities" and has tended to push the origins of the conflict further and further backward in time. From the standpoint of the present, it is surely possible to see the foundations of the great power stalemate being laid during the war, but we can also see, from the written record, at least, that it was a process to which the Research and Analysis Branch contributed respectably little. The Soviet Union must henceforth be treated as an equal, they had argued; the age of imperial dominance was over.

The Dictatorship of the Professoriate

More than one young scholar found the party line dictated by Geroid T. Robinson to be stifling. The lapsed classicist Barrington Moore, Jr., migrated from the regimented "Spartan" atmosphere of the USSR Division to continue his study of Russian occupation policies under the "Athenian" skies of the Central European Section. The economist Irving Rudd, frustrated by a hierarchy that placed fixed limits upon his influence, left R&A to take up a position in the War Production Board. Yet another researcher decided that he could serve the war effort more nobly as an ambulance driver. "Dr. Robinson rode herd," recalled one of his section chiefs. Purges were not infrequent and some of the personnel broke under the strain, "but in general, in spite of grumbling, the staff accepted the Robinsonian control and took pride in the excellent reputation that the organization enjoyed throughout the government."[40] Orthodoxy prevailed within the USSR Division, and only rarely did a political dissident such as Paul Baran have the temerity to dismiss the Chief's visions of a Soviet–American rapprochement as "ludicrous."

Robinson, it will be recalled, had based his campaign for Russian–American accord on the apparent divergence between the ideology of world revolution and Moscow's practical objective of national security. For Baran, however, "there is no contradiction between these concepts"; indeed, a revolutionary crisis in Germany would resolve both of them simultaneously: "All developments after the war which will strengthen Russia's political influence will have revolutionary implications for other countries, and all revolutionary events in other countries are bound to boost Russia's international position."[41] To conclude otherwise was to betray "a complete lack of understanding of the basic principle underlying the complicated interwoven political philosophy of the international communist movement."

In the context of the war, the scholars of the USSR Division tended to overcompensate in order to avoid the appearance of partisanship, and Baran himself normally refrained from public criticism of the Soviet Union for fear of aligning himself with critics of socialism per se.[42] As an independent Marxist, however, who had left the Plekhanov Institute of Economics in 1928 to escape the straitjacket of Stalinist orthodoxy, Baran evidently felt secure enough in his intellectual position to give voice to his misgivings, and he did so with alacrity. What Robinson had viewed as conciliatory overtures from Moscow were merely "shades and colors of the Leninist rainbow." The policy of the Kremlin, he countered, would be determined pragmatically by the balance of the opposing forces within the liberated areas; and until this configuration crystallized, any agreement concluded in advance would be "a scrap of paper." Having endured decades of isolation in order to build a socialist economy and having withstood the devastation of war to maintain it, the Soviet leadership would not at this critical juncture abandon its historic mistrust of the capitalist West. It may well have been precisely by virtue of his forthright partisanship that the Marxist Baran was able to maintain his political equanimity as the Grand Alliance broke apart and the United States and USSR hardened their positions and became locked in struggle over the future of Europe. His colleagues in the USSR Division, however, had for the most part shielded themselves from ideological controversy under the mantle of social science objectivity, which now afforded scant protection against the frigid blasts of the Cold War.

The individualistic scholars of the USSR Division had, by the end of the war, been transformed into a smoothly functioning interdisciplinary team whose methods were uniquely suited to the "interlocked and integrated" character of Soviet society. More than any other unit in R&A, this scholarly contingent recognized that "any attempt to distinguish the economic from the political, and to deal separately with one or the other, is at best unrealistic and at worst can lead to very serious misconceptions."[43] Using the tools of social science research, and compelled by wartime considerations to project a scrupulous objectivity, they pooled their disciplinary resources and approached the Soviet Union, *sine ira et studio,* as an integrated totality. On the other side of the war, however, the conception of a social totality that had served the alliance evolved easily into the adversarial model of monolithic totalitarianism, and congealed into an orthodoxy that dominated American research on Russia for two decades afterwards. Once scholarship had been pressed into service, it was not so easily discharged.

The lines that connect the discourse of postwar Sovietology to the Research and Analysis Branch are direct and tangible. During the war two members of the Carnegie Foundation had called upon Research and Analysis Chief William Langer in Washington: "My visitors were impressed by the R. and A. approach to the analysis of complicated situations," he noted, "and, in the course of lengthy discussions, raised the question of whether some similar system might not be introduced in our universities."[44] At about the same time, USSR Chief Geroid Robinson was using the respite offered by the Russian victories of fall 1943 to predict, in a letter to the Provost of Columbia University, a postwar expansion in Russian studies that would correspond to the change that he saw taking place in the distribution of world power. A few weeks later he sketched a program of training for the new generation of scholars, diplomats, and journalists who would be professionally concerned with the emergent Soviet superpower. By the end of 1945, before the ink was dry on the Presidential Order that disbanded the Office of Strategic Services, plans were secure to relocate the USSR Division in Morningside Heights, where it became the first of the nation's "area institutes" of graduate study. The Russian Institute at Columbia University opened its doors on September 25, 1946, with G. T. Robinson presiding.[45]

Motivated partly by the fear that Columbia would be branded as "red" if it too exclusively dominated the field of Russian studies in the United States, Robinson was anxious to stimulate at least one other university to participate in the area-studies venture. Harvard appeared to be the obvious choice. The largesse of the great foundations—Carnegie, Ford, Rockefeller—continued, and within another year a cadre of R&A graduates had launched Harvard University's new Russian Research Center. The sociologists Alex Inkeles and Barrington Moore, Jr., the economists Wassily Leontief, Walter Galenson, and Louis Boochever, not to mention future directors Donald McKay and William Langer, were among the first generation of R&A veterans to transfer the research enterprise begun in the USSR Division to Cambridge.[46]

The continuity of personnel indicates clearly enough the wartime roots of these two centers, but more important is the continuity of the epistemological premises on which they were founded. The guerilla warfare that had raged between regionalists and functionalists throughout the rest of the Research and Analysis Branch had been resolved in the USSR Division, and precisely this model was incorporated into the new area-studies institutes. While still insisting that its faculty and students be grounded in a traditional field of expertise, both sought to promote the principle of integrated, multidisciplinary coverage of one country. It is not too much to say that between them, Columbia's Russian Institute and the Russian Research Center at Harvard trained the first generation of professional Sovietologists.[47]

The response from Moscow to these new developments in American higher education suggests that Robinson was once again too successful in avoiding the appearance of communist sympathies in his organization. *Pravda* assailed the Russian Institute as a "hotbed of American slanderers, spies, and diversionaries," where "ignorant 'professors' deliver lectures in a course of deliberate drivel to young listeners selected on the basis of the greatest mental defectiveness and the least moral decency"; at its head stood "arch reactionaries . . . who are systematically poisoning students' minds with slander about the Soviet Union."[48] This propaganda blast bears little relation to the scholarly ambitions and achievements of these institutions. The offspring of the USSR Division by no means escaped the general tendencies of American intellectual life during the worst years of the Cold War, but they merit a more temperate examination.

The economic, statistical, and demographic research that grew out of the Research and Analysis Branch has proven notably resistant to the charges of political tendentiousness that have been leveled against American research on Russia in general. The interindustry input–output theory created by Wassily Leontief, an R&A alumnus and an Executive Director of Harvard's Russian Research Center, is an obvious case in point. Since its underlying conception is the linear relation of quantities of inputs to quantities of output to be produced, the analysis deals almost exclusively with production, and demand theory plays little or no role. Unlike conventional neoclassical theory, then, which presupposes a market economy, the Leontief Matrix is applied indifferently to the analysis of economic systems ranging from laissez-faire capitalism to the centrally planned economies of the socialist states.[49] The same can be said for the "theory-normed valuative method" which Leontief's erstwhile colleague Abram Bergson developed during his own tenure as Acting Chief of the USSR Economic Subdivision as a reliable means of interpreting Soviet national income statistics: while his work has offered little comfort to defenders of Soviet economic performance, it has never been impugned, so far as I am aware, on grounds of its political objectivity. "We must compare ideals with ideals and facts with facts," Bergson advised early on. "Participants in both sides of the debate have erred in failing to observe this elementary rule."[50]

It would be difficult to argue that the more interpretive social sciences—history, political science, sociology—have fared so well. At the outset of his career, one recent graduate of R&A acknowledged that "both his methods of research and the nature of his subject matter constantly bring the social scientist to the very edge of evaluation," and in studies of the Soviet Union the line was frequently transgressed.[51] This was perhaps inevitable as Stalin advanced on Eastern Europe and Americans fortified themselves behind impregnable ideological defenses, and the methodology of the social sciences was recalled to active duty. A senior fellow of Columbia's Russian Institute, reviewing a decade of postwar sociology, caught the ambiguity in his perplexing remark that while "the great bulk of these studies are remarkably free from ideological bias . . . the authors cannot help being ideologically engaged."[52]

Within the academic community the primary vehicle of this ideological engagement was the concept of totalitarianism—a term used on no more than a few occasions in the vast body of R&A reporting on the Soviet Union, and then in a wholly untheorized, almost casual manner. It would not be unreasonable to speculate that as an interpretive framework, Robinson found the concept to be too patently adversarial to be admissible in wartime intelligence work. In the aftermath of the war, however, the totalitarian model achieved theoretical elaboration in the works of Arendt, Friedrich and Brzezinski, and others. Stipulating a monolithic power structure that penetrates every level of social and political existence and that has been unfolding inexorably since 1917 according to an "inner totalitarian logic," it became a staple of the emerging anticommunist consensus in American political life and a virtual orthodoxy in the world of academic scholarship. "Never before has the unity of Soviet society been so monolithic," Georgii Malenkov told the Soviet Council of Ministers in 1953, and American scholars who normally scoffed at the claims of Soviet propagandists accepted this improbable metaphysic almost without demur.[53]

Although we have located the roots of academic Sovietology in the Research and Analysis Branch, it would be erroneous to assign to the veterans of the USSR Division responsibility for the directions it took in the postwar era. For one thing, they did not as a group prove to be nearly so prolific in civilian life as they had been in OSS. G. T. Robinson, though influential in the postwar decade as a teacher, an administrator, and an unrepentant Cold Warrior, became a victim of his own high standards and was never able to bring to completioin the proposed second volume of his study of rural Russia.[54] Others produced articles and monographs, some of singular value, but these authors cannot be said to have redirected the course of academic thinking in their respective disciplines; some shell-shocked veterans dropped out of sight entirely.[55]

The careers of two sociologists, however, were fundamentally recast by their wartime service in the USSR Division, and their influence both upon sociological theory and Sovietological practice has been widespread. Barrington Moore, Jr., and Alex Inkeles have both worked productively at the perimeter of mainstream Sovietology; and in a field where methodology has easily become ideology, they have done so with unusual self-reflexivity. Although one of the principal architects of the totalitarian model, Inkeles himself was the first to note the chilling effect of its hegemony over academic scholarship: "The standard dialogue has gone on for decades," he observed some twenty years after his matriculation from the Research and Analysis Branch. "I suggest we get some new themes, new ideas, new models into the discussion."[56]

It was perhaps inevitable that two sociologists should have resisted full integration into the totalitarian orthodoxy, for a model that fixated upon the regime of a party-state that imposed its will upon an inert social mass could have little use for social history or sociological theory. Inkeles' challenge could not be accepted, however, until a new generation of participants, trained in a changing ideological climate, entered the profession. Less encumbered by the orthodoxies of "consensus Sovietology," growing numbers of younger researchers have indeed begun to produce a body of scholarship on Soviet history, politics, culture, and society that has seriously eroded the totalitarian model and its effective monopoly over their respective fields.

While the early scholarship of Moore and Inkeles was frequently compromised by the discursive maneuvers of Cold War Sovietology—the invidious comparisons with selected features of the Western democracies, the substantive neglect of the global context of Soviet policy, the partisan use of punctuation ("capitalist aggression," "Western imperialism") which Foucault denounced as "the polities of inverted commas"—Moore and Inkeles have been the primary transmitters, sometimes in spite of themselves, of the legacy of the USSR Division. First, they prepared the ground for a broadening of the field by insisting upon the addition of an authentic, if eviscerated, social dimension to the narrow regime studies that have monopolized the discussion. Second, each brought with him from the USSR Division a national focus that constituted one of the earliest challenges to the institutional and process-oriented approach that had dominated American sociology up to the beginning of the war and that enabled him to perceive the USSR in systemic terms. The Soviets ceased to be the fully aberrant legatees of Bolshevist ideology, in this view, but appeared "to take over and modify for their own purposes certain beliefs and behavior patterns that had already become familiar features of industrial society elsewhere."[57] Finally, they acquired during the wartime mobilization a profound suspicion of the canons of social science objectivity that would operate in the era of crusading Sovietology as the most pernicious dogma of them all.

As literally the first American scholars to apply the theories and methods of sociological analysis to Soviet society, Barrington Moore and Alex Inkeles had ventured into an intellectual *terra incognita* which they explored with a greater openness to exception and anomaly than is easily accommodated by the totalitarian model. Significantly—and perhaps to their own chagrin!—the leading revisionist critic of the totalitarian orthodoxy has ranked them among the "few American Sovietologists [who] did stand quietly apart from the professional orthodoxy and even groped to escape it."[58]

· · ·

"This is no place for a general dissertation on Soviet society and the Soviet state," to retreat behind G. T. Robinson's standard disclaimer when a report was due before it could be brought up to his standards.[59] It seems a fitting note on which to conclude this analysis of the legacy of the USSR Division, where the apparatus of academic scholarship was displayed more proudly than anywhere else in R&A.

· SIX ·

The Critique of Modernity

*Not all great contemporary history need sound this note
of elegy. Nor does it have to have been written by someone
who has had a direct contact with large events. I think
of these merely as a kind of optimum stance toward the
material.*

H. Stuart Hughes (1964)

*The one identifiable cohesive group among the American
historians of Europe today is composed of those who applied their training to and nurtured it with the problems
raised for the United States government by the war.*

Leonard Krieger (1965)

*We too live in the stream of history, a condition that can
both enhance and impede the understanding of the past.*

Carl E. Schorske (1987)

The scholarly impulse to record history may be grounded in the urge to
intersect actively with it. Thucydides began to chronicle the Peloponne-
sian War immediately after being relieved of his command; Machiavelli
admitted that his histories helped relieve the anxiety of his dismissal
from political office; Tocqueville's historical masterwork appeared in
1856, after he too had suffered a forced retirement from public life.
Historians, like Minerva's owl, come forward only with the falling of the
dusk.

The end of the war visited upon the younger historians of OSS the
same anticlimactic withdrawal described by their classical forebears. As
anxious as they were to launch the professional careers for which they
had been trained (in many cases by the senior scholars who had recruited
them to the Research and Analysis Branch), the very events that had
delayed them now exercised a lingering claim. They would return to the
university to complete their studies or take up their first teaching positions, but the trauma of total war disrupted the continuity. The older
generation of historical thinkers—William Langer, Crane Brinton, Hajo

Holborn—had come to the OSS as mature scholars with their intellectual positions well-defined and attuned to the coherences that unify long stretches of history. Their successors, however, received there a post-graduate education that would prove profoundly disruptive but also sensitized them to disruption, disjunction, and discontinuity as the essence of the historical process. For them, the unity of history was not a secret to be discovered but a task to be achieved.

Two broadly defined vectors can be traced back to this insight. One position, represented by the campaign of Arthur Schlesinger, Jr., to preserve the "vital center" in an age of anxiety or by the masterful synthesizing narratives of Gordon Craig, saw the war as the narrow victory of Western civilization over the disintegrative forces of fascism and communism, and it affirmed with renewed commitment the liberal inheritance of reason, moderation, and the primacy of the individual. Other members of the class of '45, however, derived from their wartime *Habilitation* an insight into the cultural politics that threatened to tear the liberal order asunder from within. The dissonant voices of Nietzsche, Weber, Spengler, and Freud that were transmitted to them through their European colleagues further undermined their confidence in the orthodoxies of liberal thought. This was the legacy shared out among a generation of intellectual historians—Carl Schorske, H. Stuart Hughes, Leonard Krieger, Norman O. Brown, and others—whose research would drive them into the intellectual underworld of modernity and to disturbing reflections on the nature of history as such. The prominence of the so-called "irrationalists" in the postwar careers of these younger scholars foreshadows the final unraveling of the rationalist claims of the Enlightenment that has dominated intellectual discourse in our own time.

Gone from the work of these historians would be the Rankean credo of objectivity in which they had been trained and to which they had submitted during the war. It was not just that the discourse of pure reason was unattainable—for that seems to have been dimly suspected even by their elders—but that it was no longer even a *desideratum.* History, as they had witnessed it, experienced it, and to some degree helped to shape it, was not *der Gang Gottes in der Welt* but a brutal chronicle of caprice and irrationality in which they themselves were implicated. How could one gaze with equanimity upon such a spectacle? How could the historian *not* attempt to impose order on the chaotic past? These late modernists would find, however, that, once opened, this was not a door that could easily be closed.

The Decline of the West

"The boys of the thirties," as Stuart Hughes addressed the rising stars circling in the Oedipal constellation of higher education,[1] were drawn into the orbit of American intelligence through parallel routes. The ruling patriciate of R&A tapped the time-honored network of academic acquaintanceship for the names of promising graduate students "who have a reading knowledge of French and German or at least one of these [and] who have been trained by the European and not the American historians of your noble faculty."[2] The recruitment files of the Branch, like those of any elite graduate school, soon bulged with correspondence from prospective candidates throughout the restrictive sphere of the eastern academic mandarinate: Raymond Sontag nominated Gordon Craig from Yale, Donald McKay recruited David Pinkney from Harvard, and from the hinterland Harold Deutsch negotiated for the appointment of Franklin Ford from the University of Minnesota. The fate of the West seemed literally to hang in the balance, and progressives of the generation just coming of age heard in the rumors circulating about the new secret agency the promise of an entree into the antifascist struggle on terms they could accept politically and to which they might contribute intellectually. Once the new recruits had advanced to candidacy, however, a number of obstacles characteristically remained.

First to be allayed were the lingering political misgivings harbored by many of the young candidates themselves, schooled in the anti-interventionist polemics of the thirties and deeply suspicious of the imperial ambitions of the Western powers. Representative of this minority view was Carl Schorske, who had been preparing a thesis on the intellectual origins of Nazism under William Langer at Harvard even as he rose against his *Doktorvater* from the standpoint of a militantly anti-imperialist isolationism. The Munich Pact had represented to him the collusion of the capitalist powers, democratic and totalitarian, against a common socialist enemy, and the prospect of another war "unleashing those national hatreds that had formed such an unpleasant part of my political socialization" was too horrendous even to contemplate.[3] By the summer of 1941, however, Schorske was ready to concede that the values of social democratic radicalism and international pacifism that had been the mutually reinforcing staples of the thirties had become mutually exclusive in the forties. From Cambridge he wrote to his mentor and was readily taken on as Langer's assistant and all-round "pinch-hitter" in the fledgling Research and Analysis Branch, which then numbered barely twenty people. Schorske flourished in his new field of applied European history, and when four years later he matriculated from the Branch—*cum laude,* as it were—he was cited for a record of "outstanding leadership in directing the political intelligence work of the Europe–Africa Division."[4]

Henry Stuart Hughes, another ambitious member of the Harvard *Brüderbund,* was likewise struggling to redefine the role of the progressive intelligentsia under the weight of events. The outbreak of the war had driven him from his doctoral researches in the Bibliothèque Nationale, but he had been able to complete his thesis on "The Crisis of the French Imperial Economy" and was awaiting a commission in the Field Artillery when "the German attack on the Soviet Union ended all talk of neutrality in a struggle between two imperialisms."[5] Hughes was summoned by Donald McKay who, as a member of the R&A Board of Analysts, was vigorously recalling his former graduate students to active duty. He was transferred to Washington shortly before the new year and enrolled for a tour of duty in the Branch that would begin in Washington and lead him to distinguished service in North Africa, France, Italy, and occupied Germany before returning him to a desk in the postwar Department of State. Scion of one of the most distinguished legal families in the United States, Hughes' academic apostasy had left him especially vulnerable to the new currents of political discourse he would encounter in the Branch. To a greater extent, perhaps, than any of his peers, his wartime experience served to recast and redirect his subsequent intellectual career.

Other young scholars, however, no less imbued with the ethic of the engaged intellectual, found their paths into OSS cluttered with administrative obstacles. Leonard Krieger, whom Hajo Holborn had praised as one of the three best graduate students he had ever had, was completing a master's thesis at Yale on German liberalism in the age of unification and had been recommended for a position in R&A when he was unexpectedly drafted into the army. Languishing for thirteen months as a corporal in the Seventh Armored Division at Camp Polk, Louisiana, he found little opportunity to apply his extraordinary knowledge of German intellectual history and became a sort of test case for what Langer, in an assertive memorandum to General Donovan, described as "a large piece of business to settle with the armed forces."[6] War Secretary Stimson was leery of releasing able-bodied young men to do "civilian" work, and the lack of clout at the disposal of the infant intelligence service was a recurrent theme in its attempt to build a corps of analysts. Only after prolonged negotiations was Krieger reassigned to OSS, where his specialized academic skills found a natural outlet.[7]

Gradually, after frustrating delays brought on by security checks, uncertain budgets, and what Stuart Hughes called "suitable struggles of conscience" on the part of the young recruits themselves, the junior faculty thus began to assemble within America's first professional intelligence service. To be sure, assignment to a desk in Washington, London, or Algiers was an attractive alternative to unemployment or the perils of the front, but even for those who were ineligible for combat, R&A seemed to offer the young antifascist intellectual a respectable place in the ranks of the Grand Alliance: "It is an experience I personally would not have missed," noted Sherman Kent at the bottom of one of his regular appeals, "and that I think any young man would be only too glad to have."[8] The intellectual firepower amassed by this extraordinary academic batallion proved less decisive in the war than its accumulated curricula vita portended, but the honest sentiment he expressed was unquestionably the most powerful incentive the OSS had to offer.

The Transvaluation of Values

The generation of younger historians for whom R&A served as a professional initiation worked in a great variety of capacities, and the asymmetry of their wartime experiences resists easy generalization. But just as the careers of Leonard Krieger, Carl Schorske, and Stuart Hughes would virtually delimit the field of European intellectual history for the postwar era, so the range of their experiences as younger scholars in the Research and Analysis Branch illuminates the intellectual history of American intelligence from a particularly revealing angle. As a group they produced less of the finished political intelligence that is the basic archival legacy of the Branch than did the elder statesmen, American and European, to whom they were apprenticed. But the record is sufficient to illuminate a stage in what Schorske later called "the self-overcoming that is in the last analysis the true life of all scholarship."[9]

The three acolytes were initiated into the mysteries of intelligence work in Washington, but their careers soon diverged. With the collapse of the Wehrmacht, however, they converged on Germany, like the invading armies, from three directions. Their ambitions had been held in check throughout the war by the totems and taboos of scholarly authority embodied in the patriarchs to whom they were apprenticed, but manifestations of resistance could be detected as the work of intelligence unfolded. With the close of hostilities they erupted in a liberating act of collective intellectual patricide to which they themselves would ultimately fall victim.

·   ·   ·

The ambition of most of the researchers—of both generations—was to get into the European Theater and as close to the action as possible, and the three intellectual historians achieved this to varying degrees. Carl Schorske, Langer's right-hand man and general factotum of the Branch, remained throughout the war at his multiple posts in Washington, champing at the bit as he was pulled at the last moment from missions to London, Italy, and Moscow on account of the indispensible services he performed at headquarters: "Ever since I have been in R&A," the Chief of the London Outpost pointed out as plans for the OSS penetration of Germany began to take shape, "Carl has been concerned with matters of an administrative or semiadministrative character. He is not the only R&A analyst whose dual talents have forced him into this position, but he is the one whose inability to devote himself wholly to research and analysis has cost R&A [most] dearly in terms of output."[10] Schorske's "dual talents" for substantive and administrative work had in fact run afoul of one another in the paradox that Max Weber had identified as the fate of the West, and it was thus most appropriate for Chandler Morse to have concluded "that he deserves a better fate."

Eventually, with the collapse of German resistance, the young historian was relieved of his administrative command and sent overseas, where he spent the fall of 1945 gathering first-hand intelligence in occupied Germany. But it was really in the trenches of R&A/Washington that Schorske acquired his second graduate education. For four years he struggled there against the centrifugal forces that threatened at any given moment to reduce the Research and Analysis Branch to the condition of an unruly faculty meeting. The organization had been welded together by the wartime emergency out of disparate academic entities— humanists and social scientists, regionalists and functionalists, thesis advisors and graduate students—and it often fell to Schorske, as the ubiquitous representative of the Chief, to prevent these delicately balanced oppositions from exploding in a blaze of epistemological enmity.

Characteristically, this entailed servicing the whims of the Board of Analysts as its permanent secretary, acting as referee between the rival editorial factions, objectivist and relativist, on the Projects Committee, and translating the mutually incomprehensible idioms spoken by the economists and historians involved in the Civil Affairs program. He was regularly entrusted by Langer with heroic assignments such as reviving the Current Inteligence Staff—"the one unit that brings the entire OSS together"—where he remained only long enough to reorganize its personnel and help launch the *Political Intelligence Weekly,* which became one of OSS's most respected publications, before Langer insisted upon his return.

Schorske's aptitude for tasks of intellectual mediation reflected his education in a climate that had problematized the role of the social science intellectual and caught a generation of scholars between exactly the set of competing paradigms that comprised the rival factions of R&A. This creative tension was exemplified by his relations to Branch Chief William Langer, whom he never ceased to regard as his "advisor and mentor" despite the acute political differences between them. Politically conservative, imbued with the belief in the rationality of human judgments that lies at the heart of diplomatic history, and, as a teacher, steeped in "the prevailing nineteenth century idea of history, with its strong architecture of development and narrative structure," Langer embodied all the professional traits against which Schorske and his generation would later revolt.[11] At the same time, he recognized that the Director's authority, grounded in his uncompromising standards of scholarship and his grasp of European affairs, was even less subject to challenge in wartime Washington than it had been in the Harvard seminar room. In a relationship fraught with suppressed political ambivalence, such conflicts as did erupt provide deep insights into the intellectual dynamics of R&A and of the historical phenomenon it represents.

In January 1944 Langer delegated Harold Deutsch to conduct a fact-finding mission to London, and Schorske undertook to draft for his senior colleague a background memorandum on the growing estrangement between Washington and the London Outpost. Referring bluntly to "the inadequacy of the London leadership" and "the curse of a chaotic history," Schorske outlined a program for "bringing order, organization, and purpose into the work of the boys at Brook Street."[12]

This in-house memorandum acquired a lingering notoriety on both sides of the Atlantic when it drifted—"by devious but inevitable ways"—

into the hands of Crane Brinton, who cabled a vigorous "Apologia pro Vita Sua" in defense of his tenure as interim chief of R&A/London: "No one from Carl Schorske's position could possibly be aware of the difficulties and delicacies of our work here," he appealed directly to Langer, and continued in terms calculated to strike a sympathetic chord in his old Harvard colleague: "We cannot go to British agencies and notably to the 57 varieties of M[ilitary] I[ntelligence] with the freedom of historical scholars consulting public archives. There are a thousand strands of protocol which criss-cross in a bewildering way."[13] Given "the stickiness of the British agencies [and] the relatively *parvenu* character of our own agency in the intelligence field," Brinton cautioned, "we must not aim too high. We must continue to be in large part a sort of information bureau—an exalted information bureau, maybe, but still an information bureau."

These modest aspirations, as Schorske perceived, ran counter to the essential reality of the modern state bureaucracy, the condition of whose existence is its expansion relative to adjacent agencies—a bit of neo-Weberian sociology that R&A was to learn through painful experience. In Washington, Langer thus found himself caught between the institutional pragmatism of his prize graduate student and the laissez-faire administration of a distinguished colleague of some twenty years' standing, and was forced into one of those saturnalian decisions that were systematically unraveling the strands of authority that had governed the ordered universe of the academy. "No one could have a higher regard for him than we have," he concluded of the genial Brinton, "but we are all of the same opinion that he is not the man to act as administrative head of an organization." Langer reassured his old friend that "we have not yet reached the stage of backstairs procedures," but by the end of the month Brinton had been recalled and the pragmatic Chandler Morse—"a man of vision who is constantly seeing the problems which are likely to arise and laying plans to meet them"—was reassigned to London to weld together the political and economic sections into a single fighting unit.[14]

There can be no doubt that the principal overseas outpost of R&A required a seasoned administrator who could negotiate "the labyrinthine intelligence brothel of London" and that Brinton—who once described himself as "a moralist in the old and inoffensive sense"—lacked the administrative ruthlessness to do so.[15] More profoundly, however, the episode has the character of an early challenge to the authority of the academic patriarchy that governed the Branch. Anatomist of revolutions and historian of political thought, Crane Brinton was a respected spokesman for a movement in American intellectual historiography that aspired to a critical synthesis of internal-textual and external-biographical elements (the "method of men," as it became known). As a university scholar, Brinton demonstrated a capacity for discerning critical judgment that guided his selection of historical data, and it enabled him, as an intelligence officer, to write perceptive first-hand accounts of the competing currents of French politics that surfaced in the wake of the Allied advance.[16] A paradigm shift was quietly at work, however, that would render increasingly problematical the resistance to social history, social theory, and social science characteristic of this generation. Schorske, to be sure, had not criticized the interim chief of R&A/London on grounds of methodology or epistemology but rather because Brinton was a rotten administrator under whose guidance the London Outpost was dissipating its resources, losing ground to other intelligence agencies, and not making the contribution to the war effort of which it was capable. Still, the failure of the elder historian to achieve the "transvaluation of values" he had mocked in his last work of civilian scholarship (*Nietzsche,* 1941) symbolized the self-overcoming of the historical profession that had been under way since before the outbreak of the war.[17]

Schorske's generation, however, with its historical values still unformed, was not only challenged to adapt its academic thinking to the exigencies of war but was exposed at a critical point in its development to an intellectual spectrum that outshone that of any university. Positioned amid an extraordinary range of scholarly fields and methods, Schorske did not himself acquire a specific regional focus during his years in R&A but remained the omnicompetent one-man reserve army of the Branch. Late in the summer of 1944, when Harold Deutsch was transferred to Paris to set up an R&A outpost in the liberated capital, Schorske moved into his vacant position to serve as Acting Chief of the Europe-Africa Political Subdivision, in which capacity he coordinated the work of some 140 western and central European analysts of all disciplinary persuasions. The events of those months directed his attention especially toward France, where the explosion of repressed political energy had raised a myriad of questions of potentially great historical significance. Would the Catholic right, dormant in national politics since the Dreyfuss Affair, reemerge to play an influential role in French political life? Would De Gaulle—"the *defensor fidei* of capitalistic and nationalistic France"—

strike the same opportunistic pose in the aftermath of the Second World War that Clemenceau had assumed during the first? "My own rather romantic notion," mused the young historian, "is that France is again at one of her periodic crossroads and that what happens in the next couple of months will more or less determine her post-war social and political structure."[18] He readily admitted, however, that relative to the fast-breaking events his colleagues were able to observe first hand in Paris, "my thinking has been too much determined by historical considerations."

The survival of his historical perspective remained palpable in those months, evidenced in the historical models, methods, and metaphors with which he commented upon the political intelligence flowing or trickling into Washington. He demanded the same of the authors under his command, if only to allay "the feeling of intellectual discomfort" that disquieted him when he encountered "imprecise generalities," "historical clichés," or evidence of merely "literary" as opposed to "substantive editorship." Supervisory tasks of this sort consumed the bulk of his time in the final year of the war, but methodology passed easily into ideology in OSS and required continual scrutiny. The American-trained elders of the Branch, bound to "the reportorial tradition" of bygone days, failed to produce "a dynamic as opposed to quiescent or indifferent interpretation" of European affairs, whereas the German analysts, "brilliant but incoherent, Teutonic, and maladministered," frustrated him with their principled refusal to make concessions to their readers or to produce reports according to any criterion but "the validity of the ideas in them."[19] Caught between the American Scylla of unself-conscious narrative reportage and the European Charybdis of philosophical hyper-reflexivity, Schorske typified the generation of scholars that was acquiring during its postgraduate ordeal a sense of the elusiveness of the historical object.

With the invasion of Germany by the Allied armies and its occupation by, among others, the Office of Strategic Services, Schorske's attention narrowed increasingly to the scene of the crime, but the historian's priorities remained pronounced in his work. In March 1945 he raised with General John Magruder, Donovan's Deputy Director for Intelligence, the problem of the Bavarian Redoubt that OSS intelligence indicated the Nazis to have been planning and dwelt not upon tactics for subduing it but upon the sorts of occupation policies that could unwittingly win for it the support of traditionally irredentist movements on the German right.[20] As the occupation formally began and the threat of continued resistance faded, Schorske helped with the coordination of War Crimes work in which the Research and Analysis Branch had been enlisted. Here again, his stated objectives went beyond the legalistic documentation of the crimes of individuals to the formulation of a coherent picture of an epoch in German history: "The intention in this procedure is to make the trials an indictment of the entire Nazi system as such. It is therefore necessary, in dealing with all the specific malfeasances of the Nazi regime, to link them all together to give a rounded picture of the Nazi system, to indict it as a whole through indicting it in as many as possible of its particular aspects."[21] Neither the politics of punishment nor the jurisprudential devices that the R&A research program served appear prominently among the problems discussed in his papers of this period; rather it was the concern—an abiding, positive legacy of his apprenticeship under William Langer—to identify the long-term trends, social, institutional, and ideological, that had culminated in the catastrophe.

The survival of Nazi influences among the political forces being released by the occupation authorities—recklessly, he felt—was the final item on Schorske's agenda within the Research and Analysis Branch. In September, when little remained of the Branch to administer, he was finally able to make a belated journey to the European Theater. He arrived at the R&A Outpost in Biebrich in the waning days of the organization, but he set about immediately to apply the methodologies in which he had been trained in Cambridge and Washington to the collection of documents and interviewing of political leaders. Freed at last from administrative duties, he began to write his own reports on political parties in Frankfurt, statewide trends in Bavaria, communists in Berlin, and the recrudescence of schismatic tendencies within German Social Democracy throughout the American zone.[22] These reports, while observing the canons of political reporting developed in R&A, have much more the character of historical documentation than political analysis. They suggest, in fact, a methodological retreat in the face of a growing political disillusion, for by the end of 1945 the dusk was already falling and the chill of winter and the Cold War were already darkening the skies over Germany.

•   •   •

Much has been written about the impact of the European intellectual migration of the 1930s upon American scholarship, but in the apprenticeship of Leonard Krieger these sociological generalizations assume historical concreteness. Krieger's transfer to OSS finally came through on May 1, 1943, and even before receiving his final security clearance he was assigned to a desk in the Central European Section, where he continued his graduate education—tuition-free—among some of the most outstanding historical and political thinkers of the emigration: Franz Neumann, Hajo Holborn, and Felix Gilbert, their German-educated counterparts Walter Dorn and Eugene Anderson, and many others.

Krieger's first assignment, in the tradition of the graduate research seminar, was to conduct a review of the literature, and he quickly mastered the R&A methodology of combing published sources for details of strategic significance. Such items were sparse in the heavily censored German press, but it is the mark of a historical scholar to make the most of what one's research turns up and Krieger had been well trained. "The Fuehrer Gets Competition," he entitled a report on the death sentence handed down to a practicing fortune-teller, and suggesting that "the severity of the sentence indicates not merely the growth of the activity but also that the Nazis are getting touchy about the future."[23] Tragicomic details of this sort—like the executions of clairvoyants, rumor-mongerers, "black listeners," and defeatists upon which he regularly reported—indicated that "the Fuehrer obviously intends to brook no competition to his position as Chief Seer." Whatever may have been their value for political warfare, to the young intellectual historian they testified to "the equivalence in the Nazi mind of the criminal within and the criminal without."

Other items culled from the European press testified to the equivalence of the individual criminal and the criminality of the regime. In October Krieger reported in ambiguous language upon the arrival in Denmark of Adolph Eichmann, SS Gruppenführer and head of the Central Bureau for Jewish Relocation, to enforce the deportation order, and surmised that "the Danish pogrom is the beginning of the final campaign to rid Europe of the Jews." Under the influence of Neumann's "spearhead theory," however, he was unable to translate the "exploitation of the Jewish question" as a matter of political expediency into the physical extermination of the Jews as an end in itself: as in France, Poland, and Czechoslovakia, "the Germans have seized on the 'Jewish danger' *as a wedge* for further penetration of Danish civil life."[24] If, as he had been taught, history is rational process guided by coherent systems of thought, there must be some larger instrumentality informing Nazi Jewish policy.

The sensitivity to the disruptive forces of "cataclysm and contingency" that marked Krieger's postwar scholarship suggests that the intellectual historian, trained to search out the underlying logic of *Staatsräson,* had been blinded by the very light of reason to the pathologies upon which Nazi ideology was built.

By the end of his first year, Krieger had worked on the organization of the Wehrmacht and the SS and on political opposition within Germany. He also bore principal responsibility for at least four major reports on the German pattern of occupation, governance, and exploitation—the field in which he rapidly became the Section's acknowledged expert.[25] In these papers he demonstrated that the strategy of Nazi policy in the West was to foster divisions within the indigenous populations through a variety of measures, the effect of which was to create an identification of certain elements—"accredited with the possession of the national political will"—with the Nazi order. In the occupied East the increasingly unfavorable military position caused the Germans to use the Baltic states, White Russia, and the Ukraine for political warfare against the Soviet Union, and to cloak intensified economic exploitation under the propaganda of national liberation. Building upon his integrated interpretation of policy, politics, and propaganda, Krieger proposed measures by which the Allies might exploit the weaknesses disclosed by the analysis.

Work such as this was of the essence of U.S. intelligence during World War II, but it was less the product of an individual analyst than the culmination of a long chain of contributions. On the Continent the Secret Intelligence Branch ferreted out raw information from licit and illicit sources, R&A personnel in London, Stockholm, and elsewhere sifted and extracted from it essential data, which was cabled back to Washington where analysts fitted it to other materials, fleshed it out with background research, and shaped it into coherent analytical reports for transmission to the Departments of War and State. Typically, the grand synthesis that was performed at the end of the chain fell to the senior faculty of the Branch, and graduate assistants such as Krieger often felt a youthful longing to get closer, if not to enemy territory, then at least to the primary sources generated therein.

It was with considerable excitement, then, that Krieger learned in June 1944 that he had been awarded an OSS scholarship to complete his studies under the direction of Felix Gilbert in London. In this second phase of his intelligence career Krieger continued to develop his expertise on the organization of German controls over the occupied regions of Russia and Central Europe. But whereas his thematic concerns remained continuous, a new set of research methodologies had to be developed, suited to the greater immediacy of the sources with which he was now working: techniques of interview and interrogation rather than the analysis of transcripts of them, the discovery as distinct from the mere evaluation of documentary materials, and other front-line strategies.

The narrowing of the distance between the historian and his sources that had occurred with the move across the Atlantic only stimulated Krieger's desire to get across the Channel and begin working directly with primary sources on the European continent. The period of anticipation finally ended when he became one of the first of the R&A personnel to enter Germany. On March 31, 1945, he arrived in Cologne, via three days at the Paris Outpost where he was briefed on the different patterns of research that would be required as he advanced into the heart of the European Theater. "The job of the Paris Germanists is entirely different from ours in London," he reported back to Gilbert, "because of their even greater proximity to the sources of raw intelligence. . . . Their resulting conception was best expressed by Arthur [Schlesinger, Jr.] who characterized it as a shift from the use of intelligence for political papers to a concentration upon the acquisition of political intelligence itself."[26] In Germany, however, the historian actually found himself inside the archives, as it were, immersed in a sea of unstructured data and free at last to impose his own framework of meaning upon events. Military defeat, as Krieger put it a short while thereafter, meant the end of the Nazi party, "and the end of the Nazi party meant the collapse of most of the organizations and institutions which had given coherence to German life for a dozen years."[27]

Immediately upon his arrival, Krieger began to file reports about the controlled anarchy that attended the collapse of military resistance and civil authority—"an ironic throwback to a state of nature in which the Germans above all had never believed," he later reflected.[28] With the onset of the formal occupation he roamed through the American Zone, amid the ruins of the peculiarly German accommodation of transcendental freedom within the authoritarian state, and set to work on a variety of intelligence tasks: interviewing of local government officials, surveying the political landscape for evidence of Nazi indoctrination, reporting on the re-emergence of the trade union movement, collecting materials on internal political development and Germany's postwar international position.

Krieger's entry into Germany marked the third phase not just of his intelligence career but also of his conversion to the tradition of European political and historical theory begun at Yale under the guidance of Hajo Holborn, continued in Washington with Franz Neumann, and now culminating under the direction of Felix Gilbert, who arrived in Germany a short while after to serve as director of political research. Their activities during this period have already been to some degree recounted: in May they celebrated the demise of the Hitler regime in the Harz Mountains amid the captured archive of the German Foreign Office, and during the summer the two itinerant scholars ventured out to report on the revival of university life in Baden, where the dilemma of the German intellectual, reflected philosophically in the experiences of Karl Jaspers and Martin Heidegger, was laid out before them. Throughout the autumn months the two intellectual historians—of different nationalities and different generations—attended historic meetings of the re-emergent trade union movement and of the battered Social Democratic party organization in Hannover, Stuttgart, and Munich.[29]

This period marked the culmination of Leonard Krieger's career in the history of intelligence but the beginning of his career in the history of ideas. At the end of November, by which time an inert Germany had become a political battleground for the newly emergent superpowers, he returned to the United States, physically exhausted but intellectually invigorated by a new research agenda. The problems that would preoccupy him throughout his postwar career—the lure of enlightened absolutism, the pursuit of personal liberty through the institutions of the authoritarian state, the failure of the left opposition and the culture of secular humanism to have averted the catastrophe, and above all the tension between objective fact and existential judgment in the analysis of historical problems—testify to the unresolved paradoxes with which he had been grappling throughout the war. Like so many of his academic colleagues, Krieger had worked throughout this period as a double agent: as an enlisted man assigned to OSS, he performed the duties of an American intelligence officer, all the while serving his foreign masters— Holborn, Neumann, Gilbert—in the shadow existence of an academic scholar, observing, reflecting, and consciously or otherwise, gathering the impressions that would form the problematics of his influential postwar books.

·   ·   ·

The R&A Outpost in Germany, it may be recalled, had made its head-quarters in an abandoned champagne factory, lately owned by the Rib-bentrop family, in a suburb adjacent to Wiesbaden. The crates of champagne, like the young historians installed among them, were of high quality and in plentiful supply; but though they had aged significantly during the war, they were still not fully mature. Schorske and Krieger were stationed there, along with Franklin Ford, Hans Meyerhoff, and their battle-hardened colleague Stuart Hughes, who now presided over the dissolution of an original academic invasion force some forty profes-sors strong.

The intelligence career of H. Stuart Hughes, the last of the triumvirate of intellectual historians whom the war pried loose from the prevailing orthodoxies of the profession, proved in many respects to be the most remarkable of them all. It is reflected in his ongoing attempt to traverse the epistemological chasm that had opened up between the two gen-erations of scholars who comprised the Research and Analysis Branch and whose outlines can be faintly discerned in the series of challenges to the authority of his superiors that marked his extraordinary rise through the organization.

Having sped through a PhD at Harvard in three years, oppressed by "the staleness and flatness of graduate work in history in the late 1930s,"[30] Hughes had entered R&A, unlike Schorske and Krieger, a commissioned officer with doctorate already in hand. Perhaps for that reason, he threw himself into intelligence work with the single-mindedness of one who had no unfinished business awaiting him after the end of the war. His initial assignment, when he joined the elders of the Harvard History Department who had regrouped in R&A, recalled his graduate student days when he owed fealty to his thesis director, Donald McKay, to whom he was now reassigned. He attended McKay on the Board of Analysts for much of his first year and served on the Current Intelligence Staff, the Joint Intelligence Committee, and other seminars McKay had staffed with "an able group of young men with broad rather than specialized intellectual background."[31] These units were responsible for the dissemination of intelligence throughout the government in the form of a series of R&A publications—*The War This Week,* the *Weekly Intelligence Summary,* and others—which struggled to achieve a balance between military brevity and academic detail, schol-arly objectivity and the social democratic tendencies that had given the Branch its unsavory reputation as "a hotbed of academic radicalism."[32]

What else, wondered many an intelligence colonel, could explain their predictions of Russian survival in the face of the Wehrmacht, which until Kursk had been viewed as the model of military efficiency?

Hughes' advancement to candidacy occurred late in the afternoon of September 11, 1943, when, after an air trip of 44 hours, he landed at Algiers to begin a Mediterranean odyssey that carried him across North Africa into France, Italy, the Balkans, and finally into the heart of Germany. Apart from a six-week respite in which he reported back to Washington early in 1945, he remained in Europe throughout the duration of the war, where his career described a spectacular trajectory marked by a growing sense of independence from his elders.

OSS North Africa operations had begun with a campaign to "soften up" the region in preparation for the Allied landing in November 1942, following which the machinery of Secret Intelligence, Special Operations, and Counter-Intelligence began functioning. The rear echelon of OSS—Research and Analysis—arrived in Algiers early in May to organize a system of intelligence reporting back to Washington. This was the first time that Langer had ordered his troops into an active theater of operations—"I am almost tempted to talk of a new era," he wrote with unusual animation—and the line had not yet been defined that separated the essentially academic duties for which they had been trained from deeds of derring-do which threatened to dissipate their energies, impair their credibility, and risk their lives.

What was to become a full-scale Harvard invasion of North Africa was actually spearheaded by Rudolph Winnacker, an enterprising professor of European history from the University of Nebraska whose mission was to lay down the machinery for the transmission of spot intelligence back to Washington. It was this system that was inherited by the Cambridge contingent that arrived to relieve him in September: McKay, Executive Officer Stuart Hughes, and John Sawyer as Deputy Chief; Holborn's student Henry Roberts, although a Yale man, accompanied them to handle topographic intelligence, and a pair of cartographers rounded out the group.[33]

The R&A task force started cautiously and maintained the tradition of academic discipline for which the Branch was famous. Within a few weeks Hughes had begun to report on the resistance in southern France and ideological controversy within the French National Committee in Algeria. His academic credentials served him well in this charged environment, for as he reported back to the Western European Section in

Washington, "many of the university professors are political figures of some importance here [and] we have found it very helpful to get in touch with them in our capacity as scholars."[34] French historians, anthropologists, and political scientists guided them through the maze of resistance politics, and members of the expatriate intelligentsia smuggled them into a sixtieth anniversary celebration of the *Alliance française,* where Hughes and Sawyer heard De Gaulle deliver "a minor literary masterpiece." Its reception testified to his popularity and confirmed the R&A position that the General, supported by a coalition of leftists and intellectuals, was the political force with which the Americans would ultimately have to deal.

Later in the season, with the southern landing of the Seventh Army, Hughes had a unique opportunity to verify these estimations when he was loaned to the Civil Affairs Division with the pleasant assignment of securing political intelligence on St. Tropez, Nice, and other strategic points along the Côte d'Azur. Nominally his duties were to advise the Chief of Staff, G-5, on political developments that could affect the security of American forces, but he used this tour of duty to report also on political questions of interest to R&A. In a series of airgrams transmitted to Algiers, he drew the conclusion that "the responsible Communist leaders in Southern France were pursuing a patriotic rather than a revolutionary policy" and that, "although the Communists were in almost complete control of this critical area, they did not represent a menace to public order."[35] More generally, Hughes was able to use the transportation facilities and offical entrées accorded him by the Army to evaluate the accuracy of the intelligence reporting of the R&A staff in Algiers over the preceding year. Their steady contention that the Resistance was of primary political and military importance proved to be correct; and in predicting that De Gaulle's administration would be accepted by the great mass of the French people, "we erred only on the side of caution."[36]

Hughes' attention followed the advancing front, evidenced by his biweekly reports that were taken up increasingly with the activities of the *maquis* in Corsica, Americans in Sicily, and Partisans in Yugoslavia. With this lateral relocation came a vertical movement as well. At the end of February 1944, Langer notified Colonel Edward Glavin, commanding officer of U.S. forces in Algeria, that "professional considerations" had made it necessary for McKay to return to Harvard and that subject to the Colonel's approval, Stuart Hughes would be promoted to the rank of Major and made head of R&A operations for the whole of North Africa.[37] No longer merely a promising underling, Hughes now found that his theater of operations spread across the Mediterranean from Algeria to the Balkans, and inevitably he came to chafe under a regime that subjected him to the judgments of Branch elders some thousands of miles from the front.

Increasingly, minor policy decisions from Langer's office in Washington would feed the fires of revolt that smoldered in many of the younger officers, whose restiveness would in turn bring down upon them the weight of academic tradition and military hierarchy. On more than one occasion the Chief, threatened by perceived defilements of official totems

H. Stuart Hughes, Algiers, 1944: "Nothing is administratively normal, and life is a perpetual crisis."

and ancient academic taboos, felt impelled to remind Hughes that, even in the field, "your responsibility is primarily to me" or to issue a sternly paternalistic reprimand "that you should have been inclined to stake your judgment against ours." Langer ruled his primal intelligence horde with an iron hand; but counting on the instinctual ambivalence that years of academic training had ingrained in his young men, he never removed the velvet glove for long: "I hope you will believe me, Stuart, when I say that it is my earnest desire and aim to give the men in the field all possible lattitude."[38] More than once the prodigal sons were subdued by an authoritarian gesture with this disarmingly conciliatory tone.

Perhaps the most acute of the controversies that divided these two generations of historical scholars concerned the practical limits of intelligence work itself. On the fourth of July 1944, Hughes decided that "Algiers is no longer an exciting place to be" and that it was time to move forward into Italy. R&A had for many months been working on plans for operational bases in Italy, and with the fall of Rome a month earlier the opportunity finally arose to establish working units on the peninsula. From Rome he would coordinate—in addition to his own staff of Western and Central Europeanists—the work of R&A economists working with the Fifteenth Air Force, Balkanists peering across the Adriatic from Bari, target analysis teams in Caserta, prisoner interrogation units in Naples, and R&A "City Teams" preparing to descend upon Belgrade, Bucharest, Budapest, Prague, Vienna, and Munich to report on conditions and secure documents for future generations of historians. "In the Mediterranean," he informed Langer, "nothing is administratively normal and life is a perpetual crisis. Branch chiefs can get their work done only through a mixture of persuasion, cajolery, and occasional bursts of anger . . . Unfortunately, I am the only R&A man available who combines all these requisites."[39]

The Research and Analysis Branch, in this as in other theaters, was regarded as a wayward stepchild of the war effort, politically suspect and operating at a distant academic remove from the front. The State Department in Washington, the Army command in the field, and even the upper echelons of OSS itself threatened constantly either to coopt or to ignore it, and Hughes was scarcely exaggerating when he noted that his position often was reduced to "that of a watchdog, constantly on the alert to see that some trick is not played on his boys."[40] During his sojourn on the French Riviera, his deputy chief in Italy had yielded to the insistence of the omnivorous General Donovan upon the representation of R&A people among the forward echelons. The General's imprudent policy—"epitomized by his own phrase of "getting belly-to-belly with the enemy' "[41]—reached its inevitable fulfillment in October, when two R&A men, David Colin and George Peck, were given rudimentary military training and infiltrated into enemy-held territory in the Po Valley, to their own great excitement and the consternation and dismay of Acting Chief Frederick Burkhardt.

Hughes returned to Italy amid reports that the two adventurers had indeed fallen into enemy hands and issued an immediate directive that academic personnel were not to be assigned to missions behind enemy lines: "This request is not prompted by any desire to spare R&A men the usual hardships or dangers of war," he explained, but by a realistic concern for the special circumstances of intelligence officers.[42] It was not known how the Germans might deal with OSS personnel, in or out of uniform, but Hughes anticipated that even their PhD oral examinations might not have prepared them for what he anxiously referred to as the "unusual methods of interrogation" to which they might be subjected. He appealed, accordingly, to Langer, only to find that the Chief himself had succumbed to Donovan's vision of his professors dropping out of the skies over enemy archives. "I am not as upset as you seem to be at the thought that these men were in a position to be captured," Langer cabled back to his subordinate: "I agree that R&A men should not be used behind enemy lines unless they have had very thorough training and unless there is some special reason why they should be so used, but I do think that it is altogether legitimate for them to be far forward, and if they are far forward there is always, of course, the chance of their being captured."[43] The charismatic Donovan was by this time paying one of his flying visits to Washington, en route from the European to the Pacific Theater, and Langer may well have been enticed into his unrestrained scenario of the Axis collapsing under the relentless pressure of the Office of Strategic Services. This he likened to "two moving columns, one of which had its present headquarters at Bari and its operations directed towards the eastern half of the Mediterranean, while the second, with headquarters at Caserta, is directed west and northwest."[44] From the Italian Theater, Hughes could do no more than protest "the concerted attack on the R&A Branch, begun by the General himself," and argue that given the specific nature of their task and the specialized academic training that had prepared them for it, "this romantic point of view on R&A work has done us nearly irreparable harm."[45] But the columns continued in their inexorable march up the Italian peninsula, and in May, as Deputy Chief of R&A/Germany, Hughes found himself part of the American army of occupation.

"Stuart is turning into a veritable stakhanovite," reported Carl Schorske upon his arrival at the end of the summer, by which time Hughes had become a seasoned administrator presiding over the dissolution of the mission to Germany.[46] Of the younger scholars, Hughes had risen most rapidly through the ranks of the organization whose institutional existence was now "one big inscrutable question mark." All three, however, had in their different ways endured a trial by fire that would decisively influence their subsequent careers. In their struggle against fascism in Germany they had helped to make history, but it was their struggles with the elder historians of the Research and Analysis Branch that prepared them now to write it.

The Disenchantment of the World

In separate commentaries on the state of historical studies in the United States, Leonard Krieger and Stuart Hughes agreed that, despite the proliferation of their research interests and the gradual attenuation of their war-born camaraderie, members of "the ongoing if ever-interrupted seminar" that was R&A comprised "the one identifiable cohesive group among the American historians of Europe today."[47] This affinity applies, *a fortiori*, to the rebellious commando unit of younger intellectual historians made up of Krieger, Hughes, and Carl Schorske. Indeed, we would be more cautious about assimilating three so distinctive historical thinkers to a single project had not they themselves sought so insistently to stress the generational bond among them. The contingency of the war accentuated the oppressive weight of the historiographical patrimony this group inherited, and their duties in the Research and Analysis Branch gave point to their discontent. "Together," as Freud remarked in a somewhat different context, "they dared and accomplished what would have been impossible for them singly."

In the immediate aftermath of the war, the three political intelligence veterans moved quickly to systematize their impressions. At the request of Allen Dulles and the Council on Foreign Relations, Carl Schorske drafted in 1947 a minority opinion on *the Problem of Germany,* Leonard Krieger published his own analysis of the "inter-regnum" that culminated in the Four-Power agreement at Potsdam, while from a desk in the State Department Stuart Hughes fired off volleys of memoranda into the official void. Together, these analyses formalize the political positions with which R&A had come to be associated but whose explicit formulation had to wait until Ensign Schorske, First Lieutenant Krieger, and Lt. Colonel Hughes had been reassigned to academic life. By the mid-1940s the three had been recommissioned at the rank of Assistant Professor and were serving tours of duty at Wesleyan, Yale, and Harvard, respectively, where they were free to pose the question of modernity in a field of discourse that had been declassified and demilitarized.

The fascist state, according to their independent analyses, did not represent a profound social revolution so much as the suppression by force of the peculiar historical constellations that marked the birth of modern Germany: an intellectual culture dominated since the wars of liberation by the cult of nationalism and the unpolitical traditions of scientific objectivity and transcendental idealism; the political disenfranchisement of the progressive bourgeoisie after 1848; the intense politicization of class antagonisms since Bismarck. It followed that the mere destruction of the Nazi regime in no way ensured the consolidation of indigenous democratic forces in Germany. To the contrary, the unregulated release of suppressed political energies in the period between the Armistice and Potsdam threatened to recreate just the conditions that had invited authoritarian solutions in the past. "Germany, shattered as she is, could again become a threat to Europe if the powers do not cooperate in keeping her under close control," Schorske warned in 1947, and he continued in terms that to the conservative Council on Foreign Relations must have carried an almost subversive tone: "A united and democratic Germany, however, could also be a bridge between East and West, an arena of great power cooperation. The alternative solution, toward which the powers have been drifting, is to deal with Germany not as a common problem soluble by common international action, but as a pawn in the struggle between East and West."[48] Even before the initial combat phase of the occupation had subsided, Germany was being transformed into an ideological battleground in which the urgency of the German problem was systematically degraded to what Krieger characterized as "a specific function of general United States–Soviet relations and the foreign policies which have followed therefrom." Grimly he forecast "a lasting debit for the future."[49]

Despite the determined efforts of Langer, Sherman Kent, and others to prevent the dispersion of their corps of research analysts until a new "central intelligence agency" could be formed, Schorske and Krieger retreated back to the university as soon as they were discharged to attend to their unfinished academic business. For Stuart Hughes, however, the war had come at a transitional moment in a career already fraught with indecision, and he accordingly allowed himself to be swept along with Neumann, Marcuse, Kirchheimer, and some 900 other veterans of the defunct Research and Analysis Branch into the State Department's Interim Research and Intelligence Service. From this vantage point he observed the growing polarization of the international system along a north-south axis that ran through the middle of Germany. The bureau he headed soon became associated with a minority position that recognized the reality of superpower rivalry in Europe but sought to mitigate its dangers by building diplomatic and economic bridges to the *de facto* Soviet "sphere of influence" rather than attempting to subvert or counteract it. Thus he languished for another two years, enduring the chill of the Cold War, the departures of those of his leftist friends who were able to secure academic positions, and the mounting cynicism of those who could not. From this bureaucratic underground—"somewhere between Foggy Bottom and the Magic Mountain," he quipped—Hughes began to compose his own reflections on the implications of an American policy that seemed calculated to eradicate the social democratic center upon which a global reconciliation might yet have been founded. In 1948, by which time he felt it was no longer possible to sustain an alternative position within the government, mired "in a state of mild depression punctuated by gloomy predictions of the fate that was about to overtake the democratic left," and correspondingly less uncertain of his academic vocation, he returned to Harvard, where he took up his first regular teaching position.[50]

In a shared mood of pessimism and foreboding, each of the veterans of the left-liberal contingent of OSS thus put policy questions behind him. Even Schorske's acclaimed study of the "great schism" that had opened up between the two wings of the German Social Democratic Party could by 1955 be read as "a kind of elegy for a once creative movement that history had destroyed." Krieger situated his intellectual reconstruction of German liberalism within the morbid fascination with lost causes that preoccupied postwar historians of Europe. Hughes' contribution to a series on monographs edited by McKay on the United States and Europe was distanced from other volumes by its dark ruminations on the elite theorists Mosca and Pareto.[51] It was more than just the failed dream of a progressive polity that was being elegized, however, for when the three scholars attempted to pick up the threads of prewar historical discourse, each found his way forward blocked.

The generation to which they belonged had absorbed from its elders a characteristically American vision of enlightenment; and despite certain revisionist gestures, it retained at least the outlines of what Schorske described as "its predecessor's confidence in the progress of society and in the use of ideas both to explain and to spur that progress." Then Nietzsche planted himself in the path of Schorske's advance into the twentieth century, following whom "both rationalism and the historicist vision allied with it lost their binding power on the European cultural imagination." For Hughes it was Max Weber, Spengler, and the whole of the post-Nietzschean "reorientation of European social thought" that transvalued the rationalist and historicist ideologies that had held center stage throughout the preceding century and undermined "the capacity of Western man to cope with his spiritual environment." For Krieger it was the ghost of Ranke that had above all to be laid, and with it the use and abuse of objectivist historiography in an age heralded by the modernist mapping of the irrational.[52] The post-Nietzschean vision of modernity exposed a decentered individual whose experience was marked by fragmentation, discontinuity, and evanescence and whose actions were subject to the demands of the unruly id. It followed that history itself—even intellectual history—could no longer be seen as the collective product of rational actors who behaved in accordance with logical systems of thought, nor could the historian presume to rise above this spectacle to a realm of disinterested objectivity. The lessons of totalitarianism, the insights of the modernist protest, and their own engagement with the process of history drove the new generation of modernist historians to what Krieger described as a pervasive "disenchantment with the orderliness of things."[53]

The new intellectual history was preoccupied above all with the problem of modernity, exemplified by the furious outburst of fin-de-siècle art and ideas that Schorske characterized in terms of its self-conscious break from history and the historical consciousness per se. Fittingly, the same revolt against their cultural patrimony marked the new historians themselves, even where they paused to pay honest tribute to the antithetical tendencies that had marked the development of intellectual history during the first half of this century and which it became their final mission to transcend. First among these inheritances was a sociohistorical commitment—associated with the French *Annalistes* Bloch and Febvre and the original "New Historians" James Harvey Robinson, Charles Beard, and Carl Becker—which had sought to situate ideas within a prior context of social action in relation to which they derived their proper meaning. The alternative school of historical thought, identified in Europe with Dilthey and Croce and in America with Arthur O. Lovejoy, Perry Miller, and the History of Ideas movement, tended toward a broadly internalist position that asserted the priority of ideas in their own philosophical or aesthetic terms, in their affinities with one another, or in their autonomous development over time. The legacy, in either case, was to convey the incommensurability of text and context and to enforce a neat segregation of the realm of ideas from the realm of social action. "What is distinctive about our own generation's approaches to intellectual history?" Krieger asked rhetorically, and he suggested that it was the need to preserve both the intellectual autonomy *and* the social relevance of ideas, but to merge them within a single historical discourse that would "seek within the intellectual sphere itself the larger context."[54]

Having been swept into the maelstrom of history, the young scholars of the Research and Analysis Branch learned that even historians are embedded in the object of their study. As participant-observers by virtue of their dual citizenship in the civic republic and the republic of letters, they had acquired during the war an immediate sense not only of the social relevance of ideas but of the social responsibility of the intellectual. It is hardly surprising, then, that they should have emerged with such a profound disenchantment with the orderliness of things and a determination to legitimate their direct experience of the intersection of the social and the ideational. Underlying the disparities among them—in method, in substance, and in unit of analysis which would range from individual thinker to the intelligentsia of a city to the intellectual culture of a generation—a commitment both to the integrity but also the social relevance of ideas is palpable in their work. In Hughes' major contribution to the modernist redefinition of the field, the method of internal intellectual history automatically acquires its external relevance by virtue of its subject matter, the role of "consciousness" in "society." Schorske's indubitable achievement has been to grasp the artifact of aesthetic or intellectual culture as "a product of a life lived in a social matrix" but substantively irreducible to it.[55] In 1967 Leonard Krieger delivered a manifesto in which he challenged the intellectual historian to resist either a detached internalist or a reductive externalist position, but rather "to assess the influence of circumstance *upon* thought by pursuing the role of identifiable circumstance *in* thought."[56]

This methodological premise implied that intellectual history is, *ipso facto,* political history, even where its objects veered off into aestheticism, psychologism, or other putatively apolitical flights. Krieger protested the banishing of authorial intent by the New Critics, Schorske denounced "the ahistorical and politically neutralizing reign of the behaviorists" over the social sciences, and Stuart Hughes, calling for "the 'socialization' of ideas," broke free from the ethos of Rankean empathy in which he had been trained to a Crocean sensibility that openly permitted the political imperatives of the present to shape the questions put to the past.[57] Armed with the ethic of the engaged scholar, they imparted a moral cast to the field that enabled them to resist the encroachments of the positivist social sciences in the 1950s and weather both the radicalism of the 1960s and the quiescence of the 70s. No activists, these, but honest liberal intellectuals in the defiant sense pro-

Leonard Krieger at the London Outpost, reflecting "a pervasive disenchantment with the orderliness of things."

posed by Krieger in the aftermath of the war: "referring to that habit
of mind which manifests anxiety about the concrete organization of life,
is yet dissatisfied with current forms of organization, and is ever open
to new ideal impulses which seek to develop this organization beyond
these forms."[58]

For three decades this contextualist paradigm reigned supreme in the
field of intellectual history, refining its methods with insights derived
from the interpretive and behavioral sciences while enriching its content
with the "historical effluence" cast off by them, producing distinguished
works of scholarship, practicing an ongoing self-interrogation of its own
foundations, and challenging successive generations of students to extrapolate from the social embeddedness of ideas to the social responsibility of intellectuals. But just as history does not rest after a good
day's work, neither does historiography, and it was strictly a matter of
time before the young rebels of R&A became the new patriarchs of the
field. Inevitably, the modernist synthesis has broken apart under the
antithetical strains of a postmodern aesthetic formalism on the one hand
and a social scientific reductionism on the other, and the historians have
found themselves challenged not by the authority of their elders but by
the radical claims of the successor generation which they themselves
had sired.

The Return of the Repressed

The contextualist paradigm sought to achieve "the reciprocal illumination
of text and context" under "the sovereign aegis of time," to meet its
authors on their own rhetorical ground. In pursuit of this golden mean,
the intellectual historians had to fortify themselves along two positions:
an externalist challenge, quantitative and functionalist, that treated texts
as artifacts of cultural history and thus derivative of a prior social totality;
and an internalist position that considered them for their aesthetic, symbolic, or philosophical value. "If he neglects the first of these activities,"
Krieger noted, "the historian loses his body; if he surrenders the second
he loses his soul."[59] The craft of historical narrative suggested the strategy by which the high ground of contextualism was to be secured.

Narrative virtuosity was to be the vehicle for what Schorske described
as the "basic archetypal mental disposition to synthesize or unify forces
whose dynamics resist integration."[60] This totalizing impulse is charac-

teristic of the modernist moment generally and is the most pronounced feature both of the scholarship and the citizenship of the graduates of OSS. It also accounts for their overarching quest to reconcile the contradictory movements of text and context, structure and history, ideas and action. Through the imposition of narrative structure Schorske set about to tend the riotous garden of fin-de-siècle cultural modernism; Krieger both practiced and preached the use of narrative to preserve the autonomy of intellectual history against the claims of both linguistic formalism and sociological reductionism, arguing that "in principle our standard operating procedure is a combination of opposites";[61] and Stuart Hughes never doubted "history's traditional storytelling function," even as he pressed his colleagues to supplement it with methods borrowed from anthropology and psychoanalysis.[62]

The dialectical movement of text and context is inherently an unstable one, however. As history paints its gray in gray, the shape of modernist historiography has indeed grown old, and a new, postmodern generation has arisen to dismantle the contextualist synthesis along precisely the force lines it had sought to heal. History may or may not obey the laws of dialectical development; historiography incontrovertibly does, and the intellectual offspring of the contextualists have figured prominently in the revolt.

Narrativity lies at the heart of the "overriding preoccupation with change" that is for Krieger the "distinguishing mark of the historical discipline."[63] This emblem of its autonomy has been rendered problematical, however, by the recent resurgence of social history and its characteristic pursuit of a synchronic and often static image of past structures. While committed to a middle ground between the internalist and externalist conceptions of intellectual history, Krieger and both of his politicized contemporaries always hinted that it was safer to err on the side of the latter, for "in principle the socially-oriented varieties of intellectual history are surely on the side of the angels."[64] Of late, however, they have found themselves outflanked from the left, denounced by an ascendent generation of sociocultural historians for their restriction of the historical field to male elites and a narrativist preoccupation with the metaphysics of historical change that precludes "the complex reconstruction of vanished mind sets."[65] The editors of *Past and Present* in England, the second generation of *Annalistes* in France, and a clamorous party of social scientific historians in the United States have raised against them the battle-cry of "History from below!"

If the assumptions inherent in what Hughes called "the sweep of narrative line" have exposed the modernist historians of OSS to attack on their external flank, the forces of postmodern aesthetic formalism have been marching like a Fifth Column on their internal defenses. Hayden White is often regarded as the first intellectual historian to propose that the rhetoric of narrativity is not a transparent medium for the transmission of meaning but a "prefigurative" instrument by which contemporaries structure events and historians recast them; the intellectual historian, in this case, would be doing no more than using one allegory to explain another.[66] The ensuing investigation of the ideological strategies embodied in historical narrative has had two immediate consequences: one is an explicit critique of the contextualists' attempt to derive meaning from elements of the historical environment external to the documentary text; the corollary has been the famed "linguistic turn"—or re-turn, as I prefer—toward formal analysis in the practice of intellectual historiography. In both cases the effect has been a second transvaluation of historical values, from the hard-won ethic of political engagement practiced in R&A *through* language into a mediated engagement *with* language practiced exclusively in the university.

Stuart Hughes protested that he "never meant to belittle narrative history" even as he encouraged his students to experiment with alternative strategies for bringing order to the intellectual artifacts of a disorderly past. Unfortunately for the contextualist paradigm, they have done just that. Dominick LaCapra has argued that his mentor's penchant for "a conventional, untroubled narrative" amounts to the imposition of "a self-unifying interpretive theory"; he has taxed Schorske for his "reductive protocols of interpretation" and has paraded Leonard Krieger as the "official consciousness" of intellectual history, insensible to the apparent crisis in the subdiscipline.[67] Another student, Martin Jay, has thematized the breakdown of the typically modernist quest for totalization in his mapping of Western Marxism; and, perhaps groping toward a new synthesis, he has suggested that "the opposition between a linguistically-informed intellectual history and one indebted to traditional concepts of rationality is unnecessarily extreme."[68] Others have argued that the very "disposition to synthesize" that Schorske identified as the defining trait of his generation tends to smooth over the fissures in which genuinely oppositional tendencies take refuge.

Thus the battle-weary veterans of the Research and Analysis Branch found themselves recalled to active duty just as they thought their internalist enemies had been subdued and their externalist critics turned back at the social scientific frontiers of the discipline. In what must seem to them like the eternal return of the repressed, the high middle ground of contextualist intellectual history is being claimed by foreign legions speaking the populist dialect of *mentalités* and domestic *littérateurs* intoning the mesmerizing rhetoric of textuality. They had been offered, at a formative stage of their careers, a unique opportunity to interact directly with history, historians, and the historical consciousness, and they carried away from this encounter an ethic and an epistemology. We dare not lament the passing of the modernist synthesis, prefigured in the Research and Analysis Branch and practiced in the course of three decades of engaged scholarship. It will be the worse, however, both for history and historiography, if the impulse behind it is abandoned.

Conclusion: Intellect and Intelligence

It has recently been argued that "every historical narrative has as its latent or manifest purpose the desire to moralize the events of which it treats."[1] The foregoing study of academic scholarship in the Office of Strategic Services would seem to lend special credence to this claim, for I have conceived it from the beginning in moral terms. The Research and Analysis Branch mobilized a formidable battalion of progressive scholars whose vocation was to manipulate ideas, who understood the war in political terms, and who wanted to help. Wartime Washington was not Periclean Athens, Florence under the Medici, or Goethe's Weimar, but there remains something inspiring about it, even if the motives of particular individuals were often more pragmatic: transfers to OSS were known in the army as "cellophane commissions"—you could see right through them, but they protected you from the draft.

If my desire to moralize does not necessarily derive from the purity of individuals' motivations, neither is it prompted by the decisive role played by the Research and Analysis Branch in winning the war. The work these scholars produced was, as a general rule, of exceptionally high quality, the more so given the duress of wartime conditions and the need to forge wholly new tools of analysis and research. As any scholar knows, however, it is one thing to publish and quite another to find a receptive readership, and there is precious little evidence that the reports, analyses, and forecasts churned out in the Branch figured decisively in the determination of military or diplomatic policy. The failure of the government to utilize this unique resource to the maximum was, in my opinion, a tragic waste.

The Office of Strategic Services was dissolved by Executive Order

9620, signed by President Truman on September 20, 1945, and effective ten days later. The teams of Special Operations, Secret Intelligence, and Counter-Intelligence agents were mostly disbanded and dispersed throughout the Strategic Services Unit of the War Department, but exceptional efforts were made to preserve the Research and Analysis Branch intact.[2] Long before the war was over, General Donovan had begun to anticipate America's peacetime intelligence needs and so advised the President: "We have now in the Government the trained and specialized men needed for the task," he wrote referring specifically to R&A. "This talent should not be dispersed."[3]

The combined recalcitrance of the government and the community of scholars sabotaged the hopes of Donovan, Langer, and other OSS administrators that their organization would be permitted to evolve into a peacetime intelligence agency. Scholars who had been prepared to lend their academic skills to the war against Hitler found that with the destruction of Nazism the danger no longer seemed to be so clear and present. Some allowed themselves to be transferred to desks in the Interim Research and Intelligence Service in the State Department, others circulated proposals to channel promising graduate students into intelligence work or to induce professors to use sabbatical leaves for intelligence-gathering activities abroad, and a very few remained long enough to join Langer and Sherman Kent on the CIA's Board of National Estimates in 1950.[4] From the South-East Asia Command the anthropologist Gregory Bateson noted that even as the atomic blasts over Japan foretold the end of conventional warfare among the great powers, "already even the best personnel in O.S.S. are beginning to think that their job is finished, and powerful forces in government are already aligned to get rid of the agencies concerned with clandestine operations, psychological warfare, international economic controls, and the collecting and analysis of intelligence."[5] The great majority felt that even in R&A they had been exiled to a foreign land, forced to speak and write in a foreign tongue and to think with a foreign intelligence. In droves they shed their uniforms and returned to unfinished manuscripts and doctoral dissertations, and it cannot be gainsaid that their departure from Washington was viewed with some relief. Even William Langer conceded that "the academic is all too apt to lack elasticity. He is generally an individualist, and when he thinks he is right he is all too prone to be impatient with the difficulties."[6] But the judgment of one astute journalist may be closest to the mark: "Too many professors."

For the continuity of the Research and Analysis Branch we must look not to the State Department or the CIA but to that ultimate decentralized intelligence agency, the American academic establishment. From around the country, two generations of American and European scholars had converged upon Washington, bringing with them techniques of statistical evaluation, familiarity with the European trade union movement, fluency in regional dialects, the philosopher's grasp of ideological structures, the sociologist's expertise in content analysis. The war hardened and sharpened these skills, called forth new ones, and imparted to a community of humanist and social scientific scholars a concrete sense of the embeddedness of their ideas—and themselves—in history, which they brought back with them to their universities.

Even in academic life, however, the legacy of the Research and Analysis Branch has been attenuated over time. Shortly after the war, the anthropologist Cora DuBois told an audience at Smith College that the collaborative experience of the war, while not yet abstractly formulated, had already greatly accelerated interdisciplinary thinking: "The walls separating the social sciences are crumbling with increasing rapidity," she observed. "People are beginning to think, as well as feel, about the kind of world in which they wish to live."[7] This notice, it would seem, was premature. The blasts of war had indeed battered down the fortifications behind which the disciplines had sequestered themselves, but they have been rebuilt with a surprising sense of urgency. I think this is unfortunate, because scholarship as a whole benefits—as the epistemology of intelligence suggests—when the greatest diversity of minds, methods, and morals are thrown together, free from the surveillance of what Aby Warburg once called "the *Grenzpolizei* who patrol the borders of the disciplines."

The historian's "desire to moralize," to which I have so readily abandoned myself in these chapters, is no longer (or not yet) widely respected by historians. It seems to me an emblem, however, of the desire to escape the parochialism of the academic consciousness, to chart an intersection with the world beyond the narrow protocols of the disciplines and even of the university. This effort was called forth in the Research and Analysis Branch by the exigencies of war. It has been difficult to sustain under the exigencies of peace.

Note on Sources

Notes

Charts

Index

Note on Sources

When the Office of Strategic Services was terminated in October 1945, its records were distributed between two government agencies. The Department of State received the papers of the Research and Analysis Branch, amounting to some 1,000 cubic feet of documents, and released them to the National Archives in 1946. They were cleared in 1975–76 by a CIA declassification team, which estimates that somewhat less than 1 percent of them were withheld. Since these papers include requisitions for office furniture as well as secret intelligence reports on the Soviet Union, this figure must be weighted in terms of the significance and not merely the bulk of these materials. The remainder of the OSS papers—amounting to another 6,000 cubic feet—was transferred to the Strategic Services Unit of the War Department and then entrusted to the Central Intelligence Group. In September 1947, the newly created Central Intelligence Agency was given custody of these documents, which include operational, administrative, and support materials for all branches of OSS, including Research and Analysis. In 1980 the CIA began the process of reviewing these materials and transferring them to the National Archives, where they are being declassified, sorted, and indexed. As a scholar and as a citizen, I hope that the complete legacy can still be recovered.

All "R&A Reports" referred to in this study are in the Civil Archives Division, Legislative and Diplomatic Branch, U.S. National Archives. Textual Records of the Office of Strategic Services, R[ecord] G[roup] 226, Records of the Research and Analysis Branch, are in the Military Records Division. Except for the early years of the USSR Division, R&A Reports were generally issued unsigned and were in any case frequently collaborative and always heavily edited. In many instances, however, it has been possible, by consulting the Textual Records, to identify individuals who wrote or supervised specific reports. The sources that are the basis for these identifications are given in square brackets. I must also confess to a limited amount of editing myself. To a rushed dispatch from the Continent, a harried intelligence officer appended the following note: "Being lazy, however, we shall continue to delude ourselves that there is a natural charm about misspellings and odd phrasings which would suffer from excessive zeal in composition" (Irwin Nat Pincus to James Tyson, March 20, 1945, *Enemy Objectives Unit Report* no. 60: Papers of Charles P. Kindleberger). Suffering no such delusions myself, I have on a very few occasions taken the liberty of making minor corrections in spelling, punctuation, and grammar where I have been certain that these changes did not alter the substance of any document.

Notes

Preface

Epigraph: William L. Langer to Kermit Roosevelt, March 5, 1947: RG 226, Entry 146, Box 48, Folder 166, p. 6.

1. Hajo Holborn, "History and the Humanities," *Journal of the History of Ideas*, vol. 9, no. 1 (January) 1948), reprinted as the title essay in Holborn, *History and the Humanities* (Garden City, N.J.: Doubleday, 1972), p. 78.
2. "History of the Current Intelligence Staff": RG 226, Entry 99, Box 76, Folder 46.
3. I am aware of only three exceptions: Bradley F. Smith, *The Shadow Warriors: OSS and the Origins of the CIA* (New York: Basic Books, 1983), chap. 8; Robin Winks, *Cloak and Gown: Scholars in the Secret War, 1939–1961* (New York: Morrow, 1987), chap. 2; and Alfons Söllner, ed., *Zur Archäologie der Demokratie in Deutschland*, Band 1: *Analysen von politischen Emigranten im amerikanischen Geheimdienst, 1943–1945*, and Band 2, *Analysen von politischen Emigranten im amerikanischen Aussenministerium, 1946–1949* (Frankfurt: Fischer Verlag, 1986). The present study is, however, the only study to focus upon the full range of intellectual work produced within the R&A Branch.

1. Military Disciplines

Epigraph: William L. Langer, "Scholarship and the Intelligence Problem," *Proceedings of the American Philosophical Society,* 92 (March 1948); reprinted in *Explorations in Crisis: Papers in International History,* ed. Carl E. Schorske and Elizabeth Schorske (Cambridge: Harvard University Press, 1969), p. 333.

1. Quoted in Corey Ford, *Donovan of OSS* (Boston: Little, Brown, 1970), p. 148. The most informed treatments of the life and legend of William J. Donovan are Anthony Cave Brown, *The Last Hero: Wild Bill Donovan* (New York: Random House, 1982); Richard Dunlop, *Donovan: America's Master Spy* (Chicago: Rand McNally, 1982); and Thomas F. Troy, *Donovan and the CIA* (Frederick, Md.: University Press of America, 1981).
2. The basic published source on the creation of COI/OSS is the official *War Report of the OSS,* 2 vols., declassified July 17, 1975, and published the following year

(New York: Walker & Co., 1976). This document is based on the numerous independent branch histories submitted to Conyers Read, original director of the OSS History Project. Most of these original source materials are in the National Archives, Washington, D.C., in RG 226, Entry 99, "OSS Historical File."

3. The official documents pertaining to the creation of the COI and OSS—Donovan's "Memorandum of Establishment of Service of Strategic Information," June 10, 1941, the Presidential Order "Designating a Coordinator of Information," July 11, 1941, and the "Military Order of June 13, 1942" creating the Office of Strategic Services—are reproduced as Appendices B, C, and E to Troy, *Donovan and the CIA*. For accounts of the guerilla activities conducted between Donovan's group and other government agencies during the first year, see (in addition to Troy and Cave Brown) Bradley F. Smith, *The Shadow Warriors: OSS and the Origins of the CIA* (New York: Basic Books, 1983), pp. 55–68, and Robin Winks, *Cloak and Gown: Scholars in the Secret War, 1939–1961* (New York: Morrow, 1987), chap. 2.

4. William Langer to Kermit Roosevelt, March 5, 1947: RG 226, Entry 146, Box 48, Folder 666, p. 19. In the estimation of Bradley F. Smith, the only scholar to have lingered over the administrative record of the Board of Analysts, the system foundered on the incompatibility between the unstable enthusiasms of Colonel Donovan and the *modus operandi* of the academic research scholar: "He did not give it enough room and enough authority to do the job it had been created to do." Smith, *Shadow Warriors*, pp. 76–78.

5. Sherman Kent, "To the Staff of the Europe–Africa Division—Every Member of It," July 4, 1945: mG 226, Entry 37, Box 5.

6. William L. Langer, "Up from the Ranks" (unpublished, 1975), p. 270; obtained through the courtesy of Mr. Ray Cline, National Intelligence Study Center.

7. Edward S. Mason, "Introduction" to *Price Problems in a Defense Economy,* a collection of papers prepared for the Conference on Price Research which he chaired (privately circulated, April 1941), p. v.

8. Edward Mead Earle, *Relentless War,* Columbia Home Front Warbooks, no. 3 (New York: Columbia University Press, 1942), p. 5.

9. Edward Mead Earle, "National Defense and Political Science," *Political Science Quarterly,* vol. 55, no. 4 (December 1940), pp. 490, 487. Also his war cry, *Against This Torrent* (Princeton: Princeton University Press, 1941).

10. These resonances of the Alfred Weber–Karl Mannheim image of the *freischwebende Intelligenz*—the "free-floating intellectual"—can be discerned in Earle's paper, "National Defense and Political Science," p. 492.

11. Calvin Bryce Hoover, *Memoirs of Capitalism, Communism, and Nazism* (Durham, N.C.: Duke University Press, 1965), p. 70; see also his *Economic Life of Soviet Russia* (New York: Macmillan, 1931), *Germany Enters the Third Reich* (New York: Macmillan, 1933), and *Dictators and Democrats* (New York: Macmillan, 1937). The image of intellectual extraterritoriality is developed—coincidentally, I believe—by the German film theorist Siegfried Kracauer; see Martin Jay, "The Extraterritorial Life of Siegfried Kracauer," *Salmagundi,* 31–32 (Fall-Winter 1976), pp. 49–106.

12. William L. Langer, "The Faith of Woodrow Wilson," *New York Times Magazine*, May 4, 1941, p. 5; reprinted in *Explorations in Crisis,* pp. 263–266.
13. William L. Langer, "When German Dreams Come True," *Yale Review,* 27, no. 4 (June 1938), pp. 678–698; reprinted in *Explorations in Crisis,* pp. 277–243.
14. In addition to published sources cited, see the "Minutes of the Board of Analysts": RG 226, Entry 58, Box 1.
15. The characterization of Winnacker's Africa Secton is in RG 226, Entry 99, Box 76, Folder 45. Ralph Bunch outlined his proposed research program in a letter to Conyers Read, September 24, 1941: RG 226, Entry 146, Box 134, Folder 46: Procedural Data. For a partial list of the Washington staff at the end of 1943, see "Personnel of the Research and Analysis Branch": RG 226, Entry 145, Box 4, Folder 43. There is a "Functional Directory of Personnel as of March 1943" and an administrative schema of the Branch dated July 11, 1943, in RG 226, Entry 1, Boxes 10 and 11, respectively. At the request of Guy Stanton Ford, President of the American Historical Association, Carl Schorske prepared an annotated list of "historians who are now serving in the Office of the Coordinator of Information," Schorske to Langer, November 25, 1941; RG 226, Entry 146, Box 129, Folder 1842. AHA Presidents who served in R&A included Conyers Read (1949), William L. Langer (1957), Bernadotte Schmitt (1960), Crane Brinton (1963), Hajo Holborn (1967), John K. Fairbank (1968), David Pinkney (1980), and Gordon Craig (1982). Robin Winks has surveyed the subsequent careers of other R&A historians in *Cloak and Gown,* p. 495, n. 19. Future presidents of the American Economic Association were Calvin Hoover (1953), Edward Mason (1962), Wassily Leontief (1970), Moses Abramowitz (1980), and Charles Kindleberger (1985). Leontief won the Nobel Prize in Economics in 1973; Bunche won the Nobel Prize in 1949.
16. Letter from Paul Sweezy to the author, August 14, 1984.
17. Sherman Kent to an unnamed colleague at the University of Wisconsin: RG 226, Entry 38, Box 1: Reading File, March 1943.
18. Sherman Kent to Raymond Sontag, August 4, 1942: RG 226, Entry 38, Box 1, Recruitment File: University of California.
19. Material in this section is drawn from several files in RG 226, Entry 146, Box 143: "Institute for Social Research"; "Personnel Applications: Central European Section"; "Projects Rejected"; "Propaganda." Baxter's reservations are expressed in a memorandum to Col. G. Edward Buxton, "Possible Employment of Fritz [sic.] Neumann," June 11, 1942: RG 226, Entry 146, Box 149, Folder: Central European Section.
20. Goebbels' charming but not entirely accurate phrase, upon learning of the creation of the Coordinator of Information: Foreign Broadcasting Intelligence Service intercept, Berlin to North America, December 26, 1941 (quoted in Cave Brown, *The Last Hero,* p. 174).
21. The references to Paul Baran and Eero Saarinen are in RG 226, Entry 99, Box 76, Folders 46 and 45, respectively. Eugene Fodor's personal file turns up, for no apparent reason, in RG 226, Entry 146, Box 82, Folder 312.1/1208. Pollock and Gurland were retained by the Branch as consultants on a *per diem* basis.
22. Franz Neumann to Carl Schorske, December 19, 1944, "Document on German

Intelligence Service": RG 226, Entry 37, Box 2, Folder: Central European Section.

23. Franz Neumann to Harold Deutsch, Felix Gilbert, and R. Schmidt, July 5, 1945, "Composition of Frankfurt Committee of Lawyers": RG 226, Entry 81, Box 3: Correspondence of OSS Mission to Germany, 1944–45.

24. Felix Gilbert to Frederick Burkhardt, September 17, 1945: RG 226, Entry 81, Box 3. The allusion to Schiller's *Naive and Sentimental Poetry* was smuggled into an appraisal of a field report sent by Saul K. Padover: F[ranz] L[eopold] N[eumann] to Harold Deutsch, January 23, 1945, Eitner Papers. Beatrice Braude, secretary to Franz Neumann, recalled his Ciceronian disputation with Otto Kirchheimer in an interview in Washington, D.C., October 1985, and Anderson's quip was reported to me in an interview with Barrington Moore, Jr., Cambridge, Mass., October 26, 1987.

25. Sherman Kent: RG 226, Entry 38, Box 1: Reading File, March 1943.

26. Arthur O. Lovejoy, "Plans for an International Armed Force," a 100-page memorandum submitted to Edward Mason in March 1943 urging the creation of a postwar international authority to contain the destabilizing maneuvers of individual nation-states: RG 226, Entry 145, Box 2, Folder 22. Talcott Parsons and C. J. Friedrich, November 14, 1944, "Pattern and Dynamics of the German Social Structure," a research proposal that urged that "a carefully selected team of social scientists with a thorough knowledge of the German social structure and experience in cooperative work should proceed to Germany a few months after the armistice" to undertake a comprehensive study of the roots of German fascism: RG 226, Entry 1, Box 17, Folder: Germany.

27. John Herz, *Vom Ueberleben: Wie Ein Weltbild entstand. Autobiographie* (Düsseldorf: Droste Verlag, 1984), p. 135.

28. On R&A's perceived partiality for socialist parties and trade unions, see the correspondence of Franklin Ford and of H. Stuart Hughes: RG 226, Entry 81, Box 2. John K. Fairbank recalls the political status of OSS in the Far East in *Chinabound: A Fifty Year Memoir* (New York: Harper and Row, 1982), p. 219. On the charges of Ambassador MacVeagh, see Robert Lee Wolff to Sherman Kent, August 31, 1945: RG 226, Entry 1, Box 15: Cairo File.

29. "Functions of the Research and Analysis Branch," October 30, 1942: RG 226, Entry 145, Box 2, Folder 24.

30. John A. Wilson to William Langer, May 12, 1943: RG 226, Entry 145, Box 3, Folder 33: Director's Office.

31. Richard Hartshorne to Division and subdivision Chiefs, "Draft of Proposed Guide to Preparation of Political Reports," p. 1a: RG 226, Entry 37, Box 5, Folder: Projects Committee Correspondence. William L. Langer, "Scholarship and the Intelligence Problem," *Proceedings of the American Philosophical Society,* 92, no. 1 (March 1948), pp. 43–46, and "Preface" in *Essays in Honor of Conyers Read,* ed. Norton Downs (Chicago: University of Chicago Press, 1953), pp. vii–xiv.

32. "The problem of Objectivity in R&A Reporting": RG 226, Entry 37, Box 5: Projects Committee Correspondence.

33. Sherman Kent to Major Murray, September 15, 1945, "Contributions in the

Field of Social Sciences Made by the Research and Analysis Branch, OSS, to U.S. Stragegic Intelligence": RG 226, Entry 37, Box 5: R&A, History, Etc.

34. "The Need for Intellectual Guidance in Psychological Warfare Research," August 13, 1942, and "Psychological Warfare Planning," n.d.: RG 226, Entry 27, Box 2, PW Subcommittee.

35. Richard Hartshorne, *The Nature of Geograpahy: A Critical Survey of Current Thought in the Light of the Past,* published as vol. 29, nos. 3 and 4, of the *Annals of the Association of American Geographers* (Lancaster, Pa.: 1939), p. 32. In view of his role as guardian of the standards of positive science, it is interesting to note that Hartshorne was also the co-author, with Derwent Whittlesey and Charles C. Colby, of a critical examination of German *Geopolitik*, an ideological literature even prior to the Nazification of the universities, whose sinister implications had been missed because it had not been taken seriously by overly scientific geologists and geographers: *German Strategy of World Conquest* (New York: Farrar & Rinehart, 1942). The wartime volume carries the publisher's pertinent insignia, "Books are weapons in the war of ideas."

36. Hartshorne, "Draft of Proposed Guide to the Preparation of Political Reports," pp. 8, 10 (n. 30, *supra*). "Style Sheet for Use in the Research and Analysis Branch": RG 226, Entry 99, Box 104, Folder 97303. Also R&A 2405, "The Work of the Projects Committee," August 1, 1944. For recent theoretical discussions of these problems, see Hayden White, *The Content of the Form: Narrative Discourse and Historical Representation* (Baltimore: Johns Hopkins University Press, 1987); Roland Barthes, *Writing Degree Zero* (New York: Hill and Wang, 1968); Paolo Valesio, *Novantiqua: Rhetorics as a Contemporary Theory* (Bloomington: Indiana University Press, 1980); and Dominick LaCapra, *History and Criticism* (Ithaca: Cornell University Press, 1985), p. 219: "It is not uncommon to observe that the anti-rhetoric of plain style or, more elaborately, of 'scientificity' is itself a self-denying quest for a certain rhetoric, a rhetoric unadorned by figures, unmoved by emotion, unclouded by images, and universalistic in its conceptual or mathematical scope."

37. "Functions of the Research and Analysis Branch": RG 226, Entry 145, Box 2, Folder 24. In alluding to the fetish-character of academic disciplines which acquire a life of their own apart from the complex social world they seek to represent, I have appropriated some suggestive vocabulary from Georg Lukács' classic essay of 1922, "Reification and the Consciousness of the Proletariat, Part II: The Antinomies of Bourgeois Thought."

38. Langer to Donovan, March 15, 1944, "Social Scientists in Research and Analysis Branch": RG 226, Entry 110, Box 47, Folder 47 (notes provided for a speech by Donovan to the SSRC).

39. "Notes of Remarks Made by Mr. Schlesinger and Lt. Col. Hughes in Meeting of Tuesday, 26 June [1945], Regarding Standards of Field Reporting": RG 226, Entry 81, Box 1.

40. "Style Sheet for Use in the Research and Analysis Branch" (n. 36, *supra*).

41. "Memorandum Regarding Some Weaknesses in our System of Research and Write up with Suggestions How to Remedy": RG 226, Entry 1, Box 10: Morale File.

42. Preston E. James to William L. Langer, March 3, 1944, "Observations on Use of Social Scientists in R&A": RG 226, Entry 1: Europe–Africa Division.

43. It serves the larger argument of David Wyman's important book, *The Abandonment of the Jews* (New York: Pantheon, 1984), to claim that, although they received detailed information about the mass murder of Jews, "the OSS did nothing with it" (p. 314), but this is simply an invention on the part of the author. In preparing numerous reports such as R&A 1844, "Concentration Camps in Germany," October 3, 1944, R&A may have done all that its mandate permitted it to do (however pitiful that may have been).

44. Michel Foucault, *The Archaeology of Knowledge,* trans. A. M. Sheridan Smith (New York: Pantheon, 1972), p. 90.

45. "The Need for Intellectual Guidance in Psychological Warfare Research" (n. 33, *supra*).

46. "The Problem of Objectivity in R&A Reporting" (n. 27, *supra*), pp. 2, 4 (emphasis in original).

47. Langer, "Up from the Ranks," p. 164.

48. "Europe–Africa: The Geographic Subdivision": RG 226, Entry 99, Box 76, Folder 45, p. 73 and verso.

49. H. Stuart Hughes, "Standard Operating Procedures for Field Reports," June 28, 1945: RG 226, Entry 81, Box 1.

50. Langer to Kermit Roosevelt, March 5, 1947, pp. 9–10 (n. 4, *supra*).

51. RG 226, Entry 91, Box 7, R&A (London): *War Diary,* vol. I, p. 12. For an inspired literary romp through "this lush maze of initials," see Thomas Pynchon, *Gravity's Rainbow* (New York: Viking, 1973).

52. John A. Wilson to William Langer, May 17, 1943: RG 226, Entry 145, Box 3, Folder 33: Director's Office. Division Chiefs to The Director of the Branch, September 17, 1943: RG 226, Entry 1, Box 1: Grudge File. Richard Hartshorne to William Langer, "Branch Morale," June 8, 1943: RG 226, Entry 1, Box 1: Classified, Misc. File. It might be noted that John A. Wilson should be distinguished from Langer's special assistant for overseas outposts, John D. Wilson, and that the Africanist W. Norman Brown is not the same person as the classicist Norman O. Brown. Moreover, the Central European Section included both Franz and Robert ("der Falsch") Neumann. Finally, the economist Edgar M. Hoover is no relation to FBI Director J. Edgar Hoover, who was *persona non grata* in OSS.

53. William J. Donovan, "Introduction" to Elizabeth P. MacDonald, *Undercover Girl* (New York: Macmillan, 1947), p. vii. This charming memoir offers, if not a feminist, at least a feminine perspective on the "Sub Rosy" [sic] activities of a member of the Morale Operations Branch in the Far East Theater.

54. William Applebaum to Crane Brinton and Allen Evans, March 3, 1944, "There are Times in the Affairs of Men . . .": RG 226, Entry 1, Box 17, Folder: London 1944.

55. Emile Despres to John Ross, October 27, 1944, "Secretarial Functions": RG 226, Entry 27, Box 2, Folder: Outpost Correspondence.

56. RG 226, Entry 99, Box 76, Folder 46: Washington R&A Branch Histories, p. 9. The concept of cultural inversion comes—by way of Natalie Zemon Davis—

from the anthropologist Victor Turner, *The Forest of Symbols* (Ithaca: Cornell University Press, 1967), chap. 4.

57. Langer to Donovan, Dec. 25, 1944, "Problems of *R&A* Outposts": RG 226, Entry 107, Box 7, File 486: Memos to Col. Donovan.

58. "Personnel Situation in R&A Branch," draft, n.d.: RG 226, Entry 145, Box 3, Folder 32: Personnel (for this and the following two quotations).

2. The Frankfurt School Goes to War

An earlier version of Chapter 2 appeared in the *Journal of Modern History,* vol. 59, no. 3 (September 1987). © 1987 by The University of Chicago. All rights reserved.

Epigraph: Ens. Carl E. Schorske to Harold Deutsch, Chief, R&A/Paris, October 26, 1944: RG 226, Entry 146, Box 83.

1. The fullest historical treatment of the Frankfurt Institut für Sozialforschung is still Martin Jay, *The Dialectical Imagination: A History of the Frankfurt School and the Institute of Social Research, 1923–1950* (Boston: Little, Brown, 1972). For perspectives on the individual careers of Neumann, Marcuse, and Kirchheimer, see, respectively, Rainer Erd, ed., *Reform und Resignation: Gespräche über Franz L. Neumann* (Frankfurt am Main: Suhrkamp, 1985); H. Stuart Hughes, "Franz Neumann between Marxism and Liberal Democracy," in *The Intellectual Migration,* ed. Donald Fleming and Bernard Bailyn (Cambridge: Harvard University Press, 1969), pp. 446–462; and Alfons Söllner, "Franz Neumann," *Telos* 50 (Winter 1981–82), pp. 171–79; Barry Katz, *Herbert Marcuse and the Art of Liberation: An Intellectual Biography* (London: New Left Books, 1982); John Herz and Erich Hula, "Otto Kirchheimer: An Introduction to His Life and Work," in *Politics, Law, and Social Change,* ed. F. Burin and K. Shell (New York: Columbia University Press, 1969), pp. ix-xxxviii.

2. Franz Neumann to Max Horkheimer, September 24, 1939, reprinted in Erd, *Reform und Resignation,* p. 133.

3. From Herbert Marcuse's "Preface" to Franz Neumann, *The Democratic and the Authoritarian State: Essays in Political and Legal Theory* (New York: Macmillan, 1957), p. vii.

4. Franz Neumann, "Der Funktionswandel des Gesetzes im Recht der Bürgerlichen Gesellschaft," *Zeitschrift für Sozialforschung* (Paris, 1937), vol. 6, p. 590. Also, "Types of Natural Law," *Studies in Philosophy and Social Science,* vol. 8, no. 3 (1940), both in Neumann, *The Democratic and the Authoritarian State.*

5. Otto Kirchheimer, "The Legal Order of National Socialism," *Studies in Philosophy and Social Science,* vol. 9 (1941), pp. 456–475, reprinted in Burin and Shell, eds. (n. 1, *supra*), p. 88. Compare also Kirchheimer's essay "Changes in the Structure of Political Compromise," in Burin and Shell, eds., pp. 264–289.

6. Otto Kirchheimer, "Criminal Law in National Socialist Germany," in *Studies in Philosophy and Social Science,* vol. 8 (1939), p. 463.

7. The relevant essays are collected in Herbert Marcuse, *Schriften,* vol. 3, *Aufsätze aus der Zeitschrift für Sozialforschung, 1934–1941* (Frankfurt-am-Main: Suhr-

kamp, 1979), and in *Negations: Essays in Critical Theory*, trans. Jeremy Shapiro (Boston: Beacon Press, 1968).

8. Herbert Marcuse, "Foreword" to *Negations*, pp. xi–xii.

9. "History of the Central European Section during the Incumbency of Eugene N. Anderson as Chief," memorandum of February 17, 1945: RG 226, Entry 37, Box 5. On the recruitment of the Institute for Social Research see RG 226, Entry 38, Box 3: Reading File, March 1943, especially letters from Sherman Kent, Chief of the Europe–Africa Subdivision, to the Immigration and Naturalization Service, March 10, 1943, and to Herbert Marcuse, March 10, 1943. Alice H. Maier, former secretary to the Institute, recalled her interview with FBI agents in a letter to the author of November 2, 1985. Kirchheimer's appointment was reported to David White, R&A/London: RG 226, Entry 146, Box 86, File 1335. Pollock and Gurland are included in a roster of "Personnel of the Research and Analysis Branch": RG 226, Entry 145, Box 4, Folder 43.

10. John Herz, *Vom Ueberleben: Wie ein Weltbild entstand: Autobiographie* (Düsseldorf: Droste Verlag, 1984), p. 136.

11. Papers of the Emergency Committee in Aid of Displaced Foreign Scholars: "Correspondence with Scholars Receiving Grants or Fellowships, 1933–1945," deposited in the Archives of the New York Public Library, New York. Compare also the memoir of Steven Duggan (Director of the Committee) and Betty Drury (its Executive Secretary), *The Rescue of Science and Learning* (New York: Macmillan, 1948), and Institute of Social Research, *Ten Years on Morningside Heights: A Report on the Institute's History, 1934–1944* (privately printed, December 1944), p. 6n.

12. Rainer Erd makes the unsupported conjecture that "Neumann entered the OSS not out of political conviction but out of financial need" (Erd, pp. 10–11).

13. Franz Neumann, *Behemoth: The Structure and Practice of National Socialism* (London and New York: Oxford University Press, 1942), from the Preface, dated December 23, 1941, p. x.

14. RG 226, Entry 99, Box 76, Folder 45: Washington, R&A Branch Histories, p. 76. The historian Harold Deutsch, Chief of the Political Subdivision to which the Central European Section belonged, reported that "it did not take me even a day to recognize that Franz Neumann was by far the most significant personality among its members": letter to the author, January 10, 1986.

15. Librarian of Congress Archibald MacLeish had been instrumental in the creation of the wartime intelligence service and provided the first home for the Research and Analysis Branch in the Library Annex. See Allan Winkler, *The Politics of Propaganda: The Office of War Information, 1942–1945* (New Haven: Yale University Press, 1978), esp. chap. 2.

16. Notation to Projects Committee Submission Form, January 18, 1944, approving Civil Affairs Guide no. 4A, "The Dissolution of the Nazi Party and Its Affiliated Organizations": "To be executed by Herbert Marcuse, assisted by Francis Williamson and Louis Wiesner" (Projects Committee, 1942–1946: RG 226, Box 1: Correspondence). For the controversies attending the clearance of this Guide, see RG 226, Entry 44, Box 3, Folder III.B. The wording of the final decree— M[ilitary] G[overnment] Law No. 5: Dissolution of the Nazi Party—is virtually

identical to that proposed in the R&A "Handbook for Military Government in Germany Prior to Defeat or Surrender," Supreme Headquarters, Allied Expeditionary Force, Office of the Chief of Staff, December 1944, published in *Documents on Germany Under Occupation, 1945–1954,* ed. Beate Ruhm von Oppen (London and New York: Oxford University Press, 1955), pp. 9–13.

17. *Marx-Engels Selected Works* (Moscow: Foreign Languages Publishing House, 1962), vol. 1, p. 118.

18. "History of the Central European Section during the Incumbency of Eugene N. Anderson as Chief," p. 1 (n. 11, *supra*). Anderson's remarks on the "democratic" organization of the Section may be compared with one of the Institute's privately printed internal histories (in which he is named as one of their American sponsors): "It has been a standard practice, since the Frankfort days, to meet regularly for discussion of the various problems arising out of separate branches of investigation. Every contribution by any member of the staff, has, prior to publication, had the advantage of frequent discussion and criticism by members representing different disciplines." Institute for Social Research, "Ten Years on Morningside Heights," p. 10 (n. 13, *supra*).

19. Alfons Söllner, the most thorough analyst of this episode to date, evaluates the discourse of intelligence in terms of "an anonymous, collective process, a constitutive principle that is 'prediscursive' ": *Zur Archäologie der Demokratie in Deutschland,* vol. 1, *Analysen von politischen Emigranten im amerikanischen Geheimdienst, 1943–1945* (Frankfurt: Fischer Verlag, 1986), p. 20. As brilliantly as this approach may illuminate the objective conditions of German refugee socialists in a secret intelligence service, it may be unnecessary to displace the authorial subject in quite so radical a fashion. The process by which individual reports were written, criticized, revised, and cleared can in many cases be ascertained by consulting a large body of supporting documentation, including the weekly minutes of the Projects Committee, which would authorize a proposed report, assign it an R&A number, and name the individual(s) who would supervise and execute it.

20. For example, *Behemoth,* p. 221: "We must specifically omit culture and education."

21. Ibid., "Note on the Name Behemoth."

22. Ibid., p. 470.

23. Letter from Carl E. Schorske to the author, January 15, 1986. The preceding fragments are from the "Draft of Proposed Guide to the Preparation of Political Reports": RG 226, Entry 1, Box 9, Folder: Projects Committee.

24. R&A 1130, "Changes in the Reich Government," August 26, 1943, p. 3: Herbert Marcuse [*Political Intelligence Report* no. 23 (R&A 1113.23), section I.A.1]. Also R&A 1194, "Speer's Appointment as Dictator of the German Economy," September 13, 1943, p. 10: Franz Neumann and Paul Sweezy [RG 226, Entry 60, Box 1: Projects Committee Correspondence, Central Europe File, September 10, 1943].

25. R&A 933, "German Morale after Tunisia," June 25, 1943, p. 1: Franz Neumann [*Political Intelligence Report* nos. 6–8 (R&A 1113.6–8), section I.A.1. Also Harold Deutsch to William Langer, May 14, 1943: RG 226, Entry 38, Box 5].

26. R&A 1214, "Morale in Germany," September 16, 1943: Herbert Marcuse, assisted by Franz Neumann and Hans Heyerhoff [*Political Intelligence Report* no. 26 (R&A 1113..26), section III.D.4].

27. R&A 933, p. 1.

28. Herbert Marcuse, "Successful Experiments with Joint Employment of Tubercular and Non-tubercular Workers," October 5–11, 1943: R&A 1113.29, *Political Intelligence Report* no. 29, section II.C.5. Franz Neumann, "The Standardized Coffin," week ending May 1, 1943: R&A 1113.4, *Political Intelligence Report* no. 4, section 6.

29. R&A 1034, "Possible Changes in Nazi Germany in the Near Future," August 10, 1943: Herbert Marcuse, assisted by Eugene Drucker [*Political Intelligence Report* no. 21 (R&A 1113.21), section I.1].

30. R&A 1281, "The Significance of Prussian Militarism for Nazi Imperialism: Potential Tensions in U.N. Psychological Warfare," October 20, 1943: Herbert Marcuse and Felix Gilbert [RG 226, Entry 59, Box 1: Projects Committee, Minutes of Meetings, September 24, 1943].

31. R&A 1313.2–9, "War Profiteers," October 2–November 13, 1943: Franz Neumann [*Political Intelligence Report* no. 28 (R&A 1113.28), section II.B.6].

32. R&A 992, "The Underground Movement in Germany," September 27, 1943, p. 26.

33. R&A 1043, "German Situation in 1918 and 1943," August 13, 1943, p. 6. Also Franz Neumann and Sinclair Armstrong, "United Nations Propaganda," July 13–19, 1943, R&A 1113.17, *Political Intelligence Report* no. 17, section II.1.

34. R&A 1043, p. 6.

35. R&A 1033, "The 'Free Germany' Manifesto and the German People," August 6, 1943, p. 21: Franz Neumann [Sherman Kent to Eugene Anderson, August 10, 1943: RG 226, Entry 37, Box 2: Correspondence of Division Chief, Central Europe Folder].

36. R&A 992, "The Underground Movement in Germany," September 27, 1943.

37. R&A 1033, p. 21.

38. R&A 2387, "The Attempt on Hitler's Life and Its Consequences," July 27, 1944, p. 2: Franz Neumann [interview with Paul Zinner, San Francisco, June 17, 1985]. See also R&A 2383, "Effects of the Attempted *Coup d'état* on the Stability of the German Regime," July 28, 1944, the version that was most likely the one transmitted to the White House. There are additional materials in the "Breakers" File, Entry 1: Office of the Chief, General Correspondence.

39. Franz Neumann to Conyers Read, "Remarks to the Memorandum Prepared by Professor James K. Pollock for the Joint Chiefs of Staff, May 10, 1943, p. 3: RG 226, Entry 1, Box 1, Folder: Joint Chiefs of Staff.

40. R&A 1477, "The Process of German Collapse," December 4, 1943, p. 7: Franz Neumann, Herbert Marcuse, Felix Gilbert [*Political Intelligence Report* no. 34 (R&A 1113.34), section I.2].

41. Handwritten annotation to R&A 1547, "German Social Stratification," November 26, 1943: Herbert Marcuse [RG 226, Entry 60, Box 1: Projects Committee Correspondence, Central Europe File, December 8, 1943.

42. R&A 1549, "The Social Democratic Party of Germany," September 1, 1945:

Herbert Marcuse [RG 226, Entry 1, Box 3: Correspondence of the Division Chief, Europe–Africa Division File, Hartshorne memorandum to William Langer, July 23, 1945].

43. Letter from John Herz to the author, February 3, 1984.

44. "History of the Central European Section during the Incumbency of Eugene N. Anderson as Chief" (n. 11, *supra*), p. 3. Compare also the correspondence of General J. W. Hilldring, Director of the Civil Affairs Division of the War Department, to General Donovan, January 9, 1944: RG 226, Entry 37, Box 2: Correspondence of the Division Chiief, Civil Affairs folder: Miscellaneous Correspondence. On Holborn's role, see *Hajo Holborn: Inter-Nationes Prize*, n.a. (Bonn and Bad Godesberg: Inter-Nationes, 1969), pp. 12–13, 161–65. The standard treatment of American planning is Lutz Niethammer, *Entnazifizierung in Bayern* (Frankfurt-am-Main: S. Fischer, 1972); rev. ed., *Die Mitläuferfabrik: Die Entnazifizierung am Beispiel Bayerns* (Bonn and Berlin: Dietz, 1982), esp. pp. 31–68.

45. R&A 2500.1–2500.23, "German Military Government over Europe, 1939–1943: Methods and Organization of Nazi Controls"; R&A 1323, *Civil Affairs Handbook for Germany*.

46. "Draft of Proposed Guide to Preparation of Political Reports" (n. 25, *supra*), p. 1a.

47. R&A 2500.22, "German Military Government over Europe: The SS and Police in Occupied Europe," January 1, 1945, p. 23.

48. "Information on the Preparation of Civil Affairs Guides": RG 226, Entry 37, Box 6: Europe–Africa Division, Correspondence of the Division Chief.

49. R&A 1655.15/War Department Pamphlet 31–171, *Civil Affairs Guide:* "Adaptation of Administrative Machinery on the *Local* Level in Germany," July 22, 1944, p. 3: Otto Kirchheimer and John Herz, with G. Stewart [RG 226, Entry 60, Box 1: Projects Committee Correspondence, Central Europe File, January 18, 1944].

50. R&A 1655.14/War Department Pamphlet 31-114, *Civil Affairs Guide:* "Adaptation of Administrative Machinery on the *Regional* Level in Germany," July 22, 1944, p. 3: Otto Kirchheimer [Kirchheimer to Dean Staudinger, New School for Social Research, documenting his case for a merit increase, January 2, 1956; Kirchheimer papers, folders 2, 17, SUNY Albany].

51. R&A 1655.1/War Department Pamphlet 31-116. *Civil Affairs Guide:* "Policy toward the Revival of Old Parties and the Establishment of New Parties in Germany," July 22, 1944, p. 13: Herbert Marcuse [RG 226, Entry 60, Box 1: Projects Committee Correspondence, Central Europe File, December 10, 1943].

52. R&A 1655.2/War Department Pamphlet 31-107, *Civil Affairs Guide:* "Police and Public Safety in Germany," July 22, 1944: Franz Neumann [RG 226, Entry 60, Box 1: Projects Committee Correspondence, Central Europe File].

53. R&A 2189, "Some Criteria for the Identification of Anti-Nazis in Germany," November 15, 1944, p. 1.

54. R&A 1655.5a, *Civil Affairs Guide:* "Dissolution of the Nazi Party and Its Affiliated Organizations. Supplement: Denazification of Important Business Con-

cerns in Germany," November 27, 1944: Herbert Marcuse, assisted by Francis Williamson and Louis Wiesner [RG 226, Entry 60, Box 1: Projects Committee Correspondence, Central Europe File, September 10, 1943].

55. R&A 1655.14, p. 9.
56. R&A 1655.22/War Department Pamphlet 31–159, *Civil Affairs Guide:* "Labor Relations and Military Government," July 22, 1944, p. 7: Franz Neumann [RG 226, Entry 60, Box 1: Projects Committee Correspondence, Central Europe File, January 18, 1944, and January 29, 1944].
57. R&A 1655.1, pp. 7–8. Also Marcuse's report on "The German Communist Party," R&A 1550, July 10, 1944, pp. 62–63: "The program for the transitional period does not endanger the vested interests of any group except the Nazis and war criminals. It is based on the assumption, which has been expressed by Communist writers, that after the war the German people will not accept extremist political solutions such as the party advocated before 1933." The historian Walter Dorn of the Central European Section had already determined that even among the political exiles, "the German Communist Party is the only *émigré* party that must be taken seriously": R&A 1568, "The German Political Emigration," December 3, 1943, p. iv [R&A 992, p. 5n].
58. John Herz, "The Fiasco of Denazification in Germany," *Political Science Quarterly,* vol. 63, no. 4 (December 1948), pp. 569–594. Compare also the related article by Kirchheimer's friend Richard Schmid, a high official in the Justice administration in Stuttgart: "Denazification: A German Critique," in *American Perspective,* vol. 2, no. 5 (October 1948), pp. 231–242.
59. Neumann to Sherman Kent, April 14, 1944: RG 226, Entry 44, Box 7, "Civil Affairs Guides, Germany" Folder VIII.E.
60. Richard Hartshorne to Division and Subdivision Chiefs, n.d., "Draft of Proposed Guide to Preparation of Political Reports": RG 226, Entry 37, Box 5: Correspondence of Division Chief. Also Preston E. James to William L. Langer, March 3, 1944, "Observations on the Use of Social Scientists in R&A," and "The Problem of Objectivity in R&A Reporting," and related materials: RG 226, Entry 1, Box 9: Projects Committee Folder.
61. [Franz Neumann], "The Treatment of Germany," n.d., Gordon Stewart's "Comments on Franz's draft," October 18, 1944, and "[Felix] Gilbert's Comment on the Stewart Comment," n.d.: RG 226, Entry 37, Box 1: Europe–Africa Division, Correspondence of the Division Chief, 1942–1945; Folder: The Treatment of Germany. Subsequent drafts bore the title "How to Weaken Germany."
62. "The Treatment of Germany," p. 3.
63. Neumann to members of the Central European Section, May 3, 1945, "Plan for the Reorganization of the German and Austrian Units": RG 226, Entry 37, Box 2, Folder: Central European Section. Neumann to George Demos, "Members of the Central European Section Participating in Research on War Crimes," June 13, 1945: RG 226, Entry 37, Box 6, Folder: War Crimes Program. Neumann's determined efforts to gain for his group a hearing can be traced in his dispatches from Europe during the summer: RG 226, Entry 37, Box 6, "War Crimes Project" Folder, August 3, 1945; RG 226, Entry 1, Box 1, "Joint Chiefs of Staff" Folder, September 1, 1945. On the controversy between Donovan

and Jackson, see Bradley F. Smith, *Reaching Judgment at Nuremburg* (New York: Basic Books, 1977), pp. 270–272. This reading has been nuanced by letters to the author from Carl E. Schorske, January 15, 1986, and Telford Taylor, January 16, 1986.

64. R&A 1482, "The 'Statement on Atrocities' of the Moscow Tripartite Conference," December 10, 1943: Kirchheimer and John Herz [R&A 1113.33, *Political Intelligence Report* no. 33, section 1.3].

65. From R&A 2577.2, "Problems Concerning the Treatment of War Criminals: List of Potential War Criminals under Proposed U.S. Policy Directives," September 30, 1944. The "proposed policy directives" were developed in R&A 2577 and 2577.1.

66. Franz Neumann to Phoebe Morrison, "Comments on the Draft Memorandum on War Criminals," March 8, 1945, p. 2: RG 226, Entry 37, Box 6, Folder: War Crimes Program.

67. R&A 3110, "Leadership Principle and Criminal Responsibility," July 18, 1945, p. 14.

68. Ibid., p. 17.

69. Reported in the Monthly Progress Reports of the Europe–Africa Division: RG 226, Entry 42, Box 1, Folder: January –June, 1945.

70. R&A 3114.2, "Nazi Plans for Dominating Germany and Europe: Domestic Crimes," Draft for War Crimes Staff, August 13, 1945, p. 21: Otto Kirchheimer [Neumann to George Demos, June 13, 1945: RG 226, Entry 37, Box 6, Folder: War Crimes Program]. Further documenation is provided in Kirchheimer's "Nazi Changes in Criminal Procedure," R&A 3081, July 10, 1945 [Kirchheimer to Dean Staudinger, New School for Social Research, Januazy 2, 1956: German Émigré Collection, SUNY Albany]. Kirchheimer would dispose of these and related problems in *Political Justice: The Use of Legal Procedure for Political Ends* (Princeton: Princeton University Press, 1961), in the sections dealing with "Trial by Fiat of the Successor Regime," pp. 323–338.

71. R&A 3114.3, "Nazi Plans for Dominating Germany and Europe: The Criminal Conspiracy against the Jews," Draft for War Crimes Staff, August 13, 1945: Irving Dwork [Neumann to Demos, June 13, 1945].

72. Franz Neumann, "Anti-Semitism," May 18–24, 1943, R&A 1113.9, *Political Intelligence Weekly* no. 9, section 11.1.

73. *"Outline of R&A 3114: Nazi Plans to Dominate Europe,"* June 12, 1945, p. 17: Herbert Marcuse, supervisor [Neumann to Demos, June 13, 1945].

74. "Current Status of Anti-Semitism in Germany," n.d.: RG 226, Entry 146, Box 84, Folder 98: Neumann, Franz. *Behemoth*, p. 121. In the second edition, published in 1944 (by which time the physical extermination of the Jews had begun), Neumann wrote that in Nazi ideology and practice, "the extermination of the Jews is only [*sic*] the means to the attainment of the ultimate objective, namely the destruction of free institutions, beliefs, and groups" (London and New York: Oxford University Press), p. 551.

75. H. Stuart Hughes, "The Second Year of the Cold War," *Commentary,* vol. 48, no. 2 (August 1969), p. 27. For materials pertaining to Executive Order 9620, "Termination of the Office of Strategic Services and Disposition of Its Func-

tions," September 20, 1945, see RG 226, Entry 1, Correspondence of the Chief. I have described Marcuse's postwar years in the State Department in *Herbert Marcuse and the Art of Liberation,* pp. 130–145.

76. H. Stuart Hughes, "Franz Neumann between Marxism and Liberal Democracy" (n. 1, *supra*).

77. Franz Neumann: "Military Government and the Revival of Democracy in Germany," *Columbia Journal of International Affairs,* vol. 2, no. 1 (Winter 1948), p. 10; "Re-Educating the Germans," *Commentary,* vol. 3, no. 6 (June 1947), pp. 517–525; "Soviet Policy in Germany," *Annals of the American Academy of Political and Social Science,* vol. 263 (May 1949), pp. 165–179; "War Crimes Trials," *World Politics,* vol. 2, no. 1 (October 1949), pp. 135–147; and *German Democracy 1950* (New York: Carnegie Foundation for International Peace, 1950).

78. Franz Neumann, "Intellektuelle und politische Freiheit," speech delivered in Bonn, July 1954, trans. Peter Gay; "Notes on the Theory of Dictatorship," ed. Julian Franklin (unfinished, 1954); "Angst und Politik," lecture, Free University of Berlin, trans. Peter Gay; all in *The Democratic and the Authoritarian State.*

79. Otto Kirchheimer to Felix Gilbert and John Herz, August 29, 1945: RG 226, Entry 81, Box 3: Correspondence of OSS Mission to Germany.

80. Otto Kirchheimer, February 14, 1947: RG 59 (General Records of the Department of State), Box 6547, decimal file, FW862.4016/2-1447.

81. Kirchheimer, *Political Justice* (n. 72, *supra*), p. 341.

82. Herbert Marcuse, *One-Dimensional Man: Studies in the Ideology of Advanced Industrial Society* (Boston: Beacon Press, 1964), p. 3.

83. Herbert Marcuse, "Repressive Tolerance" (1965), in Robert Paul Wolff, Barrington Moore, Jr., and Herbert Marcuse, *A Critique of Pure Tolerance* (Boston: Beacon Press, 1969), p. 88.

84. Max Horkheimer, "Traditionelle und kritische Theorie," in *Zeitschrift für Sozialforschung,* vol. 6, no. 2 (1937), trans. Matthew O'Connell et al., in *Critical Theory* (New York: Herder and Herder, 1974), p. 214.

85. Theodor W. Adorno, *Minima Moralia: Reflections from Damaged Life* (1951), trans. E. F. N. Jephcott (London: New Left Books, 1974), p. 18; compare also his aphorisms #13 and #25.

86. The history of this criticism begins with Georg Lukács, who saw them idly reposing in the "Grand Hotel Abyss": Georg Lukács, "Preface" (1962) to *The Theory of the Novel,* trans. Anna Bostock (Cambridge: MIT Press, 1971), p. 22. It is taken up by Phil Slater, *The Frankfurt School: A Marxist Approach* (London: Routledge and Kegan Paul, 1977), who charges them with fostering a "break in the theory-praxis nexus," and argued again by Jürgen Habermas in *The Theory of Communicative Action,* vol. 1: *Reason and the Rationalization of Society,* trans. Thomas McCarthy (Boston: Beacon Press, 1984), pp. 383–386. Russell Jacoby offers a very qualified defense in *Dialectic of Defeat: Contours of Western Marxism* (Cambridge: Cambridge University Press, 1981).

87. "Marcuse: Cop-Out or Cop?" in *Progressive Labor,* vol. 6, no. 6 (February 1969), pp. 61–66. Kirchheimer's difficulties were described to me in an interview with Mrs. Anne Kirchheimer in Silver Springs, Maryland, October 5, 1985.

88. "History of the Research and Analysis Branch in the Office of Strategic Services, June 1941–September 1944": RG 226, Entry 99, Box 76, Folder 45, p. 76.

3. Historians Making History

Epigraph: Friedrich Meinecke, *Die deutsche Katastrophe* (1946), in *Werke,* Band 8: *Autobiographische Schriften* (Stuttgart, 1969); trans. Sidney Fay, *The German Catastrophe* (Boston: Beacon Press, 1963).

1. For the critical reception, see Robert A. Pois, *Friedrich Meinecke and German Politics in the Twentieth Century,* (Berkeley: University of California Press, 1972), pp. 148–151.

2. On the careers of Hajo Holborn and Felix Gilbert, see, respectively: the special issue of *Central European History,* "In Memory of Hajo Holborn, 1902–1969," vol. 3 nos. 1/2 (March–June 1970), and *Hajo Holborn: Inter-Nationes Prize, 1969* (Bonn and Bad Godesberg: Inter-Nationes, 1969), both of which contain bibliographies. Also Leonard Krieger and Fritz Stern, eds., *The Responsibility of Power: Essays in Honor of Hajo Holborn* (Garden City, N.Y.: Doubleday, 1969). A bibliography of Gilbert's writings, to 1976, is appended to his collection, *History: Choice and Commitment* (Cambridge: Harvard University Press, 1977), with a fine biographical essay by Franklin Ford.

3. On the forty-year friendship of the two Meinecke students, see Felix Gilbert, "Hajo Holborn: A Memoir," *Central European History,* vol. 3, no. 1/2 (March–June 1970), pp. 3–8; also Gilbert's recently published autobiography, *The European Past: Memoirs, 1905–1945* (New York: W. W. Norton, 1988), p. 50.

4. Friedrich Meinecke to Hajo Holborn (December 6, 1934), in Meinecke, *Werke,* Band 6, *Ausgewählter Briefwechsel* (Stuttgart, 1962), p. 143–44.

5. Letter to the author from Henry Cord Meyer, September 18, 1985. Gilbert's splendid but neglected essay, *To the Farewell Address* (Princeton: Princeton University Press, 1961), had its origins in a seminar organized by Edward M. Earle at the Institute for Advanced Study in 1939–40.

6. The literature on the post-Rankean tradition of German historiography is as large as is the number of historians indebted to it; the best guide in English is George Iggers, *The German Conception of History: The National Tradition of Historical Thought from Herder to the Present* (Middletown, Conn.: Wesleyan University Press, 1968). Felix Gilbert is himself among the most acute interpreters of the history of historiography, especially the manner in which it took place in the German universities: see especially his essays, "European and American Historiography" in John Higham et al., *History: The Development of Historical Studies in the United States* (Englewood Cliffs, N.J.: Prentice Hall, 1965); "Intellectual History: Its Aims and Methods" in *Daedalus,* vol. 100, no. 1 (Winter 1971), pp. 80–97; *Choice and Commitment,* pt. 1: "Teachers of History at the University of Berlin." Many of Hajo Holborn's best essays on historiography have been collected in the volume, *History and the Humanities* (Garden City, N.J.: Doubleday, 1972), but compare also his famous analysis of "German Idealism in the Light of Social History," trans. Robert Herzstein, in

the companion volume, *Germany and Europe: Historical Essays* (Garden City, N.J.: Doubleday, 1971), pp. 1–31.

7. Sherman Kent to Felix Gilbert, March 4, 1943: RG 226, Entry 38, Box 3: Reading File, March 1943.

8. Felix Gilbert, "Political Power and Academic Responsibility: Reflections on Friedrich Meinecke's 'Drei Generationen Deutscher Gelehrtenpolitik,' " in Krieger and Stern, eds., *The Responsibility of Power*, pp. 447–448.

9. Interview with David Pinkney, San Francisco, March 29, 1985.

10. The political reports produced by this team included: R&A 1011, "The Present Situation in Hungary," November 27, 1943; R&A 1386, "The Underground Movement in Hungary," October 22, 1943; R&A 1387, "The Means of Influencing Public Opinion in Hungary," November 27, 1943; R&A 1388, "Who's Who in Hungary from the Standpoint of United Nations P. W. Operations," November 27, 1943. Tihany was a well-known expert in Hungarian affairs; von Neumann came from a distinguished academic family whose most famous member was his brother, the mathematician John von Neumann. Professors Paul Zinner and Gordon Craig described their early experiences in R&A in discussion with the author in San Francisco, June 17, 1985, and Palo Alto, April 9, 1985, respectively.

11. Letters from Harold Deutsch, January 10, 1986, and Felix Gilbert, January 10, 1986, to the author. Information contained in the letters and personal communications with Felix Gilbert cited in these notes was offered in response to specific questions posed to him by the author; interpretations are mine and not necessarily those of Gilbert himself.

12. Hajo Holborn to Conyers Read, "Observations on J. K. Pollock's memorandum," May 9, 1943: RG 226, Entry 1, Box 1: Joint Chiefs of Staff folder.

13. R&A 1477, "The Process of German Collapse," December 4, 1943, p. 2: Felix Gilbert, Herbert Marcuse, and Franz Neumann [R&A 1113.34, November 13, 1943].

14. R&A 1483, "Possible Patterns of German Collapse," September 21, 1943, p. 9: Felix Gilbert, Herbert Marcuse, and Franz Neumann [R&A 1113.34 November 13, 1943].

15. Felix Gilbert to the author, January 10, 1986.

16. R&A 1477, "The Process of German Collapse," pp. 4–5: Felix Gilbert et al.

17. Ibid., p. 6.

18. Major General J. W. Hilldring, Director Civil Affairs Division, to General William J. Donovan, OSS, January 9, 1944: RG 226, Entry 37, Box 2: Miscellaneous Correspondence.

19. Holborn to Hilldring, August 18, 1943, and minutes of "Conference at Civil Affairs Division, Pentagon Building, September 1, 1943": RG 226, Entry 145, Box 4, Folder 41: R&A Director's Office, Civil Affairs Division.

20. Hajo Holborn, *American Military Government: Its Organization and Policies* (Washington: Infantry Journal Press, 1947). We derive his views from *The Political Collapse of Europe* (New York: Alfred A. Knopf, 1951, 1966), pp. 168–175.

21. Sherman Kent, in his militaristic memorandum, "Tactical Lessons of the German

Guide Campaign": RG 226, Entry 37, Box 2, Folder: Central European Section.

22. "History of the Economic Subdivision": RG 226, Entry 99, Box 76, Folder 45, pp. 97–98, and Emile Despres to Chandler Morse, June 6, 1944: RG 226, Entry 146, Box 83, File 312.1. The more favorable appraisal of Holborn's trials and tribulations is found in the sections of the former document dealing with R&A's work for the Civil Affairs Division, ibid., pp. 34–35.

23. For the controversy (a) with the FEA: RG 226, Entry 99, Box 76, Folder: "Branch Histories, Europe–Africa Division," pp. 99–100; (b) with the State Department, the unrevised "Notes on Minutes of January 16, 1945": RG 226, Entry 37, Box 2, Folder: Central Europe; (c) with the War Department School of Military Government in Charlottesville, Va.: RG 226, Entry 44, Box 3, Folder: "Civil Affairs Guides: Germany, III.B."

24. Penciled minutes of "Saturday meeting" to Sherman Kent from "C[arl E. Schorske]": RG 226, Entry 37, Box 2, Folder: Central European Section.

25. "Purposes of the Civil Affairs Handbooks," Introduction to Army Service Forces Manual M356, *Civil Affairs Handbook: Germany.*

26. Draft of *Civil Affairs Handbook: Germany,* section 1A: "Background of the Nazi Regime" (will become R&A 1323.1A and Army Service Forces Manual M356-1A): Felix Gilbert. References are to Gilbert's unedited draft, RG 389 (Records of the Office of the Provost Marshal General, 1941–), Entry 443, Box 842, Folder 461: Germany *Mss.*, p. 2 [correspondence with Felix Gilbert, October 25, 1985].

27. Holborn to Chandler Morse, September 4, 1944: RG 226, Entry 146, Box 82, Folder 312.1/1202: Holborn, Hajo.

28. Ibid., p. 18 (deleted from the versions finally published as R&A 1323.1A and ASFM M356-1A).

29. Harold Zink, *American Military Government in Germany* (New York: Macmillan, 1947), p. 18.

30. Colin Eisler's informative essay, "Kunstgeschichte American Style: A Study in Migration," plots the American careers of Krautheimer, Panofsky, Friedländer, Tietze, and other European émigré art historians against the modern contours of their field: Donald Fleming and Bernard Bailyn, eds., *The Intellectual Migration: Europe and America, 1930–1960* (Cambridge: Harvard University Press, 1969), pp. 544–629. Almost alone among his humanist colleagues, Krautheimer experienced the R&A episode more as an interruption than a stage in the development of his career. Apart from advising the U.S. Air Force on historical monuments of Rome to be protected from bombing—and his postwar work on the restoration of the damaged basilica of S. Lorenzo fuori le Mura—Krautheimer's art historical scholarship contributed relatively little to his work for OSS and would be largely unaffected by it.

31. R&A 1655.20 (War Department Pamphlet 31-118), *Civil Affairs Guide:* "German Elementary Schools," July 22, 1944, p. 16; Felix Gilbert and Richard Krautheimer [RG 226, Entry 60, Box 1: Projects Committee Correspondence, Central Europe, January 18, 1944].

32. R&A 1655.21 (War Department Pamphlet 31-119), *Civil Affairs Guide:* "German Higher Education and Adult Education," July 22, 1944, p. 10: Felix Gilbert

and Richard Krautheimer [RG 226, Entry 60, Box 1: Projects Committee Correspondence, Central Europe, January 18, 1944].

33. Ibid., p. 20.
34. Felix Gilbert, "Hajo Holborn: A Memoir" in *Central European History,* vol. 3, nos. 1/2 (March–June 1970), p. 3.
35. Felix Gilbert, "Introduction" to *The Historical Essays of Otto Hintze* (New York: Oxford University Press, 1975), pp. 26–28.
36. Hajo Holborn to Chandler Morse, August 18, 1944: RG 226, Entry 146, Box 82, Folder 213.1/1202. Compare also the minutes of the meetings of July 31, 1944, September 1, 1944, and September 22, 1944: RG 226, Entry 37, Box 2, Folder: "Civil Affairs—Research and Analysis Civil Affairs Committee." Members of this group were R&A Chief William Langer, Division Chiefs Edward Mason and Sherman Kent, and others, including Emile Despres, Donald McKay, Conyers Read, Preston James, Rudolph Winnacker, Richard Hartshorne, Geroid Robinson, and Carl Schorske.
37. Hajo Holborn, "American Planning of the Military Government of Germany During World War II," March 1967, published in his collection, *Germany and Europe,* p. 253.
38. The episode is the subject of a large documentary and secondary literature; for the R&A perspective, see RG 226, Entry 99, Box 76, Folder 45, pp. 96–104. Sparse details of Holborn's work on the Far Eastern Theater are contained in his report to William Langer, "Civil Affairs Staging Area, Fort Ord, California," November 6, 1944: RG 226, Entry 1, Box 14.
39. On Holborn: Crane Brinton to General Donovan, February 10, 1944: RG 226, Entry 1, Box 21 (ETO), Brinton File. On concerns over the flow of personnel from Washington to London: Carl Schorske to Harold Deutsch, January 4, 1944: RG 226, Entry 1, Box 21, Brinton File.
40. Correspondence with Felix Gilbert, February 27, 1985.
41. Crane Brinton to William Langer, January 22, 1944: RG 226, Entry 1, Box 17, London File (2).
42. William L. Langer to David E. K. Bruce (Chief of OSS/London), January 20, 1944: RG 226, Entry 1, Box 17, p. 1; see also Allen Evans' draft outline of the "four stages" through which R&A/London passed, June 19, 1944: RG 226, Entry 1, Box 21, Chandler Morse File.
43. Gilbert to Hajo Holborn et al., November 28, 1944: RG 226, Entry 73, Box 1, Folder: Central Europe, September to February 1945, Washington and London R&A Correspondence no. 1.
44. Gilbert and Hans Meyerhoff to William Langer, June 1, 1944: Central European Section, London: RG 226, Entry 146, Box 82, Folder 312.1/1186.
45. Gilbert, *The European Past: Memoirs, 1905–1945* (n. 3, *supra*), pp. 88–89.
46. Niccoló Machiavelli, *Il Principe,* chap. 8, my translation.
47. Joseph E. Persico, *Piercing the Reich* (New York: Ballantine, 1979).
48. Crane Brinton, August 29, 1944: RG 226, Entry 1, Box 18, Folder: London (2).
49. Saul K. Padover to Chandler Morse, Harold Deutsch, et al., "Report of Activities," September 11, 1944: RG 226, Entry 81, Box 18, Folder 2.

50. Lorenz Eitner to Felix Gilbert, "Cultural Department," December 22, 1944: RG 226, Entry 81, Box 2.

51. Gilbert to Franz Neumann, June 12, 1945: RG 226, Entry 1, Box 3.

52. Ibid.

53. Executive Office to General Donovan, March 31, 1945: RG 226, Entry 99, Box 106.

54. For details, RG 226, Entry 99, Box 7, Folder 25: ETO Germany. Headquarters were actually in Biebrich, a suburb south of and adjoining Wiesbaden. From Berlin Allen Dulles acted as head of the entire OSS Mission to Germany, which was itself responsible to Lucius Clay, Deputy Commanding General, U.S. Forces of Occupation.

55. Chandler Morse's notes on meeting of June 25–28: RG 226, Entry 81, Box 1, Correspondence of OSS Mission to Germany, 1944–45.

56. Gilbert to Franz Neumann, June 12, 1945: RG 226, Entry 81, Box 3 (emphasis added).

57. On Thyssen, Schlacht, and Niemöller: RG 226, Entry 81, Box 2, request of June 25, 1945. On the archives of the Foreign Office: RG 226, Entry 81, Box 1, Karl Deutsch to William Langer, June 28, 1945. On German diplomats: RG 226, Entry 99, Box 7, Folder 26: Progress Report, August 1–31, 1945. Compare also his recollections in *The European Past,* p. 216.

58. *Field Intelligence Study* no. 41, "The Liberal Universities of Baden, Part II: Heidelberg," November 13, 1945, p. 30: Felix Gilbert and Leonard Krieger [RG 226, Entry 99, Box 7, Folder 23].

59. *FIS* no. 21, "The Liberal Universities of Baden, Part I: Frieburg," supplemented by letter to the author, February 27, 1985, and Gilbert's revealing sketch of the Heidegger affair in *The European Past,* p. 207.

60. *FIS* no. 41, pp. 8, 20.

61. Ibid., p. 30.

62. Franklin Ford to Hans Meyerhoff, August 7, 1945: RG 226, Entry 81, Box 2: Correspondence of OSS Mission to Germany, 1944–45. On the recurrent theme of R&A's perceived partiality toward the German SPD, see also Stuart Hughes to Karl Deutsch and Chandler Morse, "Work Program of R&A to 15 August, 1945," July 5, 1945: RG 226, Entry 81, Box 2.

63. *FIS* no. 40, "The National Position of the Social Democratic Party," November 10, 1945, pp. 10, 7: Felix Gilbert and Leonard Krieger [correspondence with Felix Gilbert, September 18, 1985]; also their related *FIS* no. 37, "The National Conference of Social Democratic Leaders," November 3, 1945. It seems somehow odd that the SPD leaders did not remark upon the exceptionally fluent and idiomatic German spoken by this American intelligence officer.

64. *FIS* no. 44, "Current Policies of the Berlin Social Democrats," December 18, 1945, p. 8: Felix Gilbert and Franklin Ford [RG 226, Entry 99, Box 7, Folder 23: ETO Germany, Progress Reports 1–30, September 1945]; also their related *FIS* no. 33, "Observations on the Berlin Political Scene in October 1945," October 19, 1945.

65. Hajo Holborn to Conyers Read, "Observations on J. K. Pollock's Memorandum," May 9, 1943, p. 1: RG 226, Entry 1, Box 1, Joint Chiefs of Staff Folder.

66. Letter from Felix Gilbert to the author, February 27, 1945. Meinecke in turn wrote to Holborn that he had received "viel, viel zustimmende Briefe" in response to his book, and, perhaps referring to Holborn's silence, expressed his hope that a copy (already in its third edition), would reach him shortly: to Holborn, December 1, 1946, in Meinecke's *Ausgewählter Briefwechsel* (n. 4, *supra*), pp. 262–263.

67. These are, of course, the titles of two of their important postwar books: Hajo Holborn, *The Political Collapse of Europe,* and Felix Gilbert, *The End of the European Era* (New York: Norton, 1970).

68. Felix Gilbert, "Intellectual History: Its aims and Methods," *Daedalus,* vol. 100, no. 1 (Winter 1971), p. 80.

69. Letter from Franklin Ford to the author, March 21, 1985.

70. Gordon Craig and Felix Gilbert, eds., *The Diplomats* (Princeton: Princeton University Press, 1953). Fritz Stern's comment in *Dreams and Delusions: The Drama of German History* (New York: Alfred A. Knopf, 1987) was occasioned by the number of R&A alumni represented in the volume, in addition to Felix Gilbert and Hajo Holborn: Gordon Craig, Franklin Ford, H. Stuart Hughes, Henry Roberts, Carl Schorske, and Paul Zinner. *The Diplomats* may almost be thought of as closing the bracket on the R&A episode that was opened with the publication in 1943 of the famous *Makers of Modern Strategy,* edited by Edward Earle with the collaboration of Gordon Craig and Felix Gilbert (Princeton: Princeton University Press, 1943).

71. Friedrich Meinecke, "Ranke und Burckhardt" (address to the German Academy of Sciences, Berlin, 1948), in *Werke,* Band VI, *Zur Geschichte der Geschichtsschreibung* (Munich, 1968), pp. 93–110; from the abridged translation in Hans Kohn, ed., *German History: Some New German Views* (London: Allen & Unwin, 1954), p. 143.

72. Felix Gilbert, "Jacob Burckhardt's Student Years: The Road to Cultural History," *Journal of the History of Ideas,* vol. 57, no. 2 (April–June 1986), p. 253. The point is also stressed by Holborn in his fragment, "Jacob Burckhardt as Historical Thinker," published in the colllection *History and the Humanities.*

73. Leopold von Ranke, "Idee der Universalhistorie," quoted in Leonard Krieger, *Ranke: The Meaning of History* (Chicago: University of Chicago Press, 1977), p. 20. The author—also an R&A alumnus—argues that "the original Ranke was more complicated than the symbol he became."

74. Hajo Holborn, "Irrwege in unserer Geschichte?" in *Der Monat,* 2 Jahrgang, n. 17 (February 1950); the complete passage reads: "Meinecke is too much the historical realist to have understood this opposition as absolute. In his *Weltbürgertum und Nationalstaat* he felt he could still overcome the contradiction between German cultural and political values. In his *Idee der Staatsräson* written after the First World War, he threw the tension into bold relief, whereas in his most recent article, cultural values stand far above political values, but in such a way that a certain sympathy still shines over political events." Translated in part as "Misfortunes and Moral Decisions in German History" in Kohn, *German History,* p. 211, and in *History and the Humanities.* Compare Holborn"s gentle rebuke with the important essay with which Gilbert chose to honor his friend

and fellow scholar on the latter's sixtieth birthday: "Political Power and Academic Responsibility: Reflections on Friedrich Meinecke's 'Drei Generationen Deutscher Gelehrtenpolitik' " (n. 8, *supra*).

75. Meinecke, "Ranke und Burckhardt," p. 155. Further on, the 86-year-old Meinecke speaks of having lived through "the sunless side of world history," of Burckhardt's "Cassandra eyes," and of his "vision of the future, aware of its own blindness and yet with a quiet hope." In view of his own near total blindness, the visual imagery that pervades this brilliant address must have had a shattering effect on its audience.

76. Interview with Felix Gilbert, Palo Alto, February 14, 1985.

77. Friedrich Meinecke, *The German Catastrophe*, p. 120.

4. The Political Economy of Intelligence

Epigraph: Walt W. Rostow, *War Diary of the R&A Branch, OSS, London, England,* vol. 5, p. 4.

1. Commentary on economists in government begins with the AEA Presidential address by Irving Fisher, "Economists in Public Service," *American Economic Review,* vol. 9 (March 1919, Supplement), pp. 5–21; William J. Barber, "The United States: Economists in a Pluralist Society," in A. W. Coats, ed., *Economists in Government* (Durham, N.C.: Duke University Press, 1981), pp. 175–209; John Kenneth Galbraith, "How Keynes Came to America," in *Economics, Peace, and Laughter* (Boston: Houghton Mifflin, 1971), pp. 43–59; Edward S. Mason, "American Security and Access to Raw Materials," *World Politics,* vol. 1, no. 2 (January 1949), reprinted in *Economic Concentration and the Monopoly Problem* (Cambridge: Harvard University Press, 1957), pp. 224–252.

2. William N. Parker, ed., *Economic History and the Modern Economist* (Oxford: Basil Blackwell, 1986), p. 1.

3. Edward S. Mason, "Price and Production Policies of Large-Scale Enterprise," *American Economic Review,* vol. 29, no. 1 (March 1939, supplement), reprinted in Mason, *Economic Concentration and the Monopoly Problem,* pp. 55–72; also Joe S. Bain, "The Comparative Stability of Market Structures," in J. W. Markham and G. F. Papanek, eds., *Industrial Organization and Economic Development: Essays in Honor of Edward S. Mason* (New York: Houghton Mifflin, 1970), pp. 38–46.

4. Letter from E. M. Hoover to the author, May 9, 1988.

5. R&A 214A and R&A 214B, "The German Economic and Military Position" and "Summary and Conclusion" (originally *COI Monographs* no. 3 and no. 5), December 12, 1941.

6. Edward R. Zilbert, *Albert Speer and the Nazi Ministry of Arms: Economic Institutions and Industrial Production in the German War Economy* (London: Associated University Presses, 1981), p. 41: "The prompt and early recognition by the Germans of the production alternatives available to them negated the effects of Allied intelligence"; also Burton H. Klein, *Germany's Economic Preparations for War* (Cambridge: Harvard University Press, 1959). Corroborating

data was assembled in the 208 reports of the United States Strategic Bombing Survey chaired by John Kenneth Galbraith and George Ball.

7. RG 226, Entry 99, Box 76, Folder 46: "The USSR Subdivision," p. 45.

8. R&A 217A, "The German Supply Problem on the Eastern Front June 22–December 6, 1942 [sic]" (originally *COI Monograph* no. 6), March 25, 1942, p. 20.

9. [Herman Liebert,] "The Economic Group," RG 226, Entry 99, Box 76, Folder 46: Washington R&A Branch History, p. 33 [interview with Walter Levy, New York City, October 27, 1987].

10. This perspective on the history of economic thought is developed, *inter alia,* by Adolph Lowe, *On Economic Knowledge: Toward a Science of Political Economics* (New York: Harper and Row, 1965).

11. Langer to Kermit Roosevelt, March 5, 1947: RG 226, Entry 146, Box 48, Folder 606, p. 15.

12. Paul Samuelson, "A Warning to the Washington Expert," *New Republic,* vol. 111, no. 11 (September 11, 1944), p. 298: "It has been said that the last war was the chemist's war and that this one is the physicist's. It might equally be said that this is the economist's war."

13. Emile Despres to William Donovan, November 24, 1941: RG 226, Entry 27, Box 2, Folder: Strategic Memoranda.

14. R&A 217A, "The German Supply Problem on the Eastern Front" (n. 4, *supra*), p. 21. Although an Economic Subdivision undertaking, the moving spirit behind this project was a petroleum geologist, Edward Mayer.

15. R&A 388, "German Tank Strength, Production, and Losses," June 1942?.

16. Elizabeth Gilboy to Chandler Morse, "Captured German Tires," December 9, 1942: R&A 544.

17. R&A 1616, "The German Anti-Friction Bearing Position," n.d.

18. R&A 693, "German Aircraft Production, Losses, and Strength," December 24, 1942, pp. 30, 49.

19. Ibid., p. 30; Sidney Alexander to Chandler Morse, October 3, 1943: RG 226, Entry 146, Box 81, File 312.1/1140. Also Donald Wheeler to Chandler Morse, "MEW's Estimate of Foreign Workers in Germany: A Case Study of the Bits and Pieces Method," May 30, 1943: R&A 943.

20. Letter to the author from Chandler Morse, October 1, 1987.

21. R&A 413, "Estimate of German Army Casualties Derived From Published Obituaries of Officers," n.d., and R&A 2195, "Rate of Officers Killed vs. Other Ranks in the German Ground Forces," n.d.

22. Sidney Alexander, "Numbers Racket," February 20, 1945, and Sidney Alexander to Preston James, "Story of Serial Number Analysis," May 26, 1945: RG 226, Entry 27, Box 2.

23. The serial numbers story is recounted by Richard Ruggles and Henry Brodie in an article in the *Journal of the American Statistical Association,* vol. 42, no. 237 (March 1947), pp. 72–91. The episode was further clarified in a letter to the author from another OSS participant, William Parker, March 21, 1988.

24. It is most significant that Walt W. Rostow selected this passage from Santayana's *Character and Opinions in the United States* as the opening gambit in his account

of this shift: *Pre-Invasion Bombing Strategy* (Austin: University of Texas Press, 1981), p. ix. The full passage reads: "Human discourse is intrinsically addressed not to natural existing things but to ideal essences, poetic or logical terms which thought may define and play with. When fortune or necessity diverts our attention from this congenial ideal sport to crude facts and pressing issues, we turn our frail poetic ideals into symbols for those terrible irruptive things." An intellectual historian in spite of himself, Rostow explicitly situates his own study within a larger effort "to illuminate the relationship between ideas and action" at critical junctures in the war.

25. [Herman Liebert,] "The Economic Group," p. 18 (n. 5, *supra*).

26. [Walter J. Levy,] "The Paradox of Oil and War," *Fortune,* vol. 24, no. 1 (September 1941), pp. 69ff. Levy was to become one of the world's leading petroleum analysts; a selection of his papers, beginning with the above-mentioned article, has been published under the title *Oil Strategy and Politics,* ed. Melvin Conant (Boulder, Colo.: Westview Press, 1982).

27. *War Diary of R&A Branch,* OSS London, England, vol. 1, "Early History": RG 226, Entry 91, Box 7: p. 32.

28. Ibid., vol. 1, pp. 21–22.

29. Kindleberger, "Life of an Economist," p. 239; Rostow, *R&A War Diary,* vol. 5, "Economic Outpost with Economic Warfare Division," p. 2. [Professor Rostow kindly made this document available for my use, and confirmed his authorship of it.]

30. From the voluminous history of the Allied air forces I have drawn especially on Michael Sherry, *American Air Power: The Creation of Armageddon* (New Haven: Yale University Press, 1987); Ronald Schaffer, *Wings of Judgment: American Bombing in World War II* (New York: Oxford University Press, 1985); David MacIsaac, *Strategic Bombing in World War Two: The Story of the United States Strategic Bombing Survey* (New York: Garland, 1976); Wesley Frank Craven and James Lea Cate, eds., *The Army Air Forces in World War II,* 7 vols. (Chicago: University of Chicago Press, 1948–1955); Carl A. Spaatz, "Strategic Air Power: Fulfillment of a Concept," *Foreign Affairs,* 24 (April 1946), pp. 385–396.

31. The Economic Warfare Division was headed by Winfield W. Riefler and consisted of a Blockade Section and an Economic Intelligence Section. The latter contained the General Intelligence Unit and the EOU: Chandler Morse, "The Development and Work of the Enemy Objectives Unit," May 3, 1943: RG 226, Entry 145, Box 8, Folder 94: London. Although the unit was technically attached to the U.S. Embassy and most of its members, as commissioned officers, were responsible ultimately to the military command, they continued to honor the spirit of antihierarchical independence they had cultivated in OSS/Washington, writing their own orders, accepting and rejecting assignments according to their own priorities, and generally running the operation on their own terms.

32. Lt. Col. Richard Hughes to Chandler Morse, September 24, 1942, "American Study of Bombing Objectives," reproduced in R&A *War Diary,* vol. 5, pp. 17–18.

33. The OSS members of EOU were Harold Barnett, Warren Baum, Phillip Coombs,

Russell Dorr, Roselene Honerkamp, Nancy House, Mark Kahn, Carl Kaysen, Charles Kindleberger, Edward Mayer, Chandler Morse, Robert Rosa [later Roosa], William Salant, James Tyson, and Walt W. Rostow; the BEW contributed John De Wilde, Ruth Ellerman, and Irwin Nat Pincus.

34. [W. W. Rostow,] R&A *War Diary*, vol. 5, p. 30. Chandler Morse, "Visit to ICI Hydrogenation Plant, Billingham," October 19, 1942, reproduced Ibid., pp. 21–26.

35. *EOU Report* No. 1, November 13, 1942, "Siemens-Schuckert Cable works, Gartenfeld, West Berlin," reproduced in R&A *War Diary*, vol. 5, pp. 26–29. *Handbook of Target Information*: "Index to EOU File, Aiming Point Reports (as of 13 May, 1944)," papers of Charles P. Kindleberger. I am grateful to Professor Kindleberger for allowing me extended use of these materials, which will be deposited in the Truman Library.

36. William Salant, "The Selection of Industrial Bombing Targets: Some Analytical Notes," December 10, 1942, reproduced in R&A *War Diary*, vol. 5, pp. 32–37, and published in Rostow, *Pre-Invasion Bombing Strategy*. Salant was about to join the faculty of Stanford University when he was killed in an automobile accident in 1966. I have accepted the estimation of his promise volunteered by many of his former colleagues.

37. "Certain Considerations Regarding Evaluation of Industrial and Urban Bomb Targets": RG 226, Entry 77, Box 1, Folder: Target Potentiality Reports. Compare also *EOU Special Report* no. 8, March 9, 1943, "Selection of Bombing Targets: Significance of Production, Wastage, and Military Strength Ratios," and *EOU Special Report* no. 9, April 6, 1943, "Timing of Consequences of a Bombing Program" (both reproduced in R&A *War Diary*, vol. 5, pp. 38–43 (emphasis added). *EOU Target Potentiality Reports:* no. I-D, "German Fighter Aircraft," May 3, 1943; no. II-A, "The German Ball-Bearing Industry as Military Objective," n.d.; no. II-C, "Motor Components," March 9, 1943; no. II-J, "German Combat Airplane Engines," August 18, 1943; no. II-K, "Precision Grinding Wheels," July 22, 1943: papers of Charles P. Kindleberger.

38. Charles Kindleberger to Emile Despres, March 12, 1943: RG 226, Entry 145, Box 8, File 24: London. For a spirited account of the Photographic Interpretation Unit at Medmenham and its congenial relations with the EOU, see Constance Babington-Smith, *Air Spy: The Story of Photo Intelligence in World War II* (New York: Harper & Brothers, 1957).

39. Craven and Cate, *The Army Air Forces in World War II*, vol. 1, chap. 9, "The Casablanca Directive."

40. [Harold Barnett,] "The Use of Strategic Air Power after March 1, 1944. Appendix 5: Target Potentialities of Oil—March 1944," February 28, 1944, reproduced in R&A *War Diary*, vol. 5, pp. 70–80.

41. It is unnecessary to review this decision and its background, since Rostow has done so exhaustively in *Pre-Invasion Bombing Strategy*.

42. The leonine metaphor comes from F. C. Winterbotham's characterization of the stealthy cryptanalysts working for Stewart Menzies at Bletchley: *The Ultra Secret* (New York: Dell, 1974), p. 32. It is well-suited to the self-styled "code-breakers" of EOU, most of whom would rise to commanding positions in academic life and public service.

43. Solly Zuckerman, *From Apes to Warlords* (New York: Harper and row, 1978), pp. 226–245, and the exchange among Zuckerman, Kindleberger, and Rostow which followed in the pages of *Encounter*, vol. 51, no. 5 (November 1978), pp. 39–42; vol. 52, no. 6 (June 1979), pp. 86–89; vol. 55, nos. 2/3 (August–September 1980), pp. 100–102. In a letter to Rostow dated May 2, 1980, the octogenarian Zuckerman finally suggested that "with the world as it is, you and I have more serious things to do than rake over old embers" (papers of Charles P. Kindleberger).

44. [Walt Whitman Rostow,] R&A *War Diary*, vol. 5, p. 103.

45. "The Employment of Heavy Bombers against Germany: From the Present to V-Day," July 1944, reproduced in R&A *War Diary*, vol. 5, pp. 105–109, and Rostow, ibid., p. 112. Compare also Kindleberger to Henry Baily-King, January 1, 1945: papers of Charles P. Kindleberger.

46. *EOU Report* no. 57 (February 27, 1945), p. 1: papers of Charles P. Kindleberger. Also Carl Kaysen to Bill [Salant] and Phil [Coombs], *EOU Report* no. 41 (September 9, 1944): RG 226, Entry 77, Box 2, Folder: MAAF.

47. W. W. Rostow to Cols. Kingman Douglass and R. D. Hughes, June 12, 1944: papers of Charles P. Kindleberger.

48. *EOU Report* no. 65 (April 6, 1945): papers of Charles P. Kindleberger.

49. William Salant to Group Captain Luard, August 3, 1944, "Status of the Oil Attack" and "Minutes of the Mediterranean Oil Targets Committee, August 8, 1944": papers of William Salant. I am grateful to Dr. Walter Salant for granting me access to the papers of his late brother, which will be deposited in the Truman Library.

50. Kindleberger to Irwin Nat Pincus, August 18, 1944: papers of Charles P. Kindleberger. He was joined in the forward echelon of Twelfth Army Group Headquarters by two other OSS economists, Robert Rosa (later Roosa) and Peter Bernstein.

51. Kindleberger to Major Derek J. Ezra, April 13, 1945: papers of Charles P. Kindleberger. Lord Ezra later became head of Britain's nationalized coal industry.

52. R&A (London), February 1, 1946, *War Diary*, vol. 2: "Early Period of Independent Operation," January to December 1943, p. 33: RG 226, Entry 91, Box 7.

53. Paul M. Sweezy, *The Theory of Capitalist Development* (New York: Oxford University Press, 1942); from the second edition (New York: Monthly Review Press, 1956), p. 18.

54. "To understand this one has to be clear that Washington's war aims, from the beginning, went far beyond defeat of the Axis to encompass a new international economic order of free trade and free competition which would favor the U.S. as the hegemonic economic power." Letter to the author, August 14, 1984. For an extended analysis of this position, see Gabriel Kolko, *The Politics of War* (New York: Random House, 1968).

55. Paul Sweezy to Edward Mason, "American Interests in the European Settlement," April 24, 1944: RG 226, Entry 81, Box 1.

56. Ibid.

57. "Three-Power Co-Operation and the Occupation of Germany," n.d., but after

mid-July 1944: RG 226, Entry 74, Box 2: Germany—Peace. This remarkable document was written as a position paper of the members of the political and economic staffs of R&A/London with "the dual purpose of clarifying our own thinking and of giving Washington the benefit of views arrived at independently on the basis of London impressions and experiences."

58. Ibid.

59. Emile Despres, "Treatment of Germany," draft, n.d.: RG 226, Entry 74, Box 2, Folder: Germany—Peace, and his detailed response to the Mason-Sweezy memoranda, "American Interests in the European Settlement," May 5, 1944: RG 226, Entry 81, Box 1.

60. [W. W. Rostow,] *War Diary,* vol. 5, p. 50; also his memorandum, "Air Warfare and the Continental Strategy," December 10, 1943: RG 226, Entry 77, Box 3.

61. William N. Parker, letter to the author, March 21, 1988.

62. Carl Kaysen to Charles Kindleberger, June 11, 1944, "Are There Other Fish in the Aquarium Than the OCTOPUS?" Papers of Carl Kaysen, kindly loaned to the author.

63. Ronald Schaffer, *Wings of Judgment,* chap. 4, for a full analysis of this problem.

64. Letter to the author, October 1, 1987. On the pervasive influence on the field exercised by the relatively unpublished Despres, see the prefatory remarks by Gerald M. Meier, ed., *International Economic Reform: Collected Papers of Emile Despres* (New York: Oxford University Press, 1973).

65. Kindleberger, "Life of an Economist."

66. Walt W. Rostow, "Reflections on the Drive to Technological Maturity," *Banca Nazionale del Lavoro Quarterly Review,* no. 161 (June 1987), p. 117. Compare also his comments on "Neo-Newtonians and Biologists," in *Rich Countries and Poor Countries: Reflections on the Past, Lessons for the Future* (Boulder and London: Westview Press, 1987), pp. 1–18, and the introductory remarks by M. M. Postan, "Walt Rostow: A Personal Appreciation," in Charles Kindleberger and Guido di Tella, eds., *Economics in the Long View: Essays in Honor of W. W. Rostow,* vol. 1, *Models and Methodology* (New York: NYU Press, 1982), pp. 1–14. On his years in the State Department, see *The Division of Europe after World War II: 1946* (Austin: University of Texas Press, 1981), esp. chap. 4.

67. Carl Kaysen to I. N. Pincus and H. J. Barnett, "Observations on a Trip through Germany, 2 May–10 May, 1945": RG 226, Entry 1, Box 17, Folder: London 1944.

68. For a perspective on his tenure at Princeton's Institute, see Joel Shurkin, *The Lighthouse Keepers* (Boston: Ticknor and Fields, forthcoming).

69. Sidney S. Alexander, "Human Values and Economist's Values," in *Human Values and Public Policy,* ed. Sidney Hook (New York: NYU Press, 1967), p. 101. Among his other studies in the foundation of normative judgments in social policy, see especially "The Impersonality of Normative Judgements," in W. A. Eltis, et al., *Induction, Growth, and Trade: Essays in Honor of Sir Roy Harrod* (Oxford: Clarendon Press, 1970), pp. 55–64.

70. Paul Sweezy to Carl Schorske and Franz Neumann, May 24, 1945: RG 226, Entry 50, Box 1, Folder: German—Letters Out; also RG 226, Entry 99, Box 7, Folder no. 23: ETO German.

71. Charles P. Kindleberger, "Origins of the Marshall Plan" (1948), and his "apologia pro vita sua," "Towards the Marshall Plan: A Memoir of Policy Development in Germany, 1945–47," both in *Marshall Plan Days* (Boston: Allen and Unwin, 1987); Walt W. Rostow, *The Division of Europe after world War II;* Sidney S. Alexander, *The Marshall Plan,* National Planning Association, Planning Pamphlets nos. 60–61 (Washington: February 1948). Also relevant is Edward S. Mason, "The New Approach to the Role of the United States in European Economic Stabilization," in Seymour Harris, ed., *Foreign Economic Policy for the United States* (Cambridge: Harvard University Press, 1948), pp. 291–297.

72. Sidney S. Alexander, "Public Television and the 'Ought' of Public Policy," *Washington University Law Quarterly,* Winter 1968, pp. 35–70.

73. *American Economic Review, Papers and Proceedings,* vol. 75, no. 2 (May 1985), pp. 320–337; republished and expanded in William Parker, ed., *Economic History and the Modern Economist* (Oxford: Basil Blackwell, 1986).

5. Social Science in One Country

Epigraph: Philip E. Mosely, "The Growth of Russian Studies," in Harold H. Fisher, ed., *American Research on Russia* (Bloomington: Indiana University Press, 1959).

1. John S. Curtiss, "Geroid Tanquary Robinson," in *Essays in Russian and Soviet History in Honor of Geroid Tanquary Robinson,* ed. John Shelton Curtiss (New York: Columbia University Press, 1963), p. xviii. Robinson is best known for his classic, *Rural Russia under the Old Regime: A History of the Landlord-Peasant World and a Prologue to the Peasant Revolution of 1917* (London and New York: Longmans, 1932).

2. Here, as elsewhere in R&A, the personnel assigned to the various administrative positions fluctuated. The USSR Division reached full strength, with its functional subdivisions directed by Morrison, Schmitt, and Leontief, only in mid-1943; it experienced further changes before the end of the war.

3. On the recruitment of Alex Inkeles: RG 226, Entry 99, Box 76, File 46, pp. 56–59. On Paul Baran: DeWitt Poole to William Langer, August 8, 1944: RG 226, Entry 1, Box 3, Foreign Nationalities Branch File, and Paul Baran to Carl Schorske, March 22, 1945, repudiating reports in the *Washington Times Herald,* "House Unit Reveals Red Link of OSS Official": RG 226, Entry 37, Box 2. On John Scott: J. A. Morrison to William Langer, March 9, 1942: RG 226, Entry 146, Box 149, Folder 2236(21). Leonard Mins, a professionally trained engineer with expert knowledge of both "electrification and soviets," was dismissed by General Donovan after being denounced as a fellow traveler: Robinson to Langer, November 4, 1942: RG 226, Entry 145, Box 7: USSR Division.

4. J. A. Morrison to William Langer, "Official Name of New Division," January 15, 1943: RG 226, Entry 145, Box 7: USSR Division. "Political Subdivision": RG 226, Entry 99, Box 76, File 46, pp. 77, 114–115a.

5. Philip E. Mosely, "The Groowth of Russian Studies," in Harold H. Fisher, ed., *American Research on Russia* (Bloomington: Indiana University Press, 1959), p. 2.

6. G. T. Robinson, "Personnel Situation in the East-European Section," November 19, 1942: RG 226, Entry 146, Box 149, Folder 2235(20): Eastern Europe. For

a longer view of the state of prewar scholarship on the USSR, see Stephen F. Cohen, *Rethinking the Soviet Experience: Politics and History since 1917* (New York: Oxford University Press, 1985), chap. 1; Walter Laqueur, *The Fate of the Revolution: Interpretations of Soviet History* (New York: Macmillan, 1967), chap. 2; Clarence A. Manning, *A History of Slavic Studies in the United States* (Milwaukee: Marquette University Press, 1957), chaps. 6, 7.

7. In addition to sources cited in n. 3, *supra,* information on the recruitment of individual scholars comes from interviews with Barrington Moore, Jr. (Cambridge, Mass., October 26, 1987), Abram Bergson (Cambridge, Mass., October 26, 1987), and Alex Inkeles (Palo Alto, October 22, 1987) and from correspondence with Robert C. Tucker (August 12, 1988). Compare also the prefatory remarks to Inkeles' *Social Change in Russia* (Cambridge: Harvard University Press, 1968), pp. ix–xi.

8. Morrison to William Langer, June 14, 1945: RG 226, Entry 1, Box 11: OSS History File.

9. Morrison to Langer, March 5, 1943: RG 226, Entry 145, Box 7, Folder 89: USSR Division. Assorted details are in RG 226, Entry 146, Box 149, Folder 20/2235: Eastern Europe (Misc. Memos), Robinson; and in RG 226, Entry 99, Box 76, File 46, *passim.*

10. Letter to the author from Robert C. Tucker, August 12, 1988.

11. [J. A. Morrison,] "General Considerations": RG 226, Entry 99, Box 76, File 46: USSR Division, p. 123.

12. R&A 535, "The Russian–German Situation on the Russian Front," n.d., transcript of remarks by Geroid T. Robinson et al.

13. J. A. Morrison, "The Economic Subdivision," p. 101, and "Methods and Techniques," pp. 38–40; RG 226, Entry 99, Box 76, File 46. Interviews with Alex Inkeles (Palo Alto, October 22, 1987) and Abram Bergson (Cambridge, Mass., October 26, 1987).

14. Robinson to Langer, October 20, 1943, "The Chief Failure of American Intelligence": RG 226, Entry 145, Box 7, Folder 89: USSR Division.

15. Langer to William Donovan, September 1, 1943, "Representative of OSS in Moscow": RG 226, Entry 145, Box 7, Folder 89: USSR Division. Also materials from the Outpost Desk, USSR Division, R&A/Washington: RG 226, Entry 146, Box 85, Folder 1255: Ruggles, Melville. Compare also John R. Deane, *The Strange Alliance: The Story of Our Efforts at Wartime Cooperation with Russia* (New York: Viking, 1947), pp. 50–58, and Bradley F. Smith, *The Shadow Warriors,* pp. 336–346.

16. On the creation of the "Russian Mission" to London: *R&A War Diary, ETO: Early History, 1942:* RG 226, Entry 91, Box 7, vol. 1; Thomas R. Hall to Shepard Morgan, October 4, 1943: RG 226, Entry 145, Box 8, Folder 94. On Robinson's humiliating rebuff by the East European Section of MIS: Robinson to T. P. Whitney, September 4, 1943, "Relations with the War Department": RG 226, Entry 145, Box 7, Folder 89.

17. R&A 605 (COI Report no. 17), "Gains of Germany (and Her Allies) through the Occupation of Soviet Territory," March 14, 1942: G. T. Robinson [signed report].

18. R&A 810, "Russia and Germany in Winter and Spring: Allied Policy and a Separate Peace," December 23, 1941: G. T. Robinson [signed report].

19. R&A 1193, "Russian and the Question of a Separate Russo-German Peace," September 14, 1943: J. A. Morrison [RG 226, Entry 99, Box 76, File 46, p. 117].

20. The question has been examined in detail by Vojtech Mastny, "Stalin and the Prospects of a Separate Peace in World War II," *American Historical Review,* vol. 77, no. 5 (December 1972), pp. 1365–1388.

21. Bergson"s retrospective evaluation, made in an interview with the author in Cambridge (October 26, 1987). The relevant reports include R&A 523, "Political Organization and Morale of the USSR," February 23, 1943; R&A 585, "Military Position of the Soviet Union," n.d.; R&A 841, "Russian Winter Offensive, 1942–43," April 14, 1943; R&A 917, "Russian Military Potential," June 25, 1943. Material from these reports was incorporated into the final series of capabilities studies: R&A 1355, "Russian Capabilities and Prospects," November 1943; followed by R&A 1355.1 on manpower, December 1943; R&A 1355.2 on morale, December 1943; R&A 1355.3 on military supplies, January 1944; and R&A 1355.4 on basic industries, July 1944. On prevailing views of Russia's military and economic capabilities, see John Lewis Gaddis, *The United States and the Origins of the Cold War, 1941–1947* (New York: Columbia University Press, 1972), chap. 1, and Robert H. Dawson, *The Decision to Aid Russia, 1941: Foreign Policy and Domestic Politics* (Chapel Hill: University of North Carolina Press, 1959).

22. G. T. Robinson, "Strategy and Policy: Can America and Russia Cooperate?" August 20, 1943: RG 226, Entry 146, Box 125, Folder: Québec.

23. Foreign Commissar Georgi Vasilyevich Chicherin's slogan for "peaceful coexistence with other governments, no matter what they are." For its lineage, Franklyn Griffiths, "Origins of Peaceful Coexistence: A Historical Note," in Walter Z. Laqueur and Leopold Labedz, eds., *The State of Soviet Studies* (Cambridge: MIT Press, 1965), pp. 156–162.

24. R&A 1109, "The Bases of Soviet Foreign Policy," September 1, 1943, pp. i–ii.

25. R&A 1552, "The Current Role of the Communist Party in the USSR," June 12, 1944, p. viii. Curtiss and Inkeles published an overview of their findings, "Marxism in the U.S.S.R.—The Recent Revival," in *Foreign Affairs,* vol. 61, no. 3 (1946), pp. 349–364. Other reports from the Morale Section included R&A 1146, "The Scope, Content, and Intent of Soviet Foreign Broadcasts," and R&A 1197, "Soviet Domestic Shortwave Broadcasts: Their Scope and Content," September 27, 1943.

26. R&A 1109, p. 15.

27. R&A 1670, "Trends in the Status of the Russian Worker," December 22, 1943, p. 28.

28. R&A 2521, "The Relative Positions of the Communist Party and the Red Army under the Soviet Regime," October 30, 1944, p. 3.

29. R&A 2185, "The Nature of Soviet National Feeling (since June 1941)," June 15, 1944.

30. R&A 2073, "Russian Aims in Germany and the Problem of Three-Power Co-

operation," May 11, 1944, p. i: G. T. Robinson [RG 226, Entry 99, Box 76, Folder 46, p. 121].

31. Robinson to Thomas R. Hall, May 20, 1944: RG 226, Entry 146, Box 85, Folder 1252: Robinson, G. T.

32. R&A 2073, "Russian Aims in Germany and the Problem of Three-Power Co-operation," May 11, 1944, pp. 8, 19.

33. G. T. Robinson to Chandler Morse, August 28, 1944: RG 226, Entry 146, Box 85, Folder 1252: Robinson, G. T. The urgency of determining in advance a multilateral principle for the occupation and governance of Germany was being argued in those same months by their academic colleague Philip Mosely, who had succeeded George F. Kennan as Political Advisor to Ambassador John G. Winant, American representative to the European Advisory Commission. See Philip E. Mosely, "The Occupation of Germany: New Light on How the Zones Were Drawn," *Foreign Affairs*, vol. 28, no. 4 (July 1950), pp. 580–604. For guides to the vast literature on this problem, see John L. Snell, *Wartime Origins of the East-West Dilemma over Germany* (New Orleans: Hauser Press, 1959); Bruce Kuklick, *American Policy and the Division of Germany: The Clash with Germany over Reparations* (Ithaca: Cornell University Press, 1972); and John H. Backer, *The Decision to Divide Germany: American Foreign Policy in Transition* (Durham, N.C.: Duke University Press, 1978).

34. Melville Ruggles to Chandler Morse, July 8, 1944, and Ruggles to Alfred Skerpan, January 9, 1945: RG 226, Entry 145, Box 85, Folder 1255.

35. R&A 2669, "Capabilities and Intentions of the USSR in the Postwar Period," January 5, 1945, p. 37, pp. 67–70. For other OSS studies that support this general framework of analysis, see R&A 1889, "Russian War Damages and Possible Reparations Claims," May 26, 1944, and R&A 1988, "Russia's Intentions to Punish War Criminals," June 27, 1944.

36. R&A 2060, "Russian Reconstruction and Postwar Foreign Trade Developments," September 9, 1944, Wassily Leontief, Abram Bergson, et al. [Interview with Abram Bergson, October 26, 1987, and correspondence with Wassily Leontief, October 27, 1988; notes in RG 226, Entry 99, Box 76, Folder 46, p. 107: The Economic Subdivision.] R&A 2060 was the first in a series that was continued by the State Department's Interim Research and Intelligence Service.

37. R&A 2060, table 5. Their figures were: industry, −26.6%; agriculture, −32.2%; transport and communications, −23.9%; housing, −15.3%; and trade, public utilities, and public institutions, −23.6%.

38. R&A 2060, p. 17, and Appendix A, *passim*.

39. The literature on the origins of the Cold War is vast and readily accessible. Particularly helpful in connection with the themes of this study are John Lewis Gaddis, *The United States and the Origins of the Cold War* (n. 21, *supra*), and George C. Herring, *Aid to Russia, 1941–1946: Strategy, Diplomacy, the Origins of the Cold War* (New York: Columbia University Press, 1973), esp. chaps. 6–8. From the Soviet side, Vojtech Mastny, *Russia's Road to the Cold War: Diplomacy, Warfare, and the Politics of Communism, 1941–1945* (New York: Columbia University Press, 1979).

40. John S. Curtiss, "Geroid Tanquary Robinson," in Curtiss, ed., *Essays in Russian and Soviet History*, p. xvii.

41. Paul Baran, "Comments on the USSR Division paper, 'Russia's Aims in Germany' ": RG 226, Entry 27, Box 1, referring to Robinson's report, R&A 2073 (May 11, 1944).
42. Paul M. Sweezy, "Paul Alexander Baran: A Personal Memoir," in *Monthly Review*, vol. 16, no. 11 (March 1965), pp. 12–48, but compare also Baran's analysis of de-Stalinization and the "tragic and sordid" aspects of the Stalin regime: "On Soviet Themes," *Monthly Review*, July–August 1956, reprinted in Baran, *The Longer View: Essays toward a Critique of Political Economy*, ed. John O'Neill (New York: Monthly Review Press, 1971), pp. 363–373.
43. R&A 2337, "Russian Economic Policies in Germany in the Period of Military Occupation," October 28, 1944, p. 3.
44. William L. Langer, *Up from the Ranks: The Autobiography of William L. Langer* (unpublished, 1975), pp. 347–348.
45. [Geroid T. Robinson,] "The Russian Institute," in L. Gray Cowan, *A History of the School of International Affairs and Associated Area Institutes: Columbia University* (New York: Columbia University Press, 1954); G. T. Robinson, *Columbia University: The Russian Institute: Report on Research and Publication, 1946–1948, 1948–1949,* and *1949–1950.* Robinson and Abram Bergson were the first senior members of the Russian Institute. They would be joined by R&A alumni, including John S. Curtiss (1947), Oliver Lissitzyn (1947), Henry Roberts (1951), and Herbert Marcuse (1951–53).
46. Clyde Kluckhohn, "Russian Research at Harvard," in *World Politics,* vol. 1, no. 2 (January 1949), pp. 267–272; Langer, *Up from the Ranks* (n. 44 *supra*); John N. Hazard, *Reflections of a Pioneering Sovietologist* (Oceana Publications: New York, 1984), chap. 8. The Russian Institute recently celebrated its fortieth birthday.
47. McGeorge Bundy: "It is a curious fact of academic history that the first great center of Area Studies in the United States was located not in any university, but in Washington, during the Second World War, in the Office of Strategic Services. In very large numbers, the area studies programs developed in American universities in the years after the war were manned, directed, or stimulated by graduates of OSS." "The Battlefields of Power and the Searchlights of the Academy," in E. A. J. Johnson, ed., *The Dimensions of Diplomacy* (Baltimore: Johns Hopkins University Press, 1964), pp. 149–152. To be fair, we may note that a few "graduates" of the Lend-Lease Administration and the War Production Board were also present at the creation.
48. *Pravda,* July 24, 1951, and April 26, 1952, quoted in Cowan, *A History of the School of International Affairs,* p. 47.
49. Wassily Leontief, "Input–Output Analysis," *International Encyclopedia of the Social Sciences* (New York: Macmillan, 1968), vol. 7, pp. 345–354, and "Academic Economics," *Science,* vol. 217, no. 4555 (July 9, 1982), pp. 104–107; William H. Miernyk, *The Elements of Input–Output Analysis* (New York: Random House, 1965); Daniel A. Graham, "Input–Output and Linear Programming," in Sidney Weintraub, ed., *Modern Economic Thought* (Philadelphia: University of Pennsylvania Press, 1977), pp. 137–162.
50. Abram Bergson, "Socialist Economics" (1948) in *Essays in Normative Economics* (Cambridge: Harvard University Press, 1966), p. 236.

51. Alex Inkeles, *Public Opinion in Soviet Russia: A Study in Mass Persuasion* (Cambridge: Harvard University Press, 1950), p. 10.

52. Arthur S. Barron, in Fisher, ed., *American Research on Russia,* p. 80.

53. Georgii Maksimionovich Malenkov, August 8, 1953, quoted in Barrington Moore, Jr., *Terror and Progress—USSR: Some Sources of Change and Stability in the Soviet Dictatorship* (Cambridge: Harvard University Press, 1954), p. 1. The model is often traced back to the writings of Hannah Arendt, *The Origins of Totalitarianism* (New York: Harcourt Brace, 1951), and of Carl J. Friedrich and Zbegeniew Brzezinski, *Totalitarian Dictatorship and Autocracy* (Cambridge: Harvard University Press, 1956).

54. Robinson appears to have published only two minor pieces after the war: "The Ideological Combat," an occasional piece for *Foreign Affairs,* vol. 27, no. 4 (July 1949), pp. 525–539, and a sketch of "Stalin's Vision of Utopia," *Proceedings of the American Philosophical Society,* vol. 99, no. 1 (January 1955), p. 11–21.

55. A list of important postwar publications of R&A alumni on Soviet affairs would include the following: John S. Curtiss, *The Russian Church and the Soviet State, 1917–1950* (Boston: Little, Brown, 1953); Vera S. Dunham, *In Stalin's Time: Middle Class Values in Soviet Literature* (Cambridge: Cambridge University Press, 1970); Bernice Madison, *Social Welfare in the Soviet Union* (Palo Alto: Stanford University Press, 1968); J. A. Morrison, "Russia and Warm Water: A Fallacious Generalization and Its Consequences," *Proceedings of the U.S. Naval Institute,* vol. 78, no. 1 (November 1952), pp. 1169–1179. Robert C. Tucker's widely read works on Marx (1961) and Stalin (1973) should be noted, but in view of his short term of service in the USSR Division relative to his lengthy period of residence in Moscow during and after the war it would be difficult to attribute them in any significant measure to his experience in the OSS.

56. Alex Inkeles, "Models and Issues in the Analysis of Soviet Society" (1966), reprinted in *Social Change in Soviet Russia* (Cambridge: Harvard University Press, 1968), p. 422; see also Alexander Dallin, "Bias and Blunders in American Studies on the USSR," in *Slavic Review,* vol. 32, no. 3 (September 1973), pp. 560–576.

57. Moore, *Soviet Politics—The Dilemma of Power: The Role of Ideas in Social Change* (Cambridge: Harvard University Press, 1950), p. 410; Inkeles, *Social Change in Soviet Russia,* pp. ix–xi. On the dominance of the "Chicago School"— represented in R&A by Morris Janowitz and Edward Shils—see Dennis Smith, *The Chicago School: A Liberal Critique of Capitalism* (New York: St. Martin's Press, 1988).

58. Stephen F. Cohen, *Rethinking the Soviet Experience,* p. 26. The relevant books, all volumes in the Russian Research Center's *Studies,* published by Harvard University Press, are: Alex Inkeles, *Public Opinion in Soviet Russia: A Study in Mass Persuasion* (no. 1, 1950); Barrington Moore, Jr., *Soviet Politics—The Dilemma of Power: The Role of Ideas in Social Change* (no. 2, 1950); Moore, *Terror and Progress—USSR: Some Sources of Change and Stability in the Soviet Dictatorship* (no. 12, 1954); Raymond Bauer, Alex Inkeles, and Clyde Kluck-hohn, *How the Soviet System Works: Cultural, Psychological, and Social Themes*

(no. 24, 1956), and Inkeles, *The Soviet Citizen: Daily Life in a Totalitarian Society* (no. 35, 1959).

59. For instance: G. T. Robinson [signed report], R&A 605.

6. The Critique of Modernity

Epigraphs: H. Stuart Hughes, *History as Art and as Science,* p. 103; Leonard Krieger, "European History in America," p. 291; Carl E. Schorske, "A Life of Learning," p. 6.

1. H. Stuart Hughes, *An Essay for Our Times* (New York: Alfred Knopf, 1949), pp. 6–7.
2. Sherman Kent to a colleague at the University of Wisconson: RG 226, Entry 38, Box 1, Reading File: March 1943.
3. Carl Schorske, "A New Yorker's Map of Cambridge: Ethnic Marginality and Political Ambivalence," transcript of talk given from notes at a symposium on *Political Activism and the Academic Conscience,* Hobart and William Smith College, December 5 & 6, 1975, ed. John Lyndenberg (1977), pp. 8–20.
4. William Langer to William Donovan, June 18, 1975: RG 226, Entry 1, Box 1, Folder: Europe–Africa, Standard of Living.
5. Hughes, *An Essay for Our Times,* pp. 6–7.
6. Langer to Donovan, November 25, 1942: RG 226, Entry 38, Box 1, Folder: Donovan, Colonel.
7. On the recruitment of Leonard Krieger: RG 226, Entry 38, Box 1: Reading File, December 1942. Other Holborn students recruited to the Research and Analysis Branch included Henry Cord Meyer and Henry Roberts.
8. Sherman Kent to the University of Wisconsin: RG 226, Entry 38, Box 3: Reading File, March 1943.
9. Carl Schorske, in *Political Activisim and the Academic Conscience,* pp. 89–90 (n. 3, *supra*).
10. Chandler Morse to William Langer, November 10, 1944: RG 226, Entry 1, Box 18, London (III) File.
11. Carl E. Schorske, "A Life of Learning," Charles Homer Haskins Lecture to the American Council of Learned Societies, April 23, 1987, published as ACLS Occasional Paper no. 1 (Washington, 1987). Compare also the introductory essay in his tribute to Langer, *Explorations in Crisis,* ed. Carl E. Schorske and Elizabeth Schorske (Cambridge: Harvard University Press, 1969), pp. ix–xliv.
12. Schorske to Harold Deutsch, "Outpost–Home Office Relations," January 4, 1944: RG 226, Entry 1, Box 21, Brinton File. Deutsch was Chief of political research for Europe–Africa.
13. Crane Brinton to "Bill" Langer, January 22, 1944: RG 226, Entry 1, Box 17, London File.
14. William Langer to David Bruce, Chief of OSS/London, February 26, 1944: RG 226, Entry 1, Box 17, London File, and Langer to Crane Brinton, February 7, 1944: RG 226, Entry 1, Box 17, London (2) File. Additional information was provided by Harold Deutsch in a letter to the author, January 30, 1986.
15. Malcolm Muggeridge, "Book Review of a Very Limited Edition," *Esquire,* 1966,

cited by R. Harris Smith, *OSS* (New York: Dell, 1970), p. 163, contrasts well with Crane Brinton's self-description in *English Political Thought in the Nineteenth Century* (1933; reissued, New York: Harper and Row, 1962), p. 8.

16. See especially the series of "French Political Reports" Brinton wrote from Normandy and Paris in autumn 1944: RG 226, Entry 146, Box 81, Folder 16.

17. Crane Brinton, *Nietzsche* (Cambridge: Harvard University Press, 1941), where the author presents himself as "a limited critic whose values have not been properly transvalued" (p. 63). For further evidence of his self-proclaimed "epistemological naiveté," see his acclaimed study, *The Anatomy of Revolution* (New York: W. W. Norton, 1938), pp. 13, 17, 22, 29. Brinton, one of the original father-figures of the R&A Branch, resigned at the end of the year.

18. Schorske to Harold Deutsch, Chief of R&A/Paris, October 10, 1945: RG 226, Entry 146, Box 84, Folder 122.

19. See in particular Schorske to Deutsch, October 26, 1944: RG 226, Entry 146, Box 84, Folder 122.

20. Schorske to Brig. Gen. John Magruder, "Political Aspects of Possible Nazi Guerrilla Warfare," March 7, 1945: RG 226, Entry 81, Box 2.

21. Schorske to Chandler Morse, "War Crimes Work," June 29, 1945: RG 226, Entry 81, Box 2.

22. Schorske to Frederick Burkhardt, Chief, Central European Section, R&A/Germany, September 26, 1945: RG 226, Entry 81, Box 3, and H. Stuart Hughes, Progress Report, R&A/Germany, September 1–September 30, 1945: RG 226, Entry 99, Box 7, Folder 23: ETO Germany. Schorske's Field Intelligence Studies included *FIS* no. 23, "The Political Parties of Frankfurt-am-Main" (September 24, 1945), *FIS* no. 35, "Policies and Plans of the New Bavarian Ministries," October 21, 1945, and *FIS* no. 39, "Statewide Tendencies of the Bavarian Political Parties," November 8, 1945 [Progress Report, R&A/Germany, September 1–30 and November 1–30, 1945: RG 226, Entry 1, Box 16, Mission to Germany, and RG 226, Entry 81, Box 2]. Lutz Niethammer, the only historian to have studied this series, concurs with my appraisal but from a very different perspective: "In view of their grasp of the interconnections among events it is not surprising that these analyses, in their method and their substantive evaluations, stand closer to the politics of the European working class movement than to American policies in general. This makes them only slightly informative as sources for American history, but heightens their value for *German* history." See *Zwischen Befreiung und Besatzung: Analysen des US-Geheimdienstes über Positionen und Strukturen deutscher Politik 1945,* ed. Ulrich Borsdorf and Lutz Niethammer (Wuppertal: Peter Hammer Verlag, 1976), p. 16.

23. Leonard Krieger [signed article], "The Fuehrer Gets Competition," R&A 1113.12, section II.4, *Psychological Warfare: Weekly Roundup,* June 8–14, 1943; and R&A 1113.19, section IIC.10, July 27–August 2, 1943.

24. Leonard Krieger [signed article], "Germany and Denmark—The Danish Jews," R&A 1113.29, section I.1, *Psychological Warfare: Weekly Roundup* (October 5–11, 1943).

25. R&A 1342, "Further Developments in German Occupation Policy," October

1943; R&A 1756, "Development of the German Pattern of Occupation," January 27, 1944; R&A 1905, "Military Mobilization in the German Occupied East," February 25, 1944; R&A 2500.8, "German Military Governmment over Europe, 1939–1943: Ostland and the Ukraine": Leonard Krieger [RG 226, Entry 60, Box 1, Project Committee minutes of September 25 and October 1, 1943, January 7 and February 6, 1944]. See also his signed articles R&A 1113.13, "New German Policy toward Occupied Territories," June 15–21, 1943, and R&A 1113.25, "Developments in Nazi Occupation Policy," September 7–13, 1943.

26. Krieger to Felix Gilbert, April 7, 1945: RG 226, Entry 81, Box 3: Correspondence of OSS Mission to German.

27. Krieger, "The Inter-Regnum in Germany: March–August 1945," *Political Science Quarterly,* vol. 64, no. 4 (December 1949), p. 509.

28. Krieger, "The Potential for Democratization in Occupied Germany: A Problem in Historical Projection," *Public Policy,* vol. 17 (1968), p. 33.

29. Sources on Krieger's months with R&A/Germany, April through November 1945: RG 226, Entry 99, Box 7, Folder 23: ETO Germany, *passim*; Krieger to Carl Schorske and Franklin Ford, October 22, 1945: RG 226, Entry 81, Box 3: Correspondence of OSS Mission to Germany. Compare also Felix Gilbert, *A European Past,* pp. 207–216.

30. H. Stuart Hughes, "Social Theory in a New Context," in Jarrell Jackman and Carl M. Borden, eds., *The Muses Flee Hitler* (Washington: Smithsonian Institution Press, 1983), p. 114.

31. "History of the Current Intelligence Staff": RG 226, Entry 99, Box 76, Folder 46, pp. 1–15.

32. Ibid.

33. John Sawyer subsequently became President of Williams College—a major R&A enclave—and then of the Andrew W. Mellon Foundation. Other scholars who joined the mission included James Barnes, Hibbert Kline, Beverly Bowie, and Frederick Burkhardt, who would become President of the American Council of Learned Societies.

34. Hughes to Henry Hill, November 8, 1943: RG 226, Entry 145, Box 2, File 27: Algiers. Hughes was particularly concerned with the nonbelligerency of the French Communist Party following the defeat of the Germans: "The Communists and the Invasion" and "Current Line of the CP in Algiers" were among the reports he filed from Algiers, along with analyses of "The Unification of the Resistance," "The National Committee and the Invasion," and "The Debate on the Provisional Government": RG 226, Entry 99, Box 19, Folders 101–2: MEDTO Algiers, Jan.–April 1944; and RG 226, Entry 46, Box 1: Algiers—Letters and Reports.

35. Hughes' reports from southeastern France, August 30–September 30, 1944, were as follows: R&A Airgram no. 1, "The Political Situation in Nice: The Prefect and the Front Nationale," September 1; Airgram no. 2, "The Communists and the Committee of National Liberation in Marseilles," September 3; Airgram no. 3, "The Department of the Alpes-Maritimes: Committees of Liberation and Public Order," September 9; Airgram no. 4, "Political Parties

in Lyon," September 18; Airgram no. 5, "Report on Two Agricultural Regions: Dijon and Clermont-Ferrand," September 25: RG 226, Entry 1, Box 23: NATO, Stuart Hughes file.

36. Hughes and Frederick Burkhardt, "Semi-Monthly Report on R&A Branch, NATO," October 1944: RG 226, Entry 1, Box 23: NATO, Stuart Hughes File.

37. William Langer to Colonel Edward Glavin, February 26, 1944, and Langer to Hughes, March 3, 1944: RG 226, Entry 1, Box 15: Algiers, 1944.

38. The exchange between Langer and Hughes, May and June 1944, may be found in RG 226, Entry 1, Box 7: Director's Committee File; and Box 15: OSS, Algiers File. Langer's final word is a defensively paternalistic gesture full of telltale double negatives and slips of the pen.

39. Hughes to Langer, October 14, 1944: RG 226, Entry 1, Box 15: Algiers, 1944. The City Teams, it should be noted, serviced not only future generations: the document team sent into Bucharest discovered in the files of the Rumanian General Staff information that resulted in the destruction of 250 German planes. Described in the "Chronological Account of Captain Burks (Feb.–March, 1945)": RG 226, Entry 83, Box 2: Notes on History, R&A MedTO.

40. Hughes to Langer, October 14, 1944: RG 226, Entry 1, Box 15: Algiers, 1944. Robert G. Neumann, an Austrian-born political scientist attached to G-2 and R&A, described the tension between the claims of Washington upon the R&A field staffs and those of the various theater commanders: "The result was to be foreseen: it failed to become fully integrated on either side of the Atlantic." "Political Intelligence and its Relation to Military Government" in Carl J. Friedrich et al., *American Experiences in Military Government in World War II* (New York: Rinehart & Co., 1948), pp. 70–85.

41. Hughes to Langer, November 6, 1944: RG 226, Entry 1, Box 15: Algiers File.

42. Hughes to Commanding Officer, November 3, 1944, "Assignment of R&A Men to Certain Types of Missions": RG 226, Entry 1, Box 15, Algiers File. The adventures of Colin and Peck, part of an advance party out of Rome picked up near the Swiss border, are recounted in RG 226, Entry 83, Box 2: PAPAYA File.

43. Langer to Hughes, November 6, 1944: RG 226, Entry 146, Box 84, File 80: Langer.

44. "OSS Mediterranean Operations" as of July 1, 1944: RG 226, Entry 99, Box 33, Folder 164.

45. Hughes to Langer, November 6, 1944: RG 226, Entry 1, Box 15: Algiers File/ OSS.

46. Schorske to Frederick Burkhardt, September 26, 1945: RG 226, Entry 81, Box 3. The command structure of OSS in Occupied Germany was as follows: Chief of the Mission was Allan Dulles, whose office was in Berlin, responsible both to Donovan of OSS and to Lucius Clay, Deputy Commanding General, U.S. Forces of Operation. In August nine members of the Research and Analysis Branch under Chandler Morse joined Dulles in the bombed-out capital. In the American Zone, Biebrich/Wiesbaden served as headquarters for the various branches of OSS: Secret Intelligence (SI) under Frank Wisner, Counter-Intelligence (X-2), and Research and Analysis, which was directed by Harold Deutsch and, as of June 22, H. Stuart Hughes.

47. H. Stuart Hughes, "Social Theory in a New Context," p. 118 (n. 30, *supra*), and Leonard Krieger, "Europen History in America," in John Higham, Leonard Krieger, and Felix Gilbert, *History: The Development of Historical Studies in the United States* (Englewood Cliffs, N.J.: Prentice Hall, 1965), pp. 291 and 291f. Krieger continued: "They have no organized existence, take no concerted action, and have even seen their war-born camaraderie and unity of purpose attenuated by more recent cross-currents of both politics and history. And yet a complex of intellectual relations persist among them to carry on what was common in their wartime experiences." Fritz Stern, himself a shade too young to have joined the fraternity of OSS intellectual historians, concurred with this estimate in his centenary lecture to the American Historical Association (1984), "Americans and the German Past: A Century of American Scholarship," published in Stern, *Dreams and Delusions: The Drama of German History* (New York: Alfred A. Knopf, 1987), pp. 266–268.

48. Carl E. Schorske, "Social and Cultural Aspects of the German Problem," in Holt Price and Carl E. Schorske, *The Problem of Germany* (New York: Council on Foreign Relations, 1947), p. 139; compare also his paper, "The Dilemma of Germany," *Virginia Quarterly Review*, vol. 24 (Winter 1948), pp. 29–42.

49. Leonard Krieger, "The Inter-Regnum in Germany: March–August 1945," *Virginia Quarterly Review*, vol. 64, no. 4 (December 1949), pp. 507–532; compare also "The Potential for Democratization in Occupied Germany: A Problem in Historical Projection," n. 27, *supra*.

50. H. Stuart Hughes, *An Essay for Our Times* (New York: Alfred A. Knopf, 1949), and his recollections of "The Second Year of the Cold War," *Commentary*, vol. 48, no. 2 (August 1969), pp. 27–32.

51. Schorske, "A Life of Learning," p. 10, referring to his first scholarly book, *Germany Social Democracy, 1905–1917: The Development of the Great Schism* (Cambridge: Harvard University Press, 1955; Leonard Krieger, "European History in America," p. 306, referring to *The German Idea of Freedom*; H. Stuart Hughes, *The United States and Italy* (Cambridge: Harvard University Press, 1952). Although Hughes is frequently lumped together in an intellectual-historical unit with Crane Brinton, another author in this series, their perspectives are strikingly different.

52. Carl E. Schorske, *Fin-de-Siècle Vienna: Politics and Culture* (New York: Alfred A. Knopf, 1980), p. xix; H. Stuart Hughes, *Osward Spengler: A Critical Estimate* (New York: Scribner's, 1952; rev. ed., 1962) and *Consciousness and Society: The Reorientation of European Social Thought, 1890–1930* (New York: Alfred A. Knopf, 1958); Leonard Krieger, *Ranke: The Meaning of History* (Chicago: University of Chicago Press, 1977), and the antecedent study, *The German Idea of Freedom* (Boston: Beacon Press, 1957).

53. Leonard Krieger, "The Autonomy of Intellectual History," *Journal of the History of Ideas*, vol. 34, no. 4 (October–December 1973), p. 508, and "European History in America" (n. 54, *supra*); see also H. Stuart Hughes, "Contemporary Historiography: Progress, Paradigms, and the Regression toward Positivism," in Gabriel Almond, Marvin Chodorow, and Roy Harvey Pearce, eds., *Progress and Its Discontents* (Berkeley: University of California Press, 1982), pp. 240–248.

54. Krieger, "The Autonomy of Intellectual History," pp. 507, 512.
55. Transcript of Schorske's remarks in a symposium on "New Trends in History," *Daedalus,* vol. 48, no. 4 (Fall 1969), p. 930.
56. Leonard Krieger, "Culture, Cataclysm, and Contingency," expanded version of a lecture delivered on November 13, 1967, at the University of Chicago, published in *Journal of Modern History,* vol. 40, no. 4 (December 1968), p. 452.
57. Leonard Krieger, "Comments on Historical Explanation," in Sidney Hook, ed., *Philosophy and History: A Symposium* (New York: NYU Press, 1963), pp. 136–42; Schorske, *Fin-de-Siècle Vienna,* p. xx; H. Stuart Hughes, *History as Art and as Science* (New York: Harper and Row, 1962), p. 96: "I remember that at one time I really believed that the writer or teacher of history could and should attain to a sublime detachment . . . Since then an intense exposure to the ideas of Bendetto Croce has cured me of such notions; I have learned that the result of the historian's efforts to be detached has usually been the very opposite of what anyone would call great history. It has been bloodless history, with no clear focus, arising from antiquarian curiosity rather than from deep personal concern, and shot through with metaphysical and moral assumptions that are all the more insidious for being artfully concealed." Hughes generalized his own historical *Bildungsprozess* in a well-attended address to the American Historical Association, "European Intellectual History 1884–1984: The Socialization of Ideas," later published in *International Forum,* no. 9 (Seoul, 1986–87), pp. 31–40.
58. Leonard Krieger, "The Intellectuals and European Society," paper presented at Columbia University's European Institute, March 1951, published in *Political Science Quarterly,* vol. 67, no. 2 (June 1952), p. 227.
59. Leonard Krieger, "The Horizons of History," *American Historical Review,* vol. 63, no. 1 (October 1957), p. 73.
60. Schorske, "A Life of Learning," p. 15.
61. Krieger, "The Autonomy of Intellectual History," pp. 515–516; also his paper, "History and Existentialism in Sartre," where he wrestles with the same structural antinomies, namely, the attempt to encompass both "the patterns of synchronization and succession" in the common medium of time: *The Critical Spirit: Essays in Honor of Herbert Marcuse,* ed. Kurt H. Wolff and Barrington Moore, Jr. (Boston: Beacon Press, 1967), p. 266
62. Hughes, "The Sweep of Narrative Line," in *History as Art and as Science,* p. 70.
63. Krieger, "The Horizons of History," p. 69.
64. Krieger, "The Autonomy of Intellectual History," p. 515.
65. Olivier Zunz, ed., *Reliving the Past: The Worlds of Social History* (Chapel Hill: University of North Carolina Press, 1985), p. 5; Roger Chartier, "Intellectual History or Socio-Cultural History? The French Trajectories," in Dominick LaCapra and Steven Kaplan, eds., *Modern European Intellectual History: Reappraisals and New Perspectives* (Ithaca: Cornell University Press, 1982), pp. 13–46; Robert Darnton, "Intellectual and Cultural History," in Michael Kammen, ed., *The Past before Us* (Ithaca: Cornell University Press, 1980), p. 327–349. Darnton's essay is a fine example of a new genre in historical writing, the review

essay of the crisis of intellectual historiography "through which intellectual historians try to take one another's pulse" (p. 328). Recent contributions include Donald R. Kelley, "Horizons of Intellectual History: Retrospect, Circumspect, Prospect," in *Journal of the History of Ideas*, vol. 48, no. 1 (January–March 1987), pp. 143–169, and John E. Toews, "Intellectual History after the Linguistic Turn: The Autonomy of Meaning and the Irreducibility of Experience," in *American Historical Review*, vol. 92, no. 4 (October 1987), pp. 879–907.

66. Hayden White, *Metahistory: The Historical Imagination in Nineteenth Century Europe* (Baltimore: Johns Hopkins University Press, 1973), and *The Content of the Form* (Baltimore: Johns Hopkins University Press, 1987).

67. Dominick LaCapra, *History and Criticism* (Ithaca: Cornell University Press, 1985), pp. 123, 83, 22; also his widely discussed manifesto, "Rethinking Intellectual History and Reading Texts," in LaCapra and Kaplan, eds., *Modern European Intellectual History*, pp. 47–85. The critique of "narrativized thinking as a reactionary form" reaches its extreme position in Sande Cohen, *Historical Culture: The Recording of an Academic Discipline* (Berkeley and Los Angeles: University of California Press, 1986), esp. pp. 110–173.

68. Martin Jay, *Marxism and Totality: The Adventures of a Concept from Lukács to Habermas* (Berkeley and Los Angeles: University of California Press, 1984), and his inquiry, "Should Intellectual History Take a Linguistic Turn?" in LaCapra and Kaplan, eds., *Modern European Intellectual History*, p. 110.

Conclusion

1. Hayden V. White, *The Content of the Form* (Baltimore: Johns Hopkins University Press, 1987), p. 14.

2. The history of the CIA is usually written from the demise of OSS, which is the subject, accordingly, of a vast literature. For a useful guide see Thomas F. Troy, *Donovan and the CIA* (Frederick, Md.: Aletheia Press, 1981).

3. Donovan to Roosevelt, November 18, 1944, in *War Report of the OSS*, Exhibit W-43, pp. 115–116.

4. Preston James, "American Universities and Field Intelligence," August 29, 1945, and William Langer to Sherman Kent, "Committee on Relations between Government Intelligence and Research Work and the American Universities," August 31, 1945: RG 226, Entry 37, Box 2.

5. Gregory Bateson to General Donovan, "Influence of Atomic Bomb on Indirect Methods of Warfare," August 18, 1945: RG 226, Entry 1, Box 17, India/Burma Folder.

6. Langer to Kermit Roosevelt, March 5, 1947: RG 226, Entry 146, Box 48, Folder 666.

7. Cora DuBois, *Social Forces in Southeast Asia* (University of Minnesota Press, 1949), pp. 10–11.

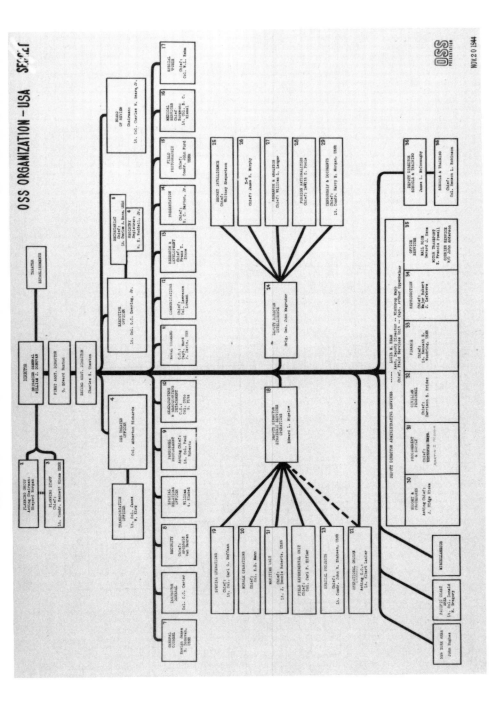

Chart 1. Organization of the Office of Strategic Services, November 20, 1944. Source: RG 226, Entry 99, Box 104.

RESEARCH AND ANALYSIS BRANCH

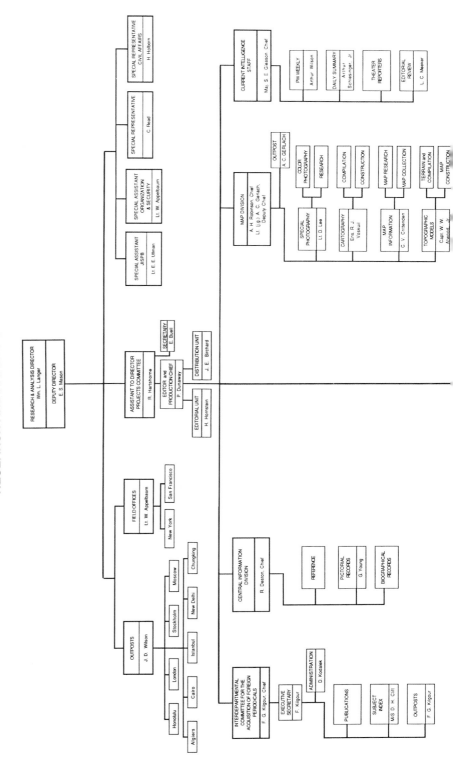

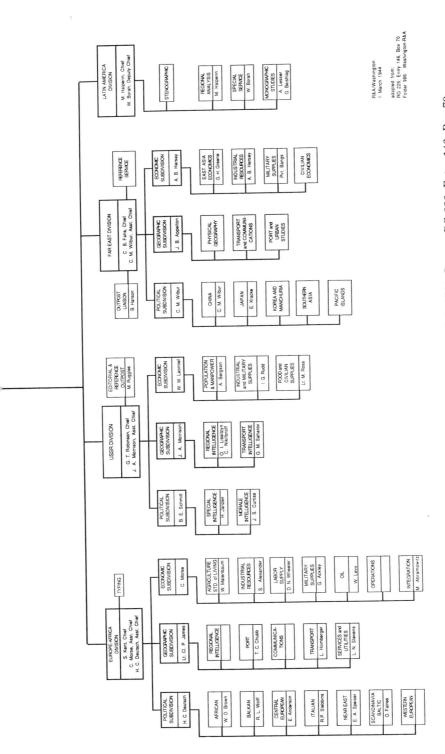

Chart 2. Organization of the Research and Analysis Branch, OSS, March 1, 1944. Source: RG 226, Entry 146, Box 70.

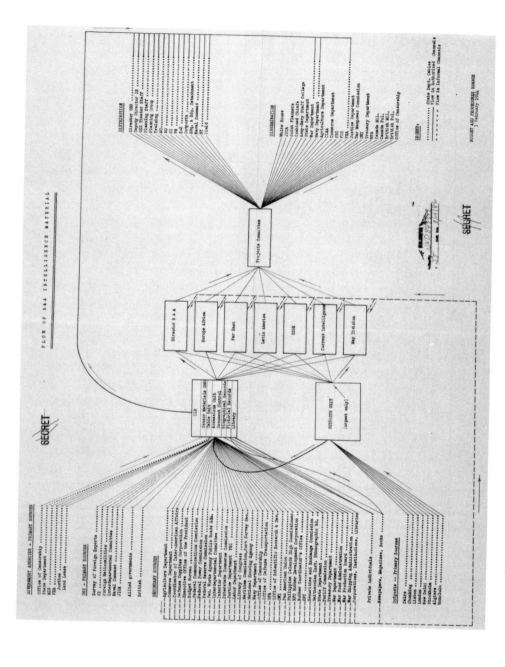

Chart 3. Flow of R&A Intelligence Material, February 1, 1944. Source: RG 226, Entry 99, Box 104.

ORGANIZATION OF RESEARCH AND ANALYSIS BRANCH, LONDON.

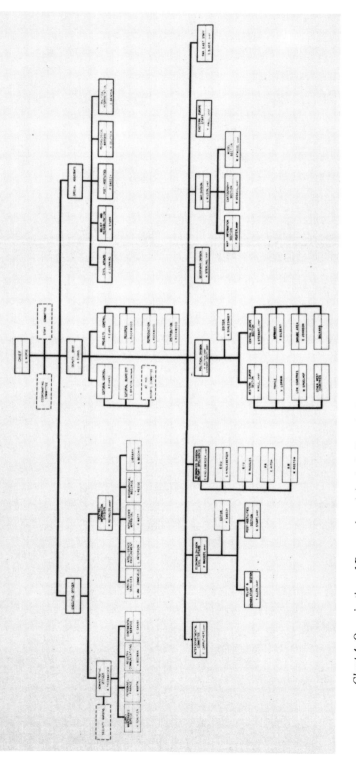

Chart 4. Organization of Research and Analysis Branch, London Outpost, June 17, 1944. Source: RG 226, Entry 1, Box 17.

Index

Journal of Modern History, 139
July 20 Movement, 42, 52, 78

Kaplan, Benjamin, 51
Kaysen, Carl, 10, 99, 115, 120, 123, 130, 132
Kellerman, Henry, 11, 51
Kent, Sherman, 8, 65, 169, 197
Kindleberger, Charles Poor, 10, 80, 99, 109, 114, 115, 129, 136; directs Enemy Objectives Unit, 118–124
Kirchheimer, Otto, 10, 67, 188; intellectual background, 29–32; joins Central European Section, 32–35; work for Civil Affairs Division, 45–47; War Crimes Research, 51–52; impact of R&A on, 59–61
Kohn, Hans, 11
Krautheimer, Richard, 11, 66, 75–76
Krieger, Leonard, 10, 80, 86, 88, 166; joins R&A Branch, 168–169; work in Washington, London, Germany, 175–179; and postwar historiography, 186–195

Lacapra, Dominick, 194
Lamprecht, Karl, 78
Langer, William L.; directs R&A Branch, 5–7; on functions of R&A, 14, 20; on organization of Branch, 21–24; relations with economists, 102–103; and USSR Division, 138; and Carnegie Foundation, 159; and Russian Research Center, 160; relations with Schorske, 167; relations with London Outpost, 171–172; and R&A/METO, 183–185; on future of R&A Branch, 197
Lend-Lease, 142–143
Leontief, Wassily, 23, 99, 139, 155–157, 160, 161
Levin, Alfred, 141
Levy, Walter, 99, 112
Library of Congress, 5, 17, 34
Lissitzyn, Oliver, 143
London Outpost, 23, 78–84, 112–128, 146, 171–173
Lovejoy, Arthur O., 13, 190
Löwenthal, Leo, 10

McKay, Donald C., 5, 23, 160, 167, 168, 180, 181
MacLeish, Archibald, 5

Magruder, John, 21, 174
Malenbaum, Wilfred, 99, 109
Marcuse, Herbert, 10, 11, 65, 67, 188; intellectual background, 29–32; joins Centeral European Section, 32–35; analysis of Nazism, 36–43; work for Civil Affairs Division, 45–47; War Crimes research, 54–55; impact of R&A on, 59–60
Marshall Plan, 132
Mason, Edward Sagendorph, 9, 21, 26; joins R&A Board of Analysts, 5–6; organizes Economic Subdivision, 98–99; and postwar reconstruction, 128; postwar career of, 129, 131
Meinecke, Friedrich, 62–65, 92, 94–96
Metzler, Lloyd, 110
Meyerhoff, Hans, 67, 86, 180
Military Government (MG). *See* Civil Affairs Division
Military Intelligence (British MI5 and MI6), 80
Miller, Margaret, 154
Miller, Perry, 9, 86, 93, 190
Ministry of Economic Warfare (British MEW), 112, 146
Mitscherlich, Alexander, 89
Monthly Review, 127, 135
Moore, Barrington, Jr., 10, 141, 158, 160, 163–164
Morale Operations Branch (MO), 81
Morgan, Shepard, 23, 112
Morgenthau, Henry, 79
Morrison, John A., 23, 139, 141, 143–145, 148
Morrison, Phoebe, 25
Morse, Chandler, 9, 22–23, 26, 80, 170, 172; as Assistant Chief of Economics Subdivision, 99; on methodology, 109; organizes R&A/London, 114–115, 125, 129; postwar career of, 131
Mosca, Gaetano, 189
Moscow Conference, 42, 52, 78
Mosely, Philip, 139, 141, 230n33

National Archives, 5
Nelson, Donald, 155
Neumann, Franz L., 65, 67, 176, 179, 188; assists in recruitment of refugee scholars, 10–12; intellectual background, 29–32; joins Central European Section, 32–35; analysis of Nazism, 36–41; research for